PROOF, PERSUASION

AND CROSS-EXAMINATION:

A Winning New Approach

In The Courtroom

Proof, Persuasion

And

Cross-Examination:

A Winning New Approach In The Courtroom

LOUIS E. SCHWARTZ

Volume One

EXECUTIVE REPORTS CORPORATION
ENGLEWOOD CLIFFS, NEW JERSEY

Library of Congress Catalog Card Number 72-11601

TO

those colorful, egocentric, brave

champions who do combat still

in the name of Truth, Justice, and/or Client—

THE TRIAL LAWYERS

PROOF, PERSUASION
AND CROSS-EXAMINATION
A Winning New Approach
In The Courtroom

VOLUME ONE

Table of Contents

SEE THE DETAILED TABLE OF CONTENTS AT THE BEGINNING OF EVERY CHAPTER

PROOF, PERSUASION
AND CROSS-EXAMINATION
A Winning New Approach
In The Courtroom

VOLUME TWO

Table of Contents

SEE THE DETAILED TABLE OF CONTENTS AT THE BEGINNING OF EVERY CHAPTER

A WORD FROM THE AUTHOR

Many years have passed since the publication of my first book, *The Trial of Automobile Accident Cases*. On comparison I find that this Guide has a diametrically opposite approach to the same objective. In both I have tried to chart a course for the guidance of trial lawyers—but each from an entirely different point of view.

Years ago I thought—if only we could know the correct questions to ask the witness and the legal significance of the possible answers—success in court must follow. I still believe this but, with the passage of time has come an awareness of the utter impossibility, in one lifetime, of acquiring sufficient knowledge to master all fields of trial work.

After a varied experience in studying and trying other types of litigation I observed that there were many points of similarity in proof and the ambitious thought occurred to me that possibly I could discover and isolate the fundamental elements that underlie *all* trials. If it were possible to reduce all questions to a few categories, then one could concentrate on these, and thus accomplish much more than by having one's attention fragmentized by the innumerable questions that might be put to all kinds of witnesses in all types of cases. By studying the atom, man has learned more about the universe than by scanning the heavens. Hopefully, the reader will agree that this Guide has brought to light the basic elements of proof and persuasion applicable to both direct and cross-examination in all trials.

I have added an ingredient that I deem essential to the trial lawyer—applied psychology—a subject rarely, if ever, taught in law school. This may serve to awaken an appreciation of the great importance of an understanding of the psychological aspects of the witness' perceptions, actions, knowledge, recollections, state of mind, and opinions—the six *Generic Questions* this Guide is all about.

I have sought to steer clear of abstract generalities and to furnish specific practical illustrations on every point. I wish to thank Matthew Bender, the publishers of my "Trial of Accident Cases," for their permission to use many such illustrations appearing in that set.

I also express my great appreciation and thanks to Mrs. Celia Blidstein, my secretary and sister-in-law, for her loyal, arduous, and patient endeavors in typing and re-typing the many drafts of the manuscript, the preparation of the Table of Cases, and the proofreading of both the text and references.

LOUIS E. SCHWARTZ

THE SIX KEYS TO TESTIMONY

TABLE OF CONTENTS

THE SIX KEYS
TO TESTIMONY

Just as there are only seven notes in the musical scale which the composer uses in infinite combinations to create all manner of music from song to symphony, similarly, all testimony can be reduced to but six basic or "generic" questions. By the knowledgeable use of these on direct or cross examination, the trial lawyer can create or demolish any legal action or defense.

§ 1:01   Existence of Fundamental Principles of Proof

Since the development of jury trials, lawyers have tried hundreds of thousands of cases of every type and description. Each case had its distinguishing features; the facts varied; the witnesses were different; the lawyers had their own distinctive styles; even the principles of law were not immutable, but shifted with the times and ever-changing mores of society. All had one thing in common—the objective of every lawyer was always the same—to produce proof and to persuade the triers of the facts to find in his client's favor.

Throughout the years much has been written in the nature of advice on the various steps in a trial, and many useful hints have been set down with reference to the selection of juries, examination and cross-examination of witnesses, addresses to the court and jury, etc. A few attempts have been made to analyse proof, notably by Moore[1] and Wigmore[2] but their approach has been from the point of view of helping the judge to evaluate the evidence rather than from the point of view of the lawyer who must produce it.

It has been assumed that every trial is unique. No one has bothered to ask whether there are any fundamental principles of proof which would have universal application and, if so, to discover and isolate them.

Every art and every science, with the exception of Advocacy, has its rudiments—its first principles. William Shakespeare, we may presume, studied the ABC's and the rules of grammar before he penned his first sonnet. Albert Einstein, no doubt, learned to count and memorized the multiplication tables as an initial step towards the eventual conception of his Theory of Relativity. Only the trial lawyer suddenly becomes eligible to practice his specialty by a mysterious process of osmosis presumed to have occurred upon his admission to the Bar.

In art, Grandma Moses, a self-taught "primitive" painter, is the exception. In law, the self-taught trial lawyer is the rule, inhibited rather than helped by the Law of Evidence which he has learned in school. He must first overcome the fears engendered by the multitudinous Rules of Exclusion (the study of what is *inadmissible*) before he will venture into the courtroom arena and there find out for himself how to use proof which is *admissible* and persuasive.

§ 1:02 Need for a "Testimonial Scale"

The work of the advocate has recently been described by Louis Nizer as the "task of weaving thousands of threads of disconnected testimony into a cloth of persuasive patterns while at the same time dexterously eliminating those strings which would spoil the design."[3] Now, it is true that thousands of threads of testimony must be woven together in the same sense that thousands of notes must be used in a symphony. But, just as there are only seven notes in the diatonic scale which the musician uses in infinite combinations, similarly the thousands of threads of testimony may be classified and reduced to a fundamental or "generic" few.

It is essential that the trial lawyer, too, have a scale—a "testimonial scale," similar to the musician's scale, as the basis for his study and experience. There presently being none, we must invent one.

It may seem impossible to isolate the elemental ingredients of testimonial proof and reduce them to a few categories. Proof, particularly testimonial proof, cannot be classified with the precision of musical notes. The subject matter of testimony is indeed broad and all-inclusive. The outpourings of the human heart and mind by witnesses on the stand are not easily reduced to a simple classification.

This "testimonial scale" must be broad enough to cover every possible type of testimony in all kinds of cases, and yet its categories must be few in number so that it will not be unwieldy. Each of its categories must be easily distinguishable from its fellows so as to permit ready and accurate classification. Furthermore, it must be arranged in a natural and logical order so that it can easily be fixed in memory and quickly recalled to mind.

§ 1:03   The Six "Notes" of the Testimonial Scale

Our proposed "testimonial scale" consists of six categories or "notes."

1. The witness' knowledge.
2. The witness' recollection.
3. The witness' perception (sight, hearing, touch, taste, smell).
4. The witness' action (by words or conduct).
5. The witness' state of mind (feelings, emotions, etc.).
6. The witness' operation of mind (opinions, conclusions, etc.).

It will be noted that each of the categories includes the words "the witness." This repetition is deliberate. *It is to emphasize the fact that we are not dealing with subjects such as "knowledge," "perception," "action," or "thought," as abstractions, but specifically in relation to the witness on the stand.*

At first blush it may be difficult to comprehend that all testimony can be contained within the confines of these six categories. We are accustomed to having Proof classified alphabetically according to an endless variety of subject matters. The difficulty is resolved by having the testimony classified, not by subject matter, but rather by the channels through which the evidence becomes available to the witness. Irrespective of the nature or subject of the testimony which a witness may give, it must pertain to his knowledge, perceptions, actions, or be a report on the state of his mind or the operation of his mind.

Ordinarily, testimony does not fit exclusively into any one single category. The categories are inter-related and overlapping, but each bit of testimony will predominately concern itself with one category rather than the others. For instance, an eyewitness to an automobile accident would testify primarily as to what he saw encompassed within the category "Perception." Actually his testimony will be an admixture of all categories: what he knows about the locale, automobiles, the rules of the road, the individuals involved; his present recollection of his original sensations: the sound of brakes, the sight of the crash; his own actions such as jumping out of the way or shouting a warning; his feeling of fright or pity for the injured; his discussions with others at the scene and elsewhere; his feeling of bias or interest in the outcome; his own thoughts or opinion or conclusion as to who was at fault. For a complete examination it may be necessary to explore all six categories in order to develop the full picture of what the witness is able to convey to the jury.

The fact that there is this overlapping does not lessen the value of the classification. It simply means that testimony must be viewed from more than one aspect. If this is done, the result will be that the testimony will not be presented as a flat dull recital but will take on many dimensions and thus become more interesting, alive, and persuasive.

§ 1:04   The Six "Generic Questions"

There are six *Generic Questions*, each of which is designed to elicit the corresponding "note" of testimony, as follows:

1. Recollection:	Q. *What do you recall as to . . .?*	
2. Knowledge:	Q. *What, if anything, do you know, of your personal knowledge, as to . . .?*	
3. Perception:	Q. *What, if anything, did you perceive (see, hear, touch, taste or smell)?*	
4. Action:	Q. *What, if anything, did you do (say or write)?*	
5. State of Mind:	Q. *What are your feelings with respect to . . .?*	
6. Operation of Mind:	Q. *What is your opinion as to . . .?*	

All possible questions which may be put to a witness are but variations and combinations of these six. A witness may have perceived one of a thousand pertinent things, and what he saw could be classified under a thousand headings. However, whenever he testifies as to something he saw, he is answering the *Generic Question, Q. What, if anything, did you perceive?*

From the advocate's point of view, there is little difference whether what the witness saw was an Abortion, Burglary, Collision, Dog, etc., from *A* to distant *Z*. The alphabetical pigeonholing of what was seen according to subject matter is relatively unimportant. What is important to the advocate is to establish that the witness knows whereof he speaks; his recollection is retentive; his sensory perceptions acute; his state of mind unbiased, to the end that the jury will be persuaded to give credence to his testimony that he indeed had perceived a certain fact, as claimed.

The advocate, on direct examination, concentrates upon establishing that the witness did, in fact, see whatever it is he is testifying to. On the other hand, the cross-examiner will concentrate on demonstrating that the witness did not or could not have correctly perceived whatever it was he claims to have seen.

The same applies to any one of the other *Generic Questions*. Recollection plays an important part in every bit of testimony given by every witness in every type of case. Nevertheless, irrespective of what it is that is being recalled, the facts which are universally important on direct examination are those which indicate that the witness undoubtedly could and did recall that to which he has testified. On the other hand, the cross-examiner should be aware of all those circumstances which tend to impair or obliterate memory so that he can explore and reveal them.

Interest or disinterest is but a state of mind. To be able to demonstrate impressively that a witness is disinterested will add greatly to the weight of his testimony. Conversely, to be able to reveal that the witness is in a state of mind which is biased or prejudiced or that his credibility is suspect is all-important to the cross examiner, be it in a civil or criminal case, representing plaintiff or defendant.

Does it really matter whether the expert witness is expressing his opinions as to ballistics, handwriting, medicine, or whatever? If you know how to frame a good hypothetical question for one type of expert, then you can do so for another. Every expert is vulnerable to the same shortcomings and limitations which can be exposed on cross-examination. The subject matter of his expertise may vary, but the direct and cross-examination can follow the same fundamental patterns set forth under the *Generic Questions* of Knowledge and Opinions.

The thesis which will be developed in the pages following is that no matter how varied the subject matter of the trial, no matter how simple or intricate the necessary proof, no matter whether representing the plaintiff or defendant, *all proof can be elicited by means of these six Generic Questions.* Furthermore, that in all questions, no matter how they are worded, *there must be, expressly or implicitly, one or more of these six Generic Questions.*

Just as the artist obtains an infinite variety of hues from the primary colors of red, black, yellow, and blue; just as the composer creates masterpieces from the few notes of the musical scale—so too, the trial lawyer may work effectively with the six *Generic Questions* and their endless combinations and variations.

§ 1:05 The Word "You" Expressed or Implied in Every Question

It will be observed that each of the six Generic Questions contains the word, "you" or "your." *Q. What, if anything, do you know, etc.? Q. What is your recollection, etc.? Q. What, if anything, did you perceive? Q. What, if anything, did you do? Q. How do you feel, with respect to . . .? Q. What is your opinion, etc.?*

The reason that every question is thus phrased is to require an answer in the first person singular, i.e., the witness on the stand must answer for himself, from his own sensory perceptions, physical faculties, or mental conceptions. We ask, *Q. What do you know, of your personal knowledge, as to . . .?* in order that the witness may answer, *A. I know thus and so.* A witness may speak only for himself. No one is competent to report anything except *his own* sensory perceptions, *his own* actions or *his own* mental conceptions. No witness is competent to testify as to the sensations, actions, or thoughts of another person and should not be asked to do so. If the word "you" is not expressly or impliedly included in the question, it will be objectionable as calling for a conclusion as to what someone else (not the witness) perceived, thought, or did.[4]

The word "you" is much more frequently implied than expressed in the questions put to a witness. One listening to testimony in court, or reading the record of a trial will find, more often than not, that the witness *Jones* is asked, *Q. What did Smith do?* or, *Q. What did Smith say?* and not, *Q. What did you see?* or, *Q. What did you hear?* and yet no one objects.

A little thought will show that the reason these questions are not objected to is that it has previously appeared, from the testimony of *Jones*, the witness on the stand, that he was in a position to see or hear what *Smith* did or said. Further, it is assumed that when the witness *Jones* is asked, *Q. What did Smith do?* he is actually being asked, *Q. What did you see Smith do?* Similarly, the question, *Q. What did Smith say?* is interpreted to mean, *Q. What did you hear Smith say?* We may be sure that, had it appeared that the witness *Jones* was not present at the time when and place where *Mr. Smith* had done the act or made the statement, the question, *Q. What did Mr. Smith do?* or *Q. What did Mr. Smith say?* would be objected to as calling for hearsay.

§ 1:06   The Generic Questions in Relation to the Trial Lawyer's Functions

The trial lawyer performs four functions at a trial, namely, (1) to produce proof (2) to object to improper evidence, (3) to cross-examine, and (4) to persuade. This book is so arranged as to correspond to the foregoing functions of the trial lawyer, with particular attention to a demonstration of how the "testimonial scale" with its six *Generic Questions* can be useful in the development and improvement of each of these functions.

PART ONE: PROOF

The chapter on proof deals with the use of the *Generic Questions* on direct examination to prove an action or defense. It also deals with how to propound the proper questions and lead the witness through the appropriate channels so as to elicit the desired testimony, as well as how to develop and strengthen each bit of testimony so as to induce persuasion.[5]

OBJECTIONS TO PROOF

After each chapter of Proof there follows a corresponding chapter of Objections to Proof to help the trial lawyer to keep the record free from error by indicating how the Rules of Exclusion apply to the various *Generic Questions*. Its objective is to enable the trial attorney to avoid improper questions and to anticipate and recognize such objectionable questions when asked by his adversary.[6]

PART TWO: CROSS-EXAMINATION

Part Two demonstrates how the understanding of the legal and psychological significance and implications of the *Generic Questions* and the answers thereto can help the attorney in the preparation of his own witnesses as well as in the cross-examination of adverse witnesses. How weaknesses in witnesses and their testimony can be discovered and revealed, and suggests persuasive argument for summation.[7]

PART THREE: PERSUASION

Part Three renews every aspect of a trial with the view of ascertaining which factors would tend to help persuade the court and jury to render a favorable verdict or decision.[8]

Chapter One

FOOTNOTES

[1] Charles C. Moore, *A Treatise on Facts* (Northport, Long Island, Edward Thompson Company, 1908).

[2] John H. Wigmore, *Principles of Judicial Proof* (Boston, Little, Brown and Company, 1913, 1931).

[3] Louis Nizer, *My Life in Court* (Garden City, N.Y., Doubleday & Company, Inc., 1961), p. 142.

[4] See Section 13.01, "Witness Incompetent to Testify as to State of Mind of Another."

[5] See Chapters 3, 5, 7, 10, 12, 14.

[6] See Chapters 4, 6, 8, 9, 11, 13, 15.

[7] See Chapters 16–22.

[8] See Chapter 24.

CREATING THREADS
OF TESTIMONY

TABLE OF CONTENTS

CREATING THREADS
OF TESTIMONY

In this chapter we will show how the Generic Questions can be used to accomplish the two important objectives of direct examination. The first is to control the flow of testimony, how to direct the witness and guide his testimony along the channels you desire in logical sequence, keeping it within proper bounds, avoiding the incompetent, irrelevant and immaterial or prejudicial. The second is how to weave the individual Generic Questions into Threads of Testimony and elicit all the favorable facts within the witness' knowledge and competence, in a manner which will produce the maximum of persuasion.

§ 2:01 Using Generic Questions to Direct the Flow of Testimony

It is, indeed, a rare witness, even among the most intelligent, who knows what facts are relevant, proper, and persuasive and what facts are better omitted. While the advocate should try to avoid using leading questions, he should never hesitate to lead the witness into and along the desired paths through what is often an intricate maze of facts. There is a difference between putting leading questions which suggest the answer and leading the witness from one line of testimony to another. The question may properly suggest a subject but not the answer.[1]

The lawyer can guide the witness from one aspect of his testimony to another by means of the *Generic Questions*. This applies not only to the routine questioning. At times, in the midst of trial, problems unexpectedly present themselves. A witness who possesses information may suddenly go mute or his answer is not responsive, or is in the form of a conclusion instead of a factual assertion, or he goes off into some undesired path of his own. What then? Just as the composer uses the musical notes to indicate what sounds he desires, the trial lawyer chooses the appropriate *Generic Question* to put the witness back into the proper channel and evoke the desired testimony.

§ 2:02 Ambiguity and Confusion Avoided by the Use of Generic Questions

By the use of the *Generic Questions*, the trial lawyer assures himself that the question is properly framed, and that the answer is more likely to be responsive and satisfactory. Of course, the examination of witnesses must never be permitted to sound stilted, repetitious, or boring as it might be if the questions were always framed in the precise verbiage of the *Generic Questions*. However, experienced counsel will learn to vary the phraseology of the questions. At times the *Generic Question* is not expressly stated, but is implied. That, however, is only when the implication is obvious to the witness. For example, the *Generic Question* for recollection or for knowledge is rarely expressly stated. One would hardly think of asking, *Q. What do you know, of your own personal knowledge as to what is your occupation?* The personal knowledge of the witness would be implicit in the question, *Q. What is your occupation?* [2]

When a question is asked in which no *Generic Question* is incorporated, either expressly or by implication, it is likely to be ambiguous if not actually misleading. To illustrate, a frequent question is *Q. What occurred?* or *Q. What happened then?* All sorts of answers are possible to such a question and the witness is given no hint by the question itself as to what is desired. It might be calling for something the witness saw, or heard, or did, or said. The question may be answered with hearsay, i.e., what he was told by someone else rather than what he himself perceived. This can be avoided by asking, *Q. What, if anything, did you see?* or *Q. What, if anything, did you do?* Such questions help the witness by giving him a cue as to what is desired. The essential thing is to make sure that the questions guide the witness to the desired responses. The use of the *Generic Questions* removes ambiguity and enables the trial lawyer to exercise greater control over the witness and thus obtain more precise and proper answers.

The advocate may purposely ask, *Q. What occurred?* rather than *Q. What, if anything, did you see?* The reason is that the answer then sounds as though the witness is stating facts rather than merely giving his own recollection of his sensory perceptions. The attorney may knowingly ask the ballistics expert, *Q. Is this the gun from which the shot was fired?* rather than *Q. In your opinion, is this the gun from which the shot was fired?* The expert's opinion will then sound like a statement of fact rather than an opinion.

It is one thing to put such ambiguous questions as a matter of strategy where the witness has been prepared and understands what is desired. It is another thing to ask such questions thoughtlessly when the effect may be to confuse and mislead the witness.

The examining attorney and his witness may understand each other even though the questions are ambiguous. Opposing counsel, however, must develop the faculty of recognizing the ambiguities. He must be able to categorize each question according to the six *Generic Questions* no matter how it is worded. He must do this if he is to make timely objections; if he is to prevent the jury from accepting a mere recollection, conclusion, or hearsay as the equivalent of the fact itself; if he is to be able to expose the weaknesses of the answers through cross-examination.

§ 2:03   Leading or Suggestive Questions [3]

A leading question is one which suggests to the witness the answer he is to deliver. Included in this category are questions which expressly or impliedly assume a material fact not theretofore testified to, so that the answer may affirm such fact. To illustrate, in an action involving an automobile, the question *Q. For how many miles would you say, was that automobile speeding?* is leading and suggestive and, therefore, improper if there is no evidence, up to that point, that the automobile had, in fact, been speeding. Instead, the witness should be asked, *Q. Did you see that automobile? Q. For how many miles did you observe it? Q. In your opinion, how fast was it traveling during the time that you observed it?*

The objection that a question is leading may be obviated by so framing the question as to give the witness a choice of answers. If the question may be answered either, "yes" or "no," then it is not generally considered leading, provided the desired answer is not suggested. The witness may be given an alternative as when asked "Whether or not" a certain thing occurred or "Was he or was he not" doing a certain act or "What, if anything" took place. Thus, the question "Was she turning to the left or to the right or was she continuing straight?" was considered proper. However, the question may be considered leading even though it calls for a "yes" or "no" answer, or the witness is asked to state "Whether or not," the test being whether the question suggests the answer.

On direct examination, leading questions are to be avoided because an examination by means of leading questions is unimpressive as well as objectionable. Jurors want to hear the testimony of the witness rather than a mere echo of the words of the attorney.

Under certain circumstances it may become necessary to put leading questions which may be allowed, in the discretion of the trial court, whenever it appears that the ends of justice will be served thereby. Thus, leading questions are permitted where:

- The subject is a non-controversial, preliminary, introductory matter.
- The witness is immature, particularly if the testimony relates to delicate matters.

- The witness lacks understanding for any reason, such as ignorance or illiteracy, or is being questioned through an interpreter, or is mentally deficient.

- The witness is reluctant, hostile, biased, and evasive.

- The witness has exhausted his memory and it is necessary to refresh it.

- The witness has taken the party by surprise because of prior contradictory statements.

- The witness is called in rebuttal to impeach an adverse witness by testimony of a prior self-contradictory statement.[4]

When used under any other circumstances, leading questions are improper, but no formal objection need be made unless the question pertains to an important, controverted fact. It is preferable to call the court's attention, by means of some comment, to the fact that counsel is testifying rather than the witness. For example, after a number of leading questions have been asked, you might say, "May I suggest that counsel himself is testifying and it would be better if he had the witness under oath do so."

If a choice must be made, it is better that the trial lawyer resort to a leading question than that he leave a hole in the fabric of his proof.

§ 2:04   Compound Questions

Often a question is so phrased that it seems to involve one *Generic Question* when it involves a few. An illustration of a question which is actually a composite of many is:

Q. *Is this photograph a correct representation of the scene as it was at the time of the accident?*

If we break this down into its components, we find at least four questions, all of which the witness must be competent to answer; otherwise the question is objectionable. The questions are:

Q. *Did you see the scene of the accident at the time the accident occurred?* [Perception]

Q. *Do you now recollect it?* [Recollection]

Q. *Do you see what is depicted on this photograph?* [Perception]

Q. *In your opinion, is what is depicted thereon a correct representation [of your present recollection] of what you saw at the time of the accident?* [Operation of Mind]

The advocate, realizing that there are not one but three *Generic Questions* (Perception, Recollection and Operation of the Mind) involved, will elicit from his witness all facts which would indicate that the witness' perception, his recollection, and his opinion are all entitled to credence.

§ 2:05   Development of Proof by Creating Threads of Testimony

If a particular bit of testimony is important, the trial lawyer dare not content himself with the bare *Generic Question* and its answer. He must try to develop the theme to a point where it changes from a mere bit of testimony to persuasive proof. The answer of a witness to one *Generic Question* can be strengthened by inferences arising from the answers to other *Generic Questions* put to the same witness. Figuratively speaking, the *Generic Question* is placed in the center of the stage and is illuminated by directing spotlights of inferences from other categories upon it.

The approach is similar to that of a musician. A composer takes a few notes as his motif, he embellishes them with harmony, scale passages, trills, arpeggios; he varies their rhythm and develops them into a movement or sonata. The advocate takes one item of testimony, combines it with other items and creates what may be called a *Thread of Testimony,* which he later combines with other related threads. The term *Thread of Testimony* is quite apt. A thread is a weak, flimsy thing. Many threads laid side by side gain but little in strength. When knitted together they can be unravelled by the loosening of one. On the other hand, they can be woven together into sturdy cloth of varied textures, patterns, and designs. Braided into strands, their strength will increase in geometric proportions. Intertwined to form ropes and cables they are capable of sustaining the greatest weight.

The analogy is obvious. One thread of testimony is a weak and flimsy thing. A case made up of many disconnected threads will still be "threadbare." When the proof is loosely knit, it may be ripped apart and torn wide open with one snip by the cross-examiner. *When, however, the threads of testimony are braided together and intertwined with many other such threads, they can form a web to enmesh, a straight-jacket to imprison, or a cloak to protect.* The choice of the threads of testimony, their infinite variety and combinations of type, substance, and presentation will reflect the skill and artistry of the weaver—the advocate.

Thus, for example, the testimony of a witness who relates what he saw in response to the question, *Q. What, if anything, did you see?* attains greater persuasiveness if, before he states what he saw, he testifies as to what he did to put himself into position where he could observe without any obstructions to his view; his state of mind, his reason or motive to observe, etc. His testimony will be further enhanced if he describes what he saw in detail and describes other things which he saw at the same time and place. Furthermore, perception may occur simultaneously by means of sight, hearing, touch, taste, and smell and his testimony as to these various sensory perceptions would corroborate each other.[5]

Should the witness be there to testify as an expert, he is not asked directly to state his opinion. The experienced trial attorney will first go into the details of the witness' qualifications (*Knowledge*), then as to what he did with respect to tests and examinations of the subject matter (*Actions*) and then the details of what he observed (*Perceptions*). Only then will he call for the opinion of the expert witness.

In creating a *Thread of Testimony*, the advocate does not limit himself to one of the six categories of testimony, but should include as many as possible. The inferences arising from the answer to any one *Generic Question* can be strengthened by the inferences flowing from others. There is, for example, harmony between a man's thoughts and deeds. When, therefore, it appears from the testimony of a witness that his sensory perceptions, his actions, and his mental conceptions were all consistent with each other, there are a great number of inferences flowing from all this testimony, pointing in the same direction, *i.e.*, towards truth and credibility.

§ 2:06   Hints for Conducting a Direct Examination [6]

- Make an outline, in advance, of the subjects to be covered by the examination.
- Unless fully experienced, prepare the questions, particularly the hypothetical questions, in advance.
- Frame the questions in simple plain language, avoiding technical terms or high sounding phrases.
- Make the questions as short as possible.
- Be sure each question is proper in form.
- Don't use such phrases as "As a matter of fact," "Isn't it fact," "Don't you mean," "That's true isn't it?"
- Arrange the questions in logical order.
- The first few questions should be designed to put the witness at his ease.
- If the witness is intelligent, let him tell his story in his own way. Interrupt him as little as possible.
- Let the witness hold the jury's attention—keep yourself in the background.
- Speak kindly, reassuringly, clearly and in a natural, unaffected manner.
- Be deliberate, weighing each question—avoid all haste or confusion.

- Keep cool, never lose your temper or allow yourself to become nervous or agitated.
- Don't show disappointment or chagrin at a disappointing or surprising answer.
- Don't cross-examine your own witness unless he is hostile.

§ 2:07 Keeping Within the Rules of Evidence

The trial lawyer has a double responsibility. He must know how to prove his facts most effectively but, at the same time, he must do so in a manner which will not run counter to any of the evidence Rules of Exclusion. When asking questions, whether on direct or cross-examination, it is essential that the attorney be ever mindful that there are bounds beyond which it is improper to go. It is poor policy to win a verdict which may be reversed because of the violation of some rule of evidence. On the other hand, when the adversary is asking the questions, the reaction to any objectionable ones or to improper answers must be instantaneous and well nigh instinctive. The objection to a question, if it is to be made at all, must be made in the split second between the completion of the question and the start of the answer. After that it may be too late.[7]

THE OBJECTIONS TO EACH GENERIC QUESTION

A theoretical knowledge of the law of evidence will not suffice in the heat of battle during trial. The practical application of the Rules of Exclusion must be so much a part of the trial lawyer as to be second nature. In order to facilitate a full understanding and mastery of the Rules of Exclusion and their practical application, we have selected illustrative problems commonly encountered, involving the Rules of Exclusion and have presented them after each of the six *Generic Questions* in the form in which they would arise at trial. By arranging the possible objections in this manner, the law of evidence assumes a more practical and meaningful form. When a witness is testifying about his perceptions—the objections to perceptions will come to mind. When the witness is about to express an opinion—all objections may be disregarded except those pertaining to opinions.

The objections are arranged uniformly under four headings for each *Generic Question,* i.e.:

(A) Objections to the *witness* as being incompetent, as by reason of interest, privilege, lack of qualifications, etc.

(B) Objections to *evidence* as being incompetent, as calling for hearsay, opinions, or matters against public policy.

(C) Objections to irrelevant evidence, i.e., that it is not logically related to the issues.

(D) Objections to evidence which is both immaterial and prejudicial.

The illustrative objections were selected as the most likely to be encountered in everyday trial practice. They are representative of what evidentiary problems are likely to arise when the proof deals with each of the *Generic Questions.*

The text which follows each objection indicates not only the general rule but also the exceptions. It discusses the circumstances which would require that the objection be sustained as well as those under which the objection would be overruled. Whenever possible, it indicates when and how the objection can be avoided as well as what may be done to circumvent the Rule of Exclusion as, by offering the evidence on a different theory or for a limited purpose, or as against one but not another party, or by reframing the question, laying a proper foundation, or calling a different witness.

§ 2:08 Outline of Chapters Following

Each chapter following under the heading of **Proof** is devoted to one of the *Generic Questions.* In each we shall study the scope, nature, psychological aspects of the *Generic Question* and how the testimony of the witness in answer to the question may be strengthened and developed into an effective *Thread of Testimony* which, when combined with others, will become persuasive proof. The underlying principles are illustrated by *Threads of Testimony* which have been carefully selected on the basis of their practical utility in every day practice. They are the forms of proof which are frequently encountered in litigation.

After each chapter of Proof there is a chapter of Objections, illustrating the possible evidentiary problems which commonly arise in connection with that particular *Generic Question.*

Chapter Two

FOOTNOTES

[1] Rausch v. Buisse (Wis. 1966), 146 N.W. 2d 801.

[2] See Section 5.01, "Definition of Personal Knowledge."

[3] Louis E. Schwartz, *Trial of Accident Cases,* 3rd ed. (New York, Matthew Bender, 1968), Section 147.

John Henry Wigmore, *Evidence* 3rd ed. (Boston, Little, Brown and Company, 1940), Section 773–79.

[4] See Section 7.23, "Effective Use of a Prior Inconsistent Statement Made by a Witness."

[5] See Chapter 7.

[6] Schwartz, *Trial of Accident Cases,* Section 152.

[7] *Ibid,* Section 190.

TECHNIQUES IN PROVING A WITNESS' RECOLLECTIONS

TABLE OF CONTENTS

TECHNIQUES IN PROVING
A WITNESS' RECOLLECTIONS

The memory or recollection of the witness is probably the most important ingredient of his testimony. While it is pervasive, it is not often expressly asked about. Rather, this chapter deals with how the witness can establish circumstantially that his recollection is dependable. It also shows how, when it becomes necessary, a witness' recollection may be refreshed or how and under what circumstances a memorandum of a past recollection may be put into evidence. Because recollection is the basis for authenticating an exhibit, the procedure to be followed in introducing exhibits in evidence is included in this chapter.

Q. WHAT DO YOU RECALL AS TO . . . ?

§ 3:01   Using Recollections Most Effectively

Practically *all* testimony of a witness consists of recollections. Every question which is phrased in the past tense clearly calls for the recollection of the witness. The question *Q. What did you see?* asks for the present recollection of what the witness saw in the past. The witness, in answering the question, is not testifying as to his sense of sight but rather as to what he *now recalls* of his original sensory perception which occurred in the past and which may have been modified or obliterated by the passage of time.

Even questions phrased in the present tense involve matters of recollection. For example, the question *Q. What do you see?* seems to call for the present sensory perception of the witness. However, by the time the witness has begun his answer, he is testifying to something which is already in the past. True, it is the immediate and not the distant past, and his recollection of it is likely to be very clear. Nevertheless, the subject matter of his testimony is no longer in the present.[1] The interval of time which is the duration of the "present" is infinitesimal.[2] The witness' eye scans the paper, an image of what he sees is registered upon the retina of each eyeball; these images are then sent to the brain for interpretation. It is this interpretation of what had been seen, and not the original sight sensation, which is embodied in the words with which the witness answers the question.[3]

Inasmuch as the witness is not testifying about the fact itself, but rather as to his *recollection* of the impression which the fact had made upon his memory, two categories of testimony are involved, one is *Recollection* and the other *Perception*.[4] This is important because testimony involving two categories can be strengthened by re-enforcing either or both of them. On the other hand, such testimony can be weakened or destroyed successfully by attacking either category i.e., either the recollection or the data allegedly perceived.

§ 3:02   The Generic Question Is Usually Implicit and Not Expressed

The *Generic Question* which serves to elicit the witness' recollection is, *Q. What do you recall as to . . .?* This question is rarely expressly stated, but is implicit in almost every question.

When a witness is called to testify as to something which took place in the past, he is usually asked at the outset, *Q. Do you recall the _____ day of _____ 19___?* (the date of the occurrence in question). Such a question is merely introductory and is put primarily for the purpose of directing the attention of the witness to the specific point in time when the events involved in the lawsuit commenced to unfold.

When the witness has once been asked whether he recalls the given date, this question is rarely, if ever, followed up by a question such as *Q. What do you recall?* The word "recall" is rarely mentioned. Rather, he is asked *Q. What did you see?* or *Q. What occurred?* The examining attorney wants the testimony to appear to be a statement of fact and does not want to emphasize that what the witness is about to state is only a trace left on his memory rather than the fact itself.

By way of illustration, compare these two questions and answers in a trial for murder. The People seek to prove that the defendant Jones stabbed the victim Smith. A witness was called by the People, and testified that he recalled the day in question and that he was present at the scene, he is then asked:

(A)

Q.   What is your present recollection as to what you saw at the time?
A.   To the best of my recollection, I saw the defendant, Jones, stab Smith.

(B)

Q.   Tell us what you saw?
A.   The defendant Jones stabbed Smith.

Which bit of testimony is more persuasive? Obviously the second. The statement, "The defendant Jones stabbed Smith," sounds like a positive assertion of fact, whereas the answer, "To the best of my recollection, I saw the defendant, Jones, stab Smith," reflects a doubt on the part of the witness. In response to either question, all the witness can do is to relate his present recollection of such impressions as had been made upon his memory which were retained there and now recalled. Recollection is never the equivalent of the original event,[5] and therefore it is unwise to call attention unnecessarily to this testimonial weakness.

§ 3:03   Enhancing the Persuasiveness of Recollection

The persuasiveness of all testimony depends in great measure upon the jury's estimation of the accuracy of the witness' recollection. Recollection is, therefore, as important, if not more important, than credibility. While the jury may assume that the ordinary witness is credible, in the absence of any reason to lead to a contrary opinion, they may not assume that he has a good memory. The most honest witness may be mistaken or inaccurate in his recollections.

What then can the advocate do to persuade the jury that the witness' recollection is an accurate one? What other facts can be elicited which will enhance the likelihood that his answers to the *Generic Question Q. What do you recall as to . . .?* will be accepted and believed? Upon what psychological basis can the attorney argue to the jury in summation that the witness' recollections should be accepted? In this connection the attorney may endeavor to show that:

(A) The witness' original impression was clear and accurate.

(B) The witness had a good memory.

(C) He had a special reason for remembering.

(D) His recollection was of something likely to be remembered.

(E) His memory was refreshed.

§ 3:04   (A) Stressing that the Original Impression was Clear and Accurate

The ability to recall depends, first of all, upon the vividness and accuracy of the original impression. There can be no recollection unless certain sensations are first received and are then transmitted to the brain and there interpreted, registered, and retained.[6] Memory is inexorably bound up with "the thing remembered."[7] Of course, this need not be necessarily a "thing." It may be any perception, sensation, action, experience, idea, attitude, opinion, or any motor or intellectual phenomena, or it may even be another recollection.[8] So closely interwoven is the recollection and "the thing remembered" that generally, the two are not distinguished, and we tend to consider the recollection as the equivalent of the matter recalled.[9] No matter what it is which is being recalled, the fact that the original impression or sensation was clear and accurate will add to the likelihood that it was correctly retained and recalled.

How then can the attorney demonstrate that the original impressions were accurate? The answer varies with the type of sensation involved. For example, if the recollection is of something the witness saw or heard or otherwise perceived, any proof which would demonstrate his perceptiveness would simultaneously increase the likelihood that what was so perceived was also remembered. For recollections in that category, reference should be made to the chapter dealing with Perception.[10] Similarly, if the recollection relates to the witness' Knowledge,[11] Actions,[12] State of Mind[13] or Opinions[14] reference should also be made to the chapter dealing with the appropriate category.

§ 3:05   (B) The Witness Had a Good Memory

At the very outset of the witness' testimony, he may be asked introductory questions designed to show that he was one whose memory was probably good. A checklist of data about the witness which might be significant in appraising his ability to recollect accurately might include the following:

1. *He does recall the event.* The assertion by the witness that he has a recollection is a statement of fact and is to be considered.[15]

2. *Good memory.* Whether a witness possesses a good memory is something as to which he may testify just as he may testify as to his own state of mind.[16]

3. *His age.* Tenacity of memory differs enormously from infancy to old age. With a child, recent happenings are likely to remain fresh in his mind but he is not too interested in recalling things in the past. With an old person the opposite is true, he will recall things of long, long ago, yet may forget what took place just a few minutes before.[17]

4. *Good Health and Sensory Acuteness.* A person who is in good health, alert, and not fatigued, is more likely to obtain a better original impression because his senses are more accurate.[18]

5. *Interest and Need to Recall.* The desire to remember, of itself, helps in the process and we remember best those things we want to remember.[19]

6. *Education and Intelligence.* An educated and intelligent person understands more and this may result in a better original impres-

sion. On the other hand, an illiterate person may be able to and will commit more to memory out of necessity.[20]

7. *Fear*. Fear arouses the senses with the result that the impression is more vivid and likely to be remembered. On the other hand, it has been thought that an identification of a suspected criminal based upon a brief observation while the witness was very frightened and upset is not entitled to much weight.[21]

8. *Disinterestedness*. The absence of bias and prejudice make for more objective impressions and recollections. However, bias may furnish an incentive for remembering such facts which tend to hurt the object of one's ill-will.[22]

9. *His Memory Was Refreshed*. If, very shortly after the event, that event was called to the attention of the witness, that, in itself, helps to impress the details upon the memory.[23]

10. *The Details Recalled*. The impressiveness of a recollection is enhanced by the extent of the details which are recalled.[24]

§ 3:06   (C) There Was a Special Reason for Remembering

Testimony as to memory is strengthened if the witness is able to refer to some special circumstance connected with the transaction or event to which he testifies, which served to impress his memory.[25] For example, a desk clerk in a hotel having a large number of guests residing there for only a short time might have no more than a faint recollection of most of them; but, if one of them was violently assaulted by another in the lobby, causing considerable noise and commotion, he could hardly forget the circumstances or the identity of the persons concerned.[26]

A reason for remembering is particularly important if the event was very ordinary and commonplace or if there has been a long interval of time between the original sensation and its recollection or, if, for some other reason, it was unlikely that the fact would be remembered.[27] Dates, for example, are very easily forgotten, and it is commonplace to fix a date by reference to some contemporaneous event. The time of day may also be fixed by recalling a particular activity of the witness.

Incidentally, in relating "the thing remembered" to some other act or occurrence, the witness may give the jury an insight into the type of person he is and add to his credibility in a manner which might not otherwise be accomplished. For example, the defense in a murder trial called, as one of his alibi witnesses, a young girl who gave, as a reason for being sure of the time the defendant had been to her home the fact that when he came to the house she was late for Mass. Undoubtedly this reason not only added credence to her recollection of the precise time, but enhanced her credibility by revealing her to be a young lady who practiced her religion.[28]

In the Rosenberg spy case, the prosecution's witness, a photographer, explained how he was able to recall with certainty that it was the defendants whom he had photographed for passports because of the fact that they had brought their two young children who were quite rambunctious in the studio and he had had great difficulty in keeping them from damaging his equipment.[29]

§ 3:07   (D) The Recollection Was of Something Likely to be Remembered

There are certain intrinsic aspects of "the thing remembered" which are recognized as being more likely to be recalled than are others. The recollection is more likely to be accurate and long lasting if it was of something:

- *Important.* If the circumstances are meaningful and significant, then they will be more quickly comprehended and longer remembered.[30]

- *Exciting or sensational.* Where the original impression is of something exciting or sensational, it will be retained in the memory for a greater length of time and will be revived without losing a detail.[31]

- *Pleasant.* We instinctively give more attention to pleasurable rather than unpleasant stimuli.[32]

- *Shameful.* Shameful and distressing experiences often make an indelible mark which require no effort of memory to recall. On the other hand, there are occasions when the mind will subconsciously block out the memory of certain unpleasant events.[33]

- *Recent.* One of the most important factors in loss of recollection of details is the passage of time.[34]

- *Duty to Report.* If the event was one as to which the witness was charged with a duty to report, this will serve as an incentive to impress it upon his memory.[35]

§ 3:08   Introductory Questions Relevant to Memory

The foregoing suggest that there are certain questions which may be asked a witness which will serve to introduce him to the jury and will also enable the jury to appreciate the circumstances with reference to his memory in general and his recollections of the occurrence in particular. These questions, together with other introductory questions designed to show that the witness was unbiased and unprejudiced, and was in a position to have a clear and accurate original impression of the event in question, should be put at the outset and before the witness is asked to relate the substance of his recollections.

ILLUSTRATIVE THREAD OF TESTIMONY

Introductory Questions Relevant to Memory

Q. *How old are you?*
A. *28 years old.*

Q. *What is your occupation?*
A. *I am a newspaper reporter.*

Q. *Do you recall the first day of October of last year?*
A. *I do.*

Q. *Where were you at about 6:30 in the afternoon of that day?*
A. *I was on Main Street.*

Q. *What were you doing at that time?*
A. *I was strolling along with my fiancee.*

Q. *What, if anything, fixes that day in your memory?*
A. *It was my first day home from the Army.*

Q. *What was the condition of your health?*
A. *I was in fine condition.*

Q. *Do you have a good memory?*
A. *An excellent one.*

Q. *Did you, at that time, witness a collision of two automobiles at First and Main Streets?*
A. *I did.*

Q. *Tell the Court and jury what occurred as you recall it.*
A. *(Witness relates the details of the occurrence).*

Q. *After the occurrence, did you speak to anyone about what had happened?*
A. *Yes.*

Q. With whom did you speak?

A. I spoke to the police officer who came to the scene and I have spoken to a man who came to see me from your office and a representative of the other driver.

Q. Have you signed any statements?

A. Yes, I signed statements for both parties.

Q. Have you spoken to me about the facts before coming to court?

A. Yes, I spoke to you yesterday.

§ 3:09   Refreshing Recollection in Court

A witness is not always aware of all the information he possesses. "It is well known that we retain much that we cannot recall."[36] Often he is not aware that he has forgotten some fact when, actually, he does possess the information but it is hidden in some mysterious crevice of his subconscious mind. Everyone has, at one time or another, something brought back to mind of which he believed that he had no knowledge whatsoever.

The law recognizes that a person may forget something he once knew and then recall it after his memory is refreshed. Therefore, whenever it appears that a witness has forgotten some fact, his memory may be refreshed.[37] To accomplish this, the witness may be asked leading questions,[38] his attention may be directed to a prior conversation, event or circumstance,[39] or he may be shown a writing,[40] or any other thing.[41] He is then asked if it refreshes his recollection. If he says it does, he may then state his recollection independently and without the aid of the reference.[42]

The experienced trial lawyer will explain this to the witness when preparing him for trial. The witness will be given to understand that should he be asked such questions as, "Is that *all* that happened?" or, "Have you told us the *entire* conversation?" he is not to answer bluntly, "Yes, it is," and thus close the door to further questioning. Rather, he should consider such a question as an indication that he has omitted something, and should answer, "That is all that I remember *now*." This will give his attorney the opportunity to refresh his recollection, to inquire further and to ask him leading questions, should that be necessary.[43]

The memory of the witness may have been refreshed by looking at certain memoranda or documents before coming to court. The witness may testify that he has done so, as this will explain how it is that he recalls many details after a long lapse of time. Or, the witness may refresh his memory while on the witness stand and in the presence of the jury. There is less likelihood of error if the recollection is refreshed while the witness is on the stand.

When a memorandum is used simply to refresh the recollection of a witness, it may be of any type of writing, public or private,[44] formal or informal,[45] complete or incomplete,[46] an original or a copy,[47] made by the witness[48] or anyone else,[49] or dictated by the witness to someone else,[50] and it may have been prepared contemporaneously with the event or later.[51] The paper or exhibit which is used to refresh recollection need not be itself admissible in evidence, and the mere fact that it was used to refresh recollection does not mean that it is to be received in evidence.[52] However, the adversary has a right, upon request, to inspect it;[53] he may offer it in evidence,[54] and cross-examine as to it.[55]

Witnesses instinctively feel that if their memory were refreshed in any way, then this would lessen the weight of their testimony and create the impression that their testimony was the result of suggestion rather than fact.[56] Psychologists, however, tell us that, if very shortly after the occurrence of an event, it is called to the attention of the witness, this, in itself, helps impress the details upon the memory. The shorter the time which elapsed between the occurrence and calling attention to the occurrence, the more likely that it will be fixed upon the memory. If we are reminded of events soon after their occurrence, that in itself becomes a reason why we should again recollect them.[57] This form of attention is frequently almost equivalent to primary or original attention as an assurance of fidelity of memory and should engender a high degree of confidence.[58]

Certainly, if the matter was unimportant to the witness, or a routine matter, and there was no special reason for it to be impressed upon his mind, it would be highly unlikely that he would be able to recall it in detail after a long lapse of time unless it was called to his attention soon after the event and he had reason to expect that he would be questioned about it.[59] Whenever it would be unlikely that the witness could or would have retained all of the details in his memory, and there is some record of the facts, it is better that the witness refresh his recollection, as in the following illustration, in which the doctor refreshes his recollection from his own records which are not in evidence.

ILLUSTRATIVE THREAD OF TESTIMONY

Doctor's Records Used to Refresh His Recollection [60]

Q. Do you, at this time, remember the details of the care and treatment of the plaintiff?

A. No.

Q. Did you keep a record of the plaintiff's care and treatment?

A. I did.

Q. *Would that record refresh your recollection of the details of the care and treatment?*

A. *It would.*

Q. *Have you that record with you?*

A. *I have.*

Q. *What was the date when you first examined this plaintiff?*
Witness: May I look at my records?
Counsel: Yes, you may refresh your recollection from your records.

A. *It was on February 1st, last year.*

§ 3:10   Itemized Lists or Memoranda

Ordinarily, a paper which has been used to refresh the witness' recollection is not received in evidence. Where, however, the paper consists of a long list of items, such as a repair bill or an accounting, which would be impossible to recall in detail, the court, in his discretion, may make an exception. The court, in such cases, may allow the witness to testify quite generally and receive the memorandum in evidence as furnishing the details, leaving to the adverse party a more minute cross-examination, if he so desires.[61]

§ 3:11   Use of Memorandum When Memory Cannot be Refreshed

It sometimes happens that the witness has completely forgotten some fact and that his memory cannot be refreshed. If, however, a memorandum had been made containing the information while his memory was fresh, it may be possible to introduce such memorandum itself in lieu of his testimony. Such a writing, if properly authenticated, is received as substantive evidence of what it contains and is known as a "memorandum of a past recollection recorded."

Before any such record will be received in evidence, it must first be authenticated by the witness. The witness, although he has forgotten the facts as set forth in the memorandum, must testify as to his recollections respecting the circumstances surrounding the making of the memorandum with respect to his personal knowledge of the facts; the contemporaneous making of the memorandum, and its accuracy.[62]

ILLUSTRATIVE THREAD OF TESTIMONY

Authenticating a Memorandum of a Past Recollection Recorded: License Number

Q. *Did you notice the license plate on that automobile?*
A. *I did.*

Q. *Did you see the license number?*
A. *I did.*

Q. *Did you take down that license number?*
A. *I did.*

Q. *On what did you write it down?*
A. *On a card I had in my pocket.*

Q. *When did you write it down?*
A. *Right away.*

Q. *Do you recall that license number now?*
A. *I do not.*

Q. *(Presenting the same) I show you this and ask you if you can identify it?*
A. *I can.*

Q. *What is it?*
A. *That is the card with the license number I wrote on it.*

Q. *Does that card refresh your present recollection of the number you saw on the automobile license plate?*
A. *No, it does not.*

Q. *Was the number correctly written down?*
A. *It was.*

Q. *What did you do with that card after you wrote that number?*
A. *I gave it to the plaintiff.*

Q. And is it now exactly the same as when you gave it to him?
A. It is.

Plaintiff's Attorney: I offer the card and the number in evidence.

§ 3:12   Recollection as the Basis for the Authentication of Exhibits

Recollection is an essential ingredient of the authentication of an exhibit so that it may be received in evidence. The witness can not possibly testify that the exhibit is correct unless he has a clear recollection of what it was or what it depicts. If, for instance, the witness is to authenticate a photograph of a scene of an accident, the weight of his authentication will depend upon the likelihood that he accurately recalls the scene. This, in turn, would depend upon many factors, including his familiarity with the place and how frequently and closely he had the opportunity to observe it. Such facts should be elicited before the witness is asked to authenticate the photograph.

GETTING A PHOTOGRAPH ADMITTED INTO EVIDENCE

There is a definite procedure to be followed in authenticating an exhibit which is almost ritualistic. The steps taken in having a photograph admitted into evidence would be as follows:

1. The exhibit should be marked for identification. This provides a convenient way in which to refer to it before it is received in evidence, and will keep the record clear. Should there be an appeal, the appellate court will know exactly what the witness was shown by its identification number. The exhibit may be used on appeal only if it was identified. The trial court has no discretion to refuse a request to mark an exhibit for identification.[63]

2. The witness should testify as to his knowledge and recollection of the exhibit or what it depicts.

3. The witness is then asked whether the photograph is a correct representation of the scene as it was at the time in issue. The photograph may have been taken at another time and by someone else, but so long as this witness can state that it correctly depicts the scene as of the time in question, that will be a sufficient foundation.

4. If there have been any changes or if the photograph differs in any way, the differences should be pointed out and the court will have to decide whether such differences make the photograph so misleading that it must be excluded.

5. The exhibit is offered in evidence and shown to the adversary for his possible objection.

6. It is then shown to the court.

7. If there is no objection, or if the objection is overruled, it is given to the court stenographer to mark in evidence.

8. The witness may then be asked to explain or mark the exhibit as required.

9. Permission should be requested to show the exhibit to the jury. It is best not to continue questioning the witness until all the jurors have had an opportunity to examine the exhibit, unless ordered by the court to proceed.

10. The exhibit number should be mentioned every time the exhibit is used or referred to.[64]

ILLUSTRATIVE THREAD OF TESTIMONY

Authentication of Photograph

Q. Do you recall the scene of the accident?
A. I do.

Q. Are you familiar with the street intersection where it occurred?
A. I am.

Q. How often have you had occasion to see that intersection?
A. I have passed there every weekday for the last five years.
Attorney (to court stenographer): *May I have this marked for identification?*
(Photograph is marked "Plaintiff's Exhibit 1 for Identification")

Q. I show you Plaintiff's Exhibit 1 for identification and ask you if you recognize it?
A. I do.

Q. What does that show?
A. That is the intersection of 1st Street and Main Street.

Q. Does that photograph, Plaintiff Exhibit 1 for Identification, correctly represent the intersection of 1st and Main Streets as it appeared on January 13, this year, the date of the occurrence involved in this litigation?
A. It does.

Q. *Does Plaintiff's Exhibit 1 for Identification show the intersection exactly as it appeared at that time?*

A. *Yes, except that there was no automobile parked near the curb then.*

Q. *With the exception of that parked automobile, is the photograph, Plaintiff's Exhibit 1 for Identification, accurate in every other respect?*

A. *It is.*

Attorney: *I offer Plaintiff's Exhibit 1 for Identification in evidence* (handing it to his adversary).

Opposing Attorney: *No objection.*

(The photograph is then handed up to the court)

The Court: (after examining the exhibit) *Let it be marked.*

(The exhibit is then given to the court stenographer.)

Court Stenographer: (Marks photograph) *Plaintiff's Exhibit 1 in evidence.*

Q. *Did you see the impact between the two vehicles?*

A. *I did.*

Q. *Would you be able to mark on Plaintiff's Exhibit 1 the point where the impact took place?*

A. *I could.*

Q. *With the court's permission, would you please mark an X at the point where the two vehicles came together?*

(Witness does so)

Attorney: *If it please your Honor, may the jury be permitted to examine the exhibit?*

Court: *Yes. Show it to the jury.*

§ 3:13   Denial of Recollection: "I Don't Remember"

Sometimes, the witness is aware that he once knew a given fact but has forgotten it. He can then truthfully state, "I don't remember." [65] The phrase should not be used as a denial of a fact. For instance, if the defendant, testifying on his own behalf, were asked, "Did you shoot John Jones?" his answer, "I don't remember," would be taken as an admission that he did shoot Jones or, at least, that he may have done so. It certainly is not the same as the blunt denial of the act, "No, I did not!"

There are times when a party may desire to persuade the jury that he has no recollection of certain facts. Thus, the plaintiff may deny that, at the time he was injured, he had any recollection of the existence of a danger which he had failed to avoid. Circumstances may exist under which forgetfulness of a known danger may, nevertheless, be consistent with due care. [66]

If the witness does deny any recollection of a certain event which he should recall, this may be viewed with suspicion unless good reason is furnished to account for the loss of memory. For example, if a blow to the head has caused unconsciousness, there may be some loss of memory for events immediately preceding the injury. This is known as retrograde amnesia. The plaintiff's memory is a blank from the time just prior to the accident until the senses are regained. In many cases, the witness will say that he "does not know what hit him." Loss of memory, after injury, may also include events which occurred after the accident, in which event it is referred to as post-traumatic amnesia. [67]

In the illustration which follows, the plaintiff testifies that she has no personal recollection of the facts of the accident. Such testimony should be corroborated by medical and other proof as to a blow upon the head.

ILLUSTRATIVE THREAD OF TESTIMONY

No Recollection Due to Amnesia [68]

Q. *Do you remember the night in question?*
A. *Yes.*

Q. *Do you remember where you were before this accident?*
A. *Yes, I was at a dance.*

Q. *Do you remember being driven home in a car?*
A. *Yes.*

Q. *Do you recall who was with you and where you were seated?*
A. *Yes. I was seated next to Jack, who was driving.*

Q. *Tell us what, if anything, you remember just prior to the accident?*

A. *I remember getting into the car and riding for a few blocks.*

Q. *Do you know along what streets this automobile was operated on the way home?*

A. *No, I don't.*

Q. *Now, you have been in court this day and you have heard testimony with regard to the accident in which you were involved, is that right?*

A. *That's right.*

Q. *Now, tell us, what is the first thing you recollect about this accident?*

A. *The first thing I knew about the accident was when I was in the hospital.*

Q. *Tell us what you remember when you woke up in the hospital?*

A. *Well, there was a doctor standing next to me and he asked me if I knew what had happened.*
Defendant's Attorney: I object to conversation.
The Court: Objection sustained. Strike out what the doctor asked.

Q. *Do you remember going to the hospital?*

A. *No.*

Q. *What else do you recall at that time?*

A. *Well, that was the time I had found out that I was in the accident, and for quite a few days I really didn't know what was going on.*

Chapter Three

FOOTNOTES

[1] "Where is it, this present? It has melted in our grasp, fled ere we could touch it, gone in the instant of becoming." William James, *Psychology, The Briefer Course* (New York, Harper and Row, 1961), p. 147.

[2] *Ibid.*, p. 148: "The moment we pass beyond a very few seconds our consciousness of duration ceases to be an immediate perception and becomes a construction more or less symbolic. To realize even an hour we must count 'Now! Now! Now!' indefinitely. Each 'now' is the feeling of a separate *bit* of time, and the exact sum of the bits never makes a clear impression on our mind. The *longest bit of duration* which we can apprehend at once so as to discriminate it from longer and shorter bits of time would seem . . . to be about 12 seconds. The *shortest* interval which we can feel as time at all would seem to be 1/500 of a second. That is, Exner recognized two electric sparks to be successive when the second followed the first at that interval."

[3] Louis E. Schwartz, *Trial of Accident Cases,* 3rd ed. (New York, Matthew Bender, 1968), Section 1547.

[4] See Chapter 7.

[5] James, *Psychology, The Briefer Course,* p. 179.
"When a witness testifies, what is he doing? He is reporting his present memory of something he observed in the past, something he saw or heard." Jerome Frank, *Courts on Trial* (Princeton, N.J., Princeton University Press, 1949), p. 17.
See also Chapter 7.

[6] Schwartz, *Trial of Accident Cases,* Section 1547.

[7] James, *Psychology, The Briefer Course,* p. 155.

[8] Alexander A. Schneider, *Introductory Psychology* (New York, Rinehart and Company, Inc., (1951), pp. 212–17.

[9] See Note 2 this chapter.

[10] See Chapter 7.

[11] See Chapter 5.

[12] See Chapter 10.

[13] See Chapter 12.

[14] See Chapter 14.

[15] When a witness remembers, it means that, in addition to having the recollection of the original fact, his mind is aware that it does remember it. William James has defined the phenomenon of memory as *"the knowledge of an event or fact, of which we have not been thinking, with additional consciousness that we have thought or experienced it before."* James, *op. cit.,* pp. 287–89.

[16] See Section 12.02, "Admissibility of Testimony of State of Mind."

[17] See Section 17.06, "The Witness' Age."

[18] See Section 17.07, "The Witness' Poor Health and Sensory Acuteness."

[19] See Section 17.02, "Circumstances Negating Recollection: No Reason to Recall."

[20] See Section 17.08, "The Witness' Education and Intelligence."

[21] People v. Bollott, (1967), 20 N.Y. 2d 600, 233 N.E. 2d 103, 286 N.Y. S 2d 1.

[22] See Section 17.09, "The Witness' Feelings and Emotions."

[23] See Section 3.09, "Refreshing Recollection In Court."

See also Section 17.11, "The Witness' Memory Was Not Refreshed as Claimed."

[24] See Section 17.13, "Exposing Inability to Recall Collateral Matters."

[25] Charles C. Moore, *A Treatise on Facts*, (Northport, L. I., Edward Thompson Co., 1908) Section 805.

People v. Strollo (1908), 191 N.Y. 42, 83 N.E. 573, 575.

[26] Moore, *op. cit.*, Section 805.

[27] *Ibid.*

[28] William W. Wilboure, *The Wheels*, (The MacMillan Company, 1968), New York, p. 271.

[29] As reported by Hy Gardner in his newspaper column, this was not brought out on direct examination but was left for the defense to elicit on cross-examination. When challenged by the defense lawyers, who sarcastically needled him about having an elephantine memory, the photographer made his point clear. "Ordinarily," he admitted, "I might not remember them. But since they came in on a Saturday when I'm usually closed, and the two children got me nervous running around and messing up the studio, they made an indelible impression on my mind."

[30] See Section 17.03, "Recollection Was of an Insignificant and Routine Matter."

[31] *Ibid.*

[32] See Section 17.09, "The Witness' Feelings and Emotions."

[33] *Ibid.*

[34] See Section 17.04, "To Show That Time Has Erased Memory: Earlier Recollection More Accurate."

[35] See Section 17.02, "Circumstances Negating Recollection: No Reason to Recall."

[36] Eston Jackson Asher, Joseph Tiffin, and Frederick B. Knight, *Introduction to General Psychology* (Boston, D. C. Heath & Company, 1953), pp. 207–09.

[37] Norris v. New York etc. R. Co. (1904), 91 N.Y.S. 16.

John Henry Wigmore, *Evidence* 3rd ed. (Boston, Little, Brown and Company, 1940), Section 758.

Schwartz, *Trial of Accident Cases,* Section 150.

[38] De Kremen v. Clothier (1905), 190 App. Div. 481, 96 N.Y.S. 525.

[39] Prentis v. Bates (1891), 88 Mich. 567, 50 N.W. 637, 93 Mich. 234, 53 N.W. 153.

O'Hagan v. Dillon (1879), 76 N.Y. 170.

[40] De Palma v. Weinman (1909), 15 N.M. 68, 103 P. 782.

Kobfalt, Inc. v. Massachusetts Bonding & Insurance Co. (Pa. Com. Pl. 1963), 77 York 121.

[41] Hinkleman v. Pasteelnick (1925), 3 N.J. Misc. 1010, 130 A. 441.

[42] Parsons v. State (Ala.), 38 So. 205.

Edlin v. Commonwealth (1921), 190 Ky. 348, 227 S.W. 462.

State v. Finley (1896), 118 N.C. 1161, 24 S.E. 495.

[43] Wigmore on Evidence, 3rd ed. Section 758.

Irving Goldstein, *Trial Technique* (Chicago, Callaghan and Company, 1935), Section 325.

Robert E. Keeton, *Trial Tactics and Methods* (Boston, Little, Brown and Company, 1954), p. 44.

[44] Millway v. Brown (Mo. App. 1946), 197, S.W. 2d 987.

Benge v. Commonwealth (1944), 298 Ky. 562, 183 S.W. 2d 631.

[45] Stetson v. Godfrey, 20 N.H. 227.

[46] Hardegree v. Riley (1929), 219 Ala. 607, 122 So. 814.

[47] State v. Murphy (1939), 345 Mo. 358 S.W. 2d 398.

United States v. Riccardi (1949), 174 F. 2d 883. But not if the original was willfully destroyed to frustrate cross-examination. People v. Betts (1947), 272 App. Div. 737, 74 N.Y.S. 2d 791.

[48] World Fire & Marine Ins. Co. v. Edmondson (1943), 244 Ala. 224, 12 So. 2d 754.

[49] Levenson v. Commonwealth Syndicate (1940), 24 N.Y.S. 2d 781.

Marti v. Standard Fire Insurance Co. (1942), 127 N.J., L. 591, 23 A. 2d 576.

[50] State v. Smith (1943), 223 N.C. 457, 27 S.E. 2d 114.

[51] Dowling Bros. Distilling Co. v. United States (6th Cir. [Ky.] 1946), 153 F. 2d 353.

[52] United States v. Rappy (2d Cir. [N.Y.] 1946), 157 F. 2d 964, 967.

Moran v. Otis Elevator Co. (1935), 291 Mass. 314, 197 N.E. 11.

Bigelow v. Hall (1882), 91 N.Y. 145.

[53] Eckhardt v. People (Colo. 1952), 250 P. 2d 1009.

People v. Schepps (1922), 217 Mich. 406, 186 N.W. 508.

Richardson v. Nassau Electric R. et al Co. (1920), 190 App. Div. 529, 180 N.Y.S. 109.

[54] State v. Brooks (1948), 136 N.J.L. 577, 57 A. 2d 34, Cf. Jurgiewicz v. Adams (1945), 71 R.I. 239, 43 A. 2d 310.

[55] United States v. Krulewitch (1944), 145 F 2d 76.

Barnard v. Cedar Rapids City Cab Co. (Iowa 1965), 133 N.W. 2d 885.

[56] See Section 17.12, "The Witness Was Coached, His Story Memorized."

[57] James, *Principles of Psychology,* vol. 1, p. 670.

[58] Moore, *op. cit.,* Section 775.

[59] See Section 17.02, "No Reason to Recall," Section 389, "Recollection Was of an Insignificant and Routine Matter."

[60] Schwartz, *Trial of Accident Cases,* Section 1180.

See Francis X. Busch, *Trial Procedure Materials* (Indianapolis, The Bobbs-Merrill Co. Inc., 1961) pp. 197–9 for an illustration of a direct examination to refresh the memory of a witness in an action for breach of contract.

[61] Howard v. McDonough (1879), 77 N.Y. 592.

[62] Papas v. Aetna Insurance Co. (1930), 111 Conn. 415, 150 A. 310.
Schwartz, *op. cit.,* Section 151.

[63] Duncan v. McTiernan (1964), 151 Conn. 469, 199 A. 2d 332.

[64] Schwartz, *op. cit.,* Section 149.

[65] James, *Psychology, The Briefer Course,* p. 287–89.

[66] Tomlinson v. Wilson & Toome Fertilizer Co. (Fla. App. 1964), 165 So. 2d 801.

Stottlemyre v. Missouri Pacific Railroad Co. (Mo. App. 1962), 358 S.W. 2d 437.

[67] Schwartz, *Trial of Accident Cases,* Section 1330.

[68] *Ibid.,* Section 607.

OBJECTIONS TO
PROOF OF RECOLLECTION

TABLE OF CONTENTS

FOUR

OBJECTIONS TO
PROOF OF RECOLLECTION

Each chapter dealing with the proof of a Generic Question is to be followed by a chapter in which the objections which may be made to such proof are delineated. In this way the examining lawyer is made aware of the bounds beyond which he may not go, and his adversary is prepared to recognize possible objections instantly and to know the grounds upon which to object and to have authoritative citations to support his objections. Illustrations are given for each type of objection.

§ 4:01 Objections to Recollections Generally

The Generic Question Q. What is your recollection as to . . . ? is unobjectionable unless the subject matter of the recollection called for is improper. For instance, if the witness is asked for his recollection of something he had heard that would be objectionable if what he heard was hearsay. Or, if he is asked for his recollection as to what he did, it might be objectionable if the answer violated the privilege of doctor and patient. Inasmuch as any recollection is inseparable from the thing recalled, any objection would therefore be addressed to the latter, i.e., if the recollection called for is something seen or heard, reference should be made to the chapter on Objections to Perceptions.[1] Similarly, if the recollection was of some action, reference should be made to Objections to Actions.[2]

There is no objection to a recollection simply because the witness' memory is poor or the recollection is not vivid. Such circumstances merely go to the weight of the testimony but would not be the basis for its exclusion.[3] There may, however, be reasons for the exclusion of evidence offered for the purpose of refreshing recollection, or the use of memoranda which is sought to be introduced into the record as independent evidence. This chapter deals exclusively with the objections which may be interposed when a witness is asked to refresh his recollection by reference to some note or memorandum, or when such a memorandum is offered into evidence.

§ 4:02   (A) Witness Incompetent: He Never Had Personal Knowledge

In defense of an action for breach of an employment contract, the defendant called a witness who was asked by defendant's attorney:

Q. *What is your occupation?*
A. *I am defendant's bookkeeper.*

Q. *How long have you been in defendant's employ?*
A. *Three months.*

Q. *Will you please look at defendant's payroll book and tell us how many days the plaintiff was absent from his job from January 1 to December 31 of last year?*

Plaintiff's Attorney: I object.

The objection should be sustained for the reason that the witness, who had only been employed by defendant for three months, obviously could have no personal knowledge of matters which took place before the commencement of his employment. Having no personal knowledge, he could have no recollection which could be refreshed and thus would be incompetent to give the desired information.[4]

What the witness is competent to do, having worked as a bookkeeper for the defendant for three months, would be to establish that the payroll book was one kept in the regular course of the defendant's business and that it was the regular course of such business to make such records regarding the employees' working hours and pay each day. Such testimony would make it possible for the book to be received under a statute admitting entries made in the regular course of business.[5]

§ 4:03   (B) Testimony Incompetent: Need for Refreshing Recollection

In a personal injury action, the defendant's employee denied on cross-examination that he had given his name either to the police officer who came to the scene or to anyone else. For rebuttal, the plaintiff called the police officer and he was asked by plaintiff's attorney:

Q. *Did you make a memorandum in your notebook after you came to the scene?*
A. *I did.*

Q. *Did you note the name of the motorman in your notebook?*
A. *I did.*

Q. *Look at your book in which you entered it, and tell us, what was the name of the motorman which was given to you at that time?*
Defendant's Attorney: I object.

It was held to be reversible error to overrule this objection and allow the witness to answer because the witness had not "expressed or indicated any loss of memory" regarding the circumstances detailed in his report.[6] A memorandum should not be used to refresh a witness' memory unless it is first ascertained whether the witness can recall the events in question without resort to memorandum.[7] He must also testify that the paper shown him does, in fact, refresh his recollection.[8] Thus, instead of the last question, the witness should be asked:

Q. *Do you now recall the name?*
A. *No, I do not.*

Q. *Would your notation refresh your recollection?*
A. *It would.*

Q. *With the court's permission, will you look at your notebook and tell us whether that refreshes your recollection?*
A. *It does.*

Q. *Now that you have refreshed your recollection, please give us the name of the motorman.*

§ 4:04   Reading From Memorandum

Action on checks. The defense was that they had been altered. The defendant testified in his own behalf and was asked by his attorney:

Q. *What, if anything, did you do when you endorsed the checks?*
A. *I made a memorandum of their dates, amounts, and when payable.*

Q. *Is this the memorandum?*
A. *It is.*

Q. *Look at this memorandum and tell us whether it refreshes your recollection?*
A. *It does.*

Q. *And you now recall the facts to which it relates?*
A. *I do.*

Q. *Will you read the entries to the jury?*
    Plaintiff's Attorney: I object.

The objection should be sustained. It having been shown that the witness' memory was refreshed and that he now has a distinct recollection of the essential facts to which it relates, there is no longer any need to have him read the memorandum, which is not in evidence, to the jury. Instead, the witness should be asked to testify from his recollection.[9]

If the witness had testified that the memorandum did not refresh his recollection, it might have been authenticated by him as a memorandum of a past recollection recorded and gone into evidence.[10] Here, however, the witness is being asked to read from a document which is not in evidence, which is improper.[11]

§ 4:05 Admissibility of the Memorandum Used to Refresh Recollection

In a personal injury action in which plaintiff was struck by an automobile, he called the police officer who came to the scene, who was asked by plaintiff's attorney:

Q. *Officer, what, if anything, did you do when you came to the scene?*
A. *I noted the position of the vehicle and I spoke to the operator of the automobile* (the defendant).

Q. *Officer, is it a part of your duties to make such a report of your investigation?*
A. *It is.*

Q. *And have you, before coming to court, refreshed your recollection by looking at your report?*
A. *I have.*

Q. *Tell us the position in which you found the vehicle.*
A. (The witness describes its position).

O. *And tell us what, if anything, the defendant said to you?*
A. (The witness states the conversation).

Q. *Officer, I show you this paper, marked Plaintiff's Exhibit 8 for identification, and ask you what it is.*

A. *That is my report of my investigation of the accident.*

Plaintiff's Attorney: I offer the report, Plaintiff's Exhibit 8 for identification, into evidence.

Defendant's Attorney: I object.

The objection should be sustained. The witness having testified from memory, the report which he used to refresh his memory is unnecessary and the mere fact that the witness had used the report to refresh his recollection does not make it admissible as original evidence.[12]

A memorandum or other exhibit used to refresh recollection need not be such as would be admissible in evidence [13] and the mere fact that the exhibit was used to refresh recollection does not make it admissible by the party using it.[14]

If the witness cannot testify from memory, but must resort to the paper, that would amount to a use of the memorandum as original evidence, in which event, the writing would have to be authenticated before it could be received as a memorandum of a past recollection recorded.

With respect to the adversary (in this case, the defendant's attorney), the rule is different. When notes or papers have been used by the witness while he is on the stand, the adversary has a right to examine such memoranda.[15] There is a difference of authority, however, as to whether the adversary may compel the production for inspection of memoranda which the witness used to refresh his recollection *outside* the courtroom before being examined. The traditional view is that this may not be done.[16] There is authority giving the judge discretion in the matter.[17] An increasing number of cases have repudiated the distinction and permit inspection of the memoranda, irrespective of when it was used to refresh recollection,[18] on the rationale that "the risk of imposition and the need of safeguard is just as great" in both situations.[19] If the adversary desires, he may have the writing produced to inspect it, to cross-examine the witness thereon and to put the memorandum in evidence insofar as it relates to the testimony of the witness for the purpose of affecting his credibility.[20]

§ 4:06 Use of Prepared Notes—Originals Must be Produced

In a criminal prosecution, a government witness testified while holding certain notes in his hand. The witness was asked by the Attorney General:

Q. *What, if anything, did you do after each and every transaction with the defendant?*

A.   I made a memorandum in my note book.

Q.   Before coming here, did you look at the memoranda?
A.   Yes.

Q.   And did you make notes, based upon the memoranda, before coming here?
A.   I did.

Q.   And does that paper you are now holding in your hand contain those notes made by you based on the memoranda?
A.   Yes.

Attorney General: Refer to your notes to refresh your recollection and tell us about those transactions.

Defense Counsel: I object to the use of those notes by the witness and ask that the original memoranda be produced.

It has been held to be reversible error to permit notes, based upon other memoranda, to be used when the originals are not produced or their absence accounted for.[21] Opposing counsel may demand inspection of the original, and, if it exhibits erasures, alterations, or other irregularities, the jury's attention may be called thereto.[22] If the witness were allowed to testify from notes he made based on other writings, without producing them, "it would be possible for a corrupt witness to withhold the original memorandum and use notes purporting to be copies, fixed in such way as to make a much more favorable showing than that made by the original; the opposing party would be powerless to protect himself against such false showing."[23] Where the witness who has no independent recollection of the facts has, shortly before trial, prepared a memorandum specifically for the purpose of providing a basis for his testimony, the memorandum does not stimulate his memory. Therefore he may not authenticate its accuracy and it would be improper to permit him to testify from the memorandum.[24]

However, a summary prepared by the witness from his own multitudinous daily reports covering a long period of time may be used to refresh the recollection of the witness when the originals have been made available to the adversary for his study and use on cross-examination.[25]

§ 4:07   When Original Notes Were Deliberately Destroyed

Defendant was on trial for conspiracy to resell tickets at excessive prices. The People's Witness had "tapped" the defendant's wires for four days and overheard nineteen conversations, and could identify the voice of each of the four defendants as he heard it over the telephone. He was questioned by the District Attorney:

Q. Did you dictate the complaint against the defendants?
A. I did.

Q. Did you read the complaint after it was typed by the complaint clerk?
A. I did.

Q. Was the complaint in accord with your recollection of what you heard on the telephone?
A. Yes, it was.

Q. Do you have an independent recollection of the conversations by each of the defendants?
A. No.

Q. Would the complaint refresh your recollection of the conversation?
A. Yes.

Q. Will you please use the complaint to refresh your recollection and tell us the substance of those conversations?

Defense attorney asked for and obtained leave to conduct a preliminary cross-examination. He asked:

Q. Did you make any notes at the time you listened in to those conversations?
A. I did. I took them down in shorthand.

Q. What did you do with the shorthand notes?
A. I transcribed them in longhand every day and then destroyed the shorthand notes.

Q. What did you do with the longhand notes?
A. I used them to dictate the complaint and then I destroyed them.

Q. As an experienced detective, didn't you know that you would be called upon to testify as to those conversations?
A. I did.

Q. And you were aware of the fact that the defendants had a right to cross-examine you about your notes?

A. Yes.

Q. And you don't have any independent recollection of those conversations, except for what you read in the complaint, isn't that so?

A. Yes.

Q. Did you destroy both the original shorthand and the longhand transcript of your notes?

A. Yes, I did.

Q. Did you do that deliberately?

A. Yes.

Q. Did you destroy your notes in order to avoid such cross-examination as to their accuracy?

A. Frankly, yes.

Defense Attorney: I object to the use of the complaint in view of the fact that the original records were deliberately destroyed.

While, ordinarily, any paper may be used to refresh recollection, it has been held that, where the original record was deliberately destroyed to frustrate cross-examination, the court should not permit a transcript to be used. Under the circumstances appearing in the illustration, it would be incredible that the witness could recall the details of many conversations, which had taken place on different days a long time prior to the trial, without using a written record. In effect, this is more than merely refreshing the recollection of the witness and is the equivalent of using the record itself. This being so, the original should be used or its absence accounted for. It being clear that the police officer has no independent recollection and depends upon transcripts based upon original notes which he has deliberately destroyed, he should not be allowed to read such rehashed transcripts into the record.[26]

§ 4:08   Use of Copies of Records Made by Others

On a trial for income tax evasion, a witness for the government testified that he had made certain payments to the defendant. He was then asked by the Attorney General:

Q. *Do you recall the exact dates and amounts you paid the defendant?*
A. *No.*

Q. *I show you these photostats of records, look them over, and tell us if they refresh your recollection?*
A. *They do.*

Q. *Please refer to those records and give us the dates and amounts?*

    Defense Counsel: May I have a voir dire?
    Court: Yes.

Q. *Did you make those photostats?*
A. *No.*

Q. *Were they made under your direction?*
A. *No.*

Q. *Do you have an independent recollection of the dates and amounts, now that you have looked at the photostats, so that you can testify without looking at them again?*
A. *No, I would have to refer to them.*

    Defense Counsel: I object to the use of the photostats.

It has been held to be reversible error to allow copies of records to be used when the copies were made by someone other than the witness and not under his direction. While the witness might use the copies to refresh his recollection, he may not testify directly from the photostats.[27] The witness should not bring into court specially prepared, extensive testimonial notes to use instead of the original records.[28]

§ 4:09 Use of Memorandum as Independent Evidence

A witness was asked on direct examination:

Q. *Do you have a present recollection of the details?*
A. *I do not.*

Q. *I show you these photostatic records and ask you if they contain the details?*
A. *They do.*

Attorney: I offer the photostats in evidence.

Adversary: I object.

The objection should be sustained. It is one thing to awaken a slumbering recollection of an event, but quite another to use a memorandum of a recollection as independent evidence. "In the former case it is quite immaterial by what means the memory is quickened; it may be a song, or a face, or a newspaper item, or a writing of some character. It is sufficient that by some mental operation,   however mysterious, the memory is stimulated to recall the event, for when so set in motion, it functions quite independently of the actuating cause." [29] In the illustration given, the witness' memory is not being refreshed, and he has no independent recollection, and therefore the documents used are actually being used as independent evidence without first being properly authenticated and are, therefore, objectionable.[30]

A memorandum can be introduced as original evidence of a past recollection which was recorded provided the following facts first appear:

- That the witness once had personal knowledge of the facts contained in the memorandum.

- That the memorandum does not now refresh his recollection and that he is unable to recollect the facts even after looking at the memorandum.[31]

- That the memorandum was made contemporaneously with the event or nearly so.[32]

- That it was made by the witness,[33] or under his direction,[34] or was verified by him when made.[35]

- That the witness knows that it was correct when made[36] and accurately represents his own past knowledge[37] and that the statements are true.[38]

Chapter Four

FOOTNOTES

[1] See Chapters 8 and 9.
[2] See Chapter 11.
[3] State v. Poulos (Kan. 1966), 411 P. 2d 694.

[4] Kaplan v. Gross (1916), 223 Mass. 152, 111 N.E. 853.

Kirschner v. Hirschberg (1904), 90 N.Y.S. 351.

[5] CPLR.

[6] U.S. Homes, Inc. v. Yates (Iowa 1970), 174 N.W. 2d 402, a witness should not be allowed to see or use a memorandum, as a present memory refresher, unless it appears he is unable to testify without it.

John Henry Wigmore, *Evidence* 3rd ed. (Boston, Little, Brown and Company, 1940), Section 758.

[7] City of Minneapolis v. Price (1969). 280 Minn. 429, 159 N.W. 2d 776.

[8] National Labor Relations Board v. Federal Dairy Co. (2d Cir. [N.Y.] 1962), 297 F. 2d 487.

[9] National Ulster Bank v. Madden (1889), 114 N.Y. 280.

[10] See Section 3.11, "Use of Memorandum When Memory Cannot Be Refreshed."

[11] See Section 6.06, "Contents of a Writing."

[12] National Labor Relations Board v. Hudson Pulp & Paper Corp. (5th Cir. [Fla.], 1960), 273 F. 2d 660.

Rogalsky v. Plymouth Homes, Inc. (1968), 100 N.J. Super. 501, 242 A. 655.

Howard v. McDonough (1879), 77 N.Y. 592, 593.

Leach v. State (Tenn. 1967), 420 S.W. 2d 641.

[13] State v. Sletta (Minn. 1967), 155 N.W. 2d 392.

Maryfield Plantation, Inc. v. Harris Gin Co. (1967), 116 Ga. App. 744, 159 S.E. 2d 125; while memorandum as to telephone conversation with party was inadmissible, witness could use such memoranda to refresh his memory.

U.S. Homes, Inc. v. Yates, any document regardless of authorship may be employed to revive present memory.

[14] Mercer v. Department of Labor and Industries (Wash. 1968), 442 P. 2d 1000.

Wigmore on Evidence, (3rd ed.), Section 763.

[15] Shell Oil Co. v. Pou (Miss. 1967), 204 So. 2d 155.

Falcone v. New Jersey Bell Telephone Co. (1967), 98 N.J. Super. 138, 236 A. 2d 394.

[16] Morton v. Carelli (Alaska 1968), 437 P. 2d 335.

People v. Gezzo (1954), 307 N.Y. 385, 121 N.E. 2d 380.

Tibbetts v. Sternberg (1870), 66 Barb (N.Y.), 201.

State v. Taylor (1947), 83 Ohio App. 76, 77 N.E. 2d 279.

Wigmore on Evidence, (3rd ed), Section 762, Note 1.

[17] Goldman v. United States (1942), 316 U.S. 129.

Peters v. State (Ark. 1970), 450 S.W. 2d 276, the matter of requiring a witness, who has refreshed his memory before testifying by an out-of-court inspection of memoranda or records, but who does not use them in court, to produce them for inspection, lies within sound discretion of the trial court.

Needleman v. United States (5th Cir. [Fla.] 1958), 261 F. 2d 802, cert. dismissed 362 U.S. 600, rehearing denied 363 U. S. 858, Annot. 82 ALR 2d 473 and 7 ALR 3d 181, 247.

State v. Audette (Vt. 1970) 264 A. 2d 786, rulings authorizing or refusing production of memoranda used off the stand for purposes of refreshing recollection are properly made as discretionary rulings, made in promotion of fairness and justice, according to the circumstances of the case.

[18] People v. Scott (1963), 29 Ill. 2d 97, 193 N.E. 2d 814.

State v. Mucci (1957), 25 N.J. 423, 136 A. 2d 761.

State v. Hunt (1958), 25 N.J. 514, 138 A. 2d 1.

State v. Deslovers (1917), 40 R.I. 89, 100 A. 64.

[19] *Wigmore on Evidence,* (3rd ed), Section 762.

[20] *Ibid.,* Section 763.

Proposed Rules of Evidence for the United States District Courts and Magistrates, Rule 6.12.

[21] U.S. Homes, Inc. v. Yates, it is not permissible for a witness to testify or refresh his recollection from a copy of, or notes made from, an original record or memorandum, where it is possible to produce the original writing.

[22] Jewett v. United States (9th Cir. [Wash.] 1926), 15 F. 2d 955, 956.

[23] *Ibid.*

[24] Great Atlantic & Pacific Tea Co. v. Nobles (Fla. App. 1967), 202 So. 2d 603.

[25] O'Quinn v. United States (10th Cir. [Okla.] 1969), 411 F. 2d 78.

[26] People v. Betts (1947), 272 App. Div. 737, 74 N.Y.S. 2d 791.

[27] Delaney v. United States (3d Cir. [N.J.] 1935), 77 F. 2d 916, 917.

[28] National Labor Relations Board v. Federal Dairy Co. (2d Cir. [N.Y] 1962), 297 F. 2d 487.

cf. Thompson v. United States (5th Cir. [Fla.] 1965), 342 F. 2d 137.

[29] Jewett v. United States (9th Cir. [Wash.] 1926), 15 F. 2d 955.

[30] *Ibid.,* p. 956,

[31] United States v. Kelly (2d Cir. [N.Y.] 1965), 349 F. 2d 720.

Noumoff v .Rotkvich (1967), 88 Ill. App. 2d 116, 232 N.E. 2d 107, 82 ALR 2d 473, 520.

[32] United Sand & Material Corp. v. Florida Industrial Commission (Fla. 1967), 201 So. 2d 451.

Mercer v. Department of Labor and Industry (Wash. 1968), 442 P. 2d 1000.

[33] Brown v. Provident Loan Soc. (1940), 282 N.Y. 453, 26 N.E. 2d 975.

[34] Walsh v. Chicago Rys. et al. (1922), 303 Ill. 339, 135 N.E. 709.

[35] State v. Ehlers (1922), 98 N.J.L. 236, 119 A. 15, 25 ALR 999.

[36] McElhaney v. Rouse (1966), 197 Kan. 136, 145 P. 2d 241.

[37] Dahl-Beck Electric Co. v. Rogge (Cal. App. 1969), 80 Cal. Rptr. 440; if based on hearsay statements of others, it is inadmissible.

[38] *In re* Fink's Estate (1941), 343 Pa. 65, 21 A. 2d 883.

PROOF OF
PERSONAL KNOWLEDGE

TABLE OF CONTENTS

PROOF OF
PERSONAL KNOWLEDGE

A witness who testifies to matters within his knowledge is testifying from his recollection of such matters. What then is the distinction between Knowledge and Recollection? This chapter points out the distinction and shows how the witness may better persuade the jury that he does, in fact, possess the knowledge of the facts to which he has testified.

Q. WHAT DO YOU KNOW OF YOUR PERSONAL KNOWLEDGE AS TO . . . ?

§ 5:01 Definition of Personal Knowledge

The *Generic Question Q. What do you know of your personal knowledge as to . . .?* is all inclusive. A witness could testify to anything and everything in response to such a question. Any witness is competent to testify who has evidentiary facts within his personal knowledge.[1] Whenever a witness testifies to a fact, unless there is some indication to the contrary, the presumption is that he is testifying from personal knowledge even though the question does not specifically call for it. The phrase, "of your personal knowledge," incorporated in the question is not, however, mere surplusage, for not all knowledge is personal knowledge.[2] Personal knowledge is such as was gained by the witness through his senses[3] and is not mere hearsay or speculation.

Of course, if the information being asked for is obviously within the witness' personal knowledge, the formal question is not stated in full. For example, a witness is not asked *Q. What do you know of your personal knowledge as to your occupation?* A person's occupation is something within his own personal knowledge and he may testify thereto if it is relevant to the case.[4] The witness is asked directly, *Q. What is your name? Q. Where do you reside? Q. What is your occupation? etc.* If the full formal question was to be put each and every time a witness is asked for some data within his knowledge, the questions would become unnecessarily irritating and time consuming. Nonetheless, there are occasions when the matter is obviously not within the personal knowledge of the witness and the incorporation of the phrase, "of your personal knowledge," in the question will add to the weight of the answer and lessen the possibility of an objection being interposed on the ground that the question calls for hearsay.

§ 5:02 Knowledge and Recollection Distinguished

There are two types of knowledge. One might be called "general knowledge" and the other "specific recollections." Obviously, a witness cannot testify as to what he "knows" unless he also "recalls" it. The difference is this: if the witness is aware not only of the data itself, but in addition, has a recollection of when, where, and how he came to acquire the information, as, for example, that it was something he saw, heard, sensed, or experienced, at a certain time and place, his testimony is then not "general knowledge" but a "specific recollection."

Every witness has a vast store of information or general knowledge which he has accumulated over the years, the exact source of which he would be unable to trace, nor is it always essential that he be able to do so. This chapter deals with such general knowledge.

Even though the witness speaks from personal knowledge this does not always mean that he can or will be asked to recall precisely when or where or under what circumstances he acquired such knowledge. It is only when the assertion is both important and controverted that the witness is likely to be called upon to state the exact source of his information and to pinpoint the precise time, place, or circumstance under which he learned the particular fact.

§ 5:03 Enhancing the Weight of Testimony Based Upon Personal Knowledge

In determining what additional facts are to be elicited from the witness, or what arguments may be advanced in summation to persuade a jury that the witness did, in fact, possess the knowledge he lays claim to, the following items should be considered:

- The witness' identity and background.
- The witness' capacity to know and understand.
- The accessibility of the information to the witness.
- The witness' knowledge of collateral details.

§ 5:04 The Identity and Background of a Lay Witness

Any statement of "fact" is only as credible as its source.[4] For this reason, the identity and background of the witness is of the greatest importance. In spite of this, the courts strictly limit the extent to which an attorney is permitted to question a witness to develop his background and antecedents. Thus, testimony by a witness on direct examination for the purpose of demonstrating that he is a person of good character is generally not allowed.[6] The rationale of this limitation is said to be that evidence of the witness' good qualities is immaterial unless his character has first been attacked.[7] Some testimony along these lines, however, is allowed. The witness is permitted to establish his identity, age, education and occupation and other similar data when this is offered for some reason other than to show good character. The adverse party has a right to know the true name and identity of every witness.[8] At times, the identity of a person may be the very issue on trial, in which event the subject may be gone into in great detail.[9]

It is recognized that the age of a witness may affect his perception, understanding, and recollection of what he has perceived [10] and that the witness is competent to testify as to his own age.[11] So, too, the testimony of a witness as to his antecedents and background is acceptable to demonstrate that a witness is competent to understand the nature of an oath,[12] or, if the witness is an expert, this testimony is received to show that he is qualified to express expert opinions.[13]

§ 5:05   The Witness Has the Capacity to Know and Understand

The occupation, profession, and learning of the witness is always competent, as it may indicate the opportunity he had to obtain the knowledge he claims to possess, as well as his capacity to understand the facts to which he testifies.[14] One who is interested in a certain field acquires and retains much information in that field which would go unnoticed by another.[15] Through learning, "perceptions carry meanings far beyond what is given directly to the senses." [16] From the fact that the witness has successfully completed certain schooling or training, we can infer that he has the requisite intelligence to do so. "The degree of credit to be given to a witness must chiefly depend upon his means of knowing the facts testified to; upon his general understanding and intelligence together with the integrity and truth with which he is supposed to narrate them." [17]

§ 5:06   The Expert's Background and Qualifications

The expert witness, by contrast, is permitted to testify as to his background in detail. The preliminary examination of a witness produced as an expert with respect to his capacity to know and understand is directed toward showing *in detail* his professional education, learning, and experience, and whether he possesses that knowledge which will qualify him to express expert opinions and which will indicate that his opinions are based on a sufficient knowledge and correct interpretation of the pertinent facts.[18] For example, should it be a medical witness who is about to testify, the mere fact that the witness is a licensed physician is *prima facie* sufficient to qualify him to express medical opinions, but no trial lawyer would be content merely with that. The adversary may even offer to concede the doctor's qualifications. If so, the attorney will thank him for the offer but politely insist upon having the expert's qualifications stated upon the record. He cannot be compelled to accept such a concession[19] and should take advantage of this opportunity to elicit the details of the background, learning, experience, and accomplishments of his learned witness.

Before trial the attorney will question his witness to discover all of his qualifications so that they may be spread upon the record. If the witness is a doctor, he will be questioned as to his being licensed to practice, the medical school he attended and date of graduation, his internships, his various degrees, hospital connections, affiliations with medical societies and academies, his special studies here and abroad, his specialty, the extent of his private practice, any governmental service, his experience in his specialty, his teaching experience, and books and articles he has published.

ILLUSTRATIVE THREAD OF TESTIMONY

Qualifying a Neurosurgeon[20]

Q. *Are you a duly licensed and practicing physician of this state?*
A. *I am.*

Q. *You are a graduate of what recognized medical institution?*
A. *_____ Medical College.*

Q. *In what year did you graduate?*
A. *That was in 19__.*

Q. *After that did you do any other institutional work?*
A. *I was an intern at the _____ Hospital. Then went to the _____ for neurology and neurosurgery.*

Q. *Did you receive a certain degree in neurology from the University of _____?*
A. *Yes, I received an M.S., in neurology and Doctor of Philosophy in neurology.*

Q. *And what did you do after that?*
A. *After my internship I went into private practice in the field of neurology and neurosurgery in this city, where I have been ever since, ex-*

*cept for a period of three and one half years when I served in the
United States Army.*

Q. When you say that you were in the medical services for the United
    States Government, you omitted to tell us what rank you came out with.
A. The rank of Lieutenant Colonel.

Q. What is your specialty?
A. My specialty is neurosurgery.

Q. And briefly for the record, what is neurosurgery?
A. That deals with the diseases of the nervous system which are amenable
    to surgical treatment, as the brain, the spinal column, the peripheral
    nerves, and as they can be benefited or treated by operation.

Q. Are you presently connected with any of the local hospitals?
A. Yes.

Q. What is your connection with them, and what hospitals?
A. I am attending neurosurgeon at the _____ Hospital and a consult-
    ing neurosurgeon at the _____ Hospital and the _____ Hospi-
    tal and the _____ Hospital.

Q. Are you a member of any medical or surgical societies, and what are
    they?
A. Well, there is the County Medical Society here and the American Medi-
    cal Association, the Academy of Neurologists, the American College of
    Surgeons.

Q. And in that connection, in your experience as a neurological surgeon,
    or specializing in surgical neurology, have you performed many opera-
    tions upon the human skull?
A. Yes.

Q. Now Doctor, have you for many years done operative procedure on the
    skull?
A. Yes, for about 25 years.

Q. In that connection have you done a great number of operations?
A. I suppose I have done as many as the next man. Yes, I have done many.

Q. In recent years have you made a study of the blood vessels of the brain and the causes and effects of cerebral hemorrhages?

A. Yes.

Q. Will you tell us about your research?

A. Ever since my training period I have been especially interested in the blood vessels of the brain as the source or mechanism of the disorders of the nervous system. In the last nine years I have made a special study of the arteries and veins of the brain as seen in x-ray film. We inject dyestuff in the artery going to the brain and see the blood vessels of the brain in various disorders.

Q. And in that period, can you tell me how many cases you have studied in specific instances of brain hemorrhage and their causes and consequences?

A. In the last seven years I have had about 80 cases of cerebral hemorrhage where I have studied them with special tests and other methods generally used.

Q. Do you teach the subject?

A. Yes, I teach neurosurgery at _____ Medical School.

Q. Now, have you written any books which have been published dealing with your specialty?

A. Yes, I have two books.

Q. What are their titles and by whom published?

A. They are _____ and _____, published by the _____ Company and they deal with the brain.

Q. Have you had any other published articles in your particular specialty?

A. Yes, about fifty-five published papers on the nervous system.

§ 5:07 The Information Was Accessible to the Witness

At times, it is perfectly obvious that the knowledge asked for would be known to the witness. At other times, the information called for is such as is not commonly known and would not be known to the witness unless he had been exposed to it, or it was accessible to him.[21] It may be something he learned through special study or experience. In such event it is important to show that the knowledge, not known to all, was accessible to the witness.

§ 5:08   Character Witness' Knowledge of Reputation

In those instances when character evidence is admissible,[22] it is not character (what a person is) but rather, reputation (what people think he is).[23] The character witness is not permitted to state what the reputation of the person is unless and until he shows that he moved in the circles or lived in the community where the matter would likely be discussed and that he had access to others from whom he could obtain such knowledge.[24] His own personal knowledge or opinion of the person's character is generally unacceptable.[25] Theoretically, it is not the witness' own evaluation that counts, but rather that of the community. Nevertheless, the witness usually will give the details of his own contact with the individual in question and the jury will naturally infer that his own opinion coincides with that of the community.

ILLUSTRATIVE THREAD OF TESTIMONY

Knowledge of Reputation of Defendant in a Criminal Case

Q.   *What is your age?*
A.   *I am nineteen years of age.*

Q.   *What is your occupation?*
A.   *I am a college student.*

Q.   *Do you know the defendant?*
A.   *I do.*

Q.   *For how many years do you know him?*
A.   *Approximately ten years.*

Q.   *Under what circumstances do you know him?*
A.   *I first met him in the Boy Scouts—we lived near each other. We have many mutual friends. In high school we played on the same basketball team. We attended the same church.*

Q.   *And has your association with him continued?*
A.   *Yes, sir.*

Q.   *Do you live in the same neighborhood as he does?*
A.   *I do.*

Q. Do you know other people in the community who know him?

A. Yes, I do.

Q. And have you had occasion to speak to other people in the community about the defendant?

A. Yes, many times.

Q. And do you know his reputation in the community for being a law abiding person?

A. Yes, sir, I do.

Q. What is his reputation for being a law abiding person?

A. It is very good.

§ 5:09 Added Information Accessible to Skilled Witness

There are witnesses who are not to be deemed "expert" witnesses nor mere "laymen." They occupy a status between these two and are called "skilled witnesses." They may be called upon to express opinions but, primarily, they are called upon to enlighten the jury as to the facts. These witnesses have had access to knowledge not accessible to the ordinary witness and, as a result of such specialized knowledge or expertise, are enabled to aid the jury by furnishing added depth to the subject under consideration and to illuminate obscure details, and make them more meaningful and persuasive. For example, any ordinary layman has knowledge enough to recognize an object as being made of wood, although there are some materials which so closely imitate wood as might mislead the layman but not the carpenter. The ordinary witness might not be able to identify the type of wood as being pine, oak, or maple, whereas the carpenter could do so. One who has made a close study of wood can observe many more facts about it of which even a carpenter would be oblivious. In the Lindbergh kidnapping case, for example, there was the testimony of such a person, who was able to demonstrate, from the design of the grains of the wood in a ladder found at the scene, that the wood from which the ladder was constructed came from the attic of the defendant's home.[26]

At times, the line of demarcation between an expert and a skilled witness is indistinct. Either type of witness is permitted to testify as to his background, access to, and ability to interpret data in his specialty.

The skilled witness, when he calls attention to, and explains obscure facts, is neither giving expert opinions, nor is he "usurping" the function of the jury. On the contrary, he is furnishing factual evidence which enables the jury to function more intelligently. For example, a witness may not express a legal conclusion, but should an issue arise involving foreign law which the court cannot judicially notice, a witness who has the requisite knowledge of such foreign law may testify to it. Such foreign law is then a factual matter and not a legal consideration.

ILLUSTRATIVE THREAD OF TESTIMONY

Knowledge of Foreign Language and Law

Q. *What is your profession?*
A. *Lawyer.*

Q. *Are you a member of the bar of this state?*
A. *I am.*

Q. *Were you formerly a resident of Poland?*
A. *I was.*

Q. *What was your profession while in Poland?*
A. *I was a lawyer.*

Q. *Were you connected with any legal institution while in Poland?*
A. *Yes. I was professor of Law at Warsaw University.*

Q. *How long did you practice law in Poland?*
A. *20 years.*

Q. *So that you have, if we lay modesty aside, quite an exhaustive knowledge of Polish law?*
A. *I believe so.*

Q. *I take it that you are familiar with the Polish language?*
A. *I am.*

Q. *Have you had experience in translating documents?*
A. *Yes. I have had extensive experience in translating Polish documents, court records and other writings.*

Q. *I show you a document marked Exhibit 1 for Identification and ask you what that purports to be?*
A. *A Polish record of marriage.*

Q. *Have you at my request examined the document carefully and translated it into English?*

A. *I have.*

Q. *Are you familiar with the form of record of marriage permitted by Polish law in 19—?*

A. *I am.*

Q. *Is that document in the form permitted by Polish law?*

A. *It is.*

Q. *Can you state whether that record Exhibit 1 for Identification is certified in accordance with Polish law?*

A. *I can.*

Q. *Is the certificate properly attested in accordance with Polish law?*

A. *It is.*

Q. *Under what signature and seal is it attested?*

A. *It is attested under the signature and seal of the official in charge of vital statistic records.*

Q. *Under Polish law would such a certificate as Exhibit 1 for Identification be conclusive evidence of a marriage?*

A. *It would.*

Q. *I show you a document marked Exhibit 2 for Identification, and ask you whether it is a true and correct translation prepared by you of the Polish document, Exhibit 1 for Identification?*

A. *It is.*
    Attorney: I now offer the certified record of marriage, Exhibit 1 for Identification together with its translation, Exhibit 2 for Identification into evidence.

§ 5:10   Knowledge of Custom or Usage

Evidence of custom or usage is properly admissible when the subject matter is not of common knowledge.[27] Proof of custom and usage is sometimes mistakenly thought of as opinion evidence to be given by an expert. This is not so. The witness telling the jury what is the custom and usage is testifying as to a matter within his personal knowledge and is not expressing an expert opinion.[28]

Custom and usage may only be proven by one who is familiar with what is customary and usual and uniformly followed under similar circumstances, time, and place. The background and experience of the witness may be shown whenever that would make it more likely that he would have the requisite knowledge of the pertinent custom and usage. Formal education is not essential. His knowledge may have been acquired by study or experience. Thus, a witness was permitted to testify as to the custom and usage of the trade with respect to the installation of safety releases on the inside of the doors of insulated truck bodies, notwithstanding that the witness had no more than a high school education and had never drafted any plans for truck body construction but had been in the business of building truck bodies (including the insulated type) for 35 years and had studied literature concerning such construction.[29]

Proof of custom and usage is used in many ways.[30] Often, the proof of what is uniformly done is offered as evidence of what was probably done in the case at bar. For example, proof of mailing. An individual who mailed a letter can testify from his recollection as to his actions in mailing the particular letter.[31] However, should it become necessary for an insurance company to prove the mailing of a specific notice of premium when thousands are mailed daily, it would be impossible for anyone to recall mailing one particular notice. In such a situation, the custom and usage followed in mailing the notices may be described and this will give rise to an inference that the notice at issue was mailed in accordance with such custom.[32]

Most frequently the proof of what is customarily, usually, and uniformly done and was the approved practice is offered as evidence of what should have been done in the case at bar. Thus, proof of what safety measures are customarily taken in a given trade may furnish the basis for the jury's finding that similar measures should have been taken in the case at bar and that a failure to do so amounts to an absence of due care, negligence, or malpractice.

To illustrate, let us take the case of a child who has been badly burned by contact with a hot return pipe which was not insulated. The mere proof that the pipe was uncovered and uninsulated would not, necessarily, constitute negligence but, should it appear that custom and usage called for such insulation, a *prima facie* case of negligence would be made out.[33] However, proof of custom and usage would not be permitted without first laying a foundation by showing that there was, in fact, a recognized custom and that the witness had knowledge that there was such a usage and what it was.

The witness called to establish the existing custom and usage may be questioned as to his background and experience insofar as that would bear upon his access to information and knowledge about the usage in the trade. His examination is similar to that of an expert.[34] So, he may be asked about his business or profession, the details of his experience in his field, his educational background, licenses held, affiliations with technical organizations or societies, his specialized reading and study, his familiarity with the custom and usage, what it is, and what would usually be done in compliance with such practice.

ILLUSTRATIVE THREAD OF TESTIMONY

Custom and Usage as to Heating Pipes

Q. *What is your business or occupation?*
A. *Registered architect, City of New York, State of New York.*

Q. *How long have you been an architect in the state?*
A. *Thirty-one years.*

Q. *And where do you have your office?*
A. ―――――――――――――――――.

Q. *Now, to your knowledge, was there a custom and usage in the architectural field in 19__ with respect to return pipes such as these shown on these photographs, Plaintiff's Exhibits 1 and 2?*

Defendant's Attorney: I object to that as being incompetent, irrelevant, and immaterial.

The Court: Objection overruled.

The Witness: Yes.

Q. *And what was the custom and usage?*

Defendant's Attorney: I object to that in that there is no foundation. That evidence of alleged custom and usage, of little value as it is, should never be permitted unless the identical conditions are first established.

The Court: Counselor, I am going to sustain the objection only in view of the fact that a foundation has not been properly laid as yet, in the Court's opinion. You should inquire into his experience with multiple dwellings of a similar character and nature.

Plaintiff's Attorney: Of course I had in mind that we are dealing with a professional who carries a license.

The Court: A man may be an architect constructing bridges and edifices like the Grand Central Palace and museums and a lot of buildings that are not comparable.

Plaintiff's Attorney: That is quite true.

Q. And have you at any time been affiliated with the City of New York?
A. Yes.

Q. In what capacity?
A. As architect for the City of New York, Department of Hospitals, Department of Public Works.

Q. Are you a member of any society of architects?
A. Yes, American Institute of Architects.

Q. And have you attended meetings of that society and conversed with other members of your profession on these subjects?
A. I have.

Q. In addition to your own work having to do with being the architect for certain buildings in New York City, have you kept up with the literature on this subject?
A. I have.

Q. And have you drawn plans and specifications for apartment houses here in the City of New York?
A. I have.

Q. And in addition to that have you from time to time had anything to do with alterations and changes in apartment houses?
Defendant's Attorney: I object.
The Court: Objection overruled. I take it that the purpose is not to show all the buildings but to show his contact, knowledge, and association gained from having such kind of work.
A. Yes, sir.

Q. *And are you familiar with practices and customs with respect to the maintenance of steam pipes and heating pipes in apartment houses within the City of New York in 19___?*

A. *I am.*

Q. *Are you familiar with heating arrangements particularly with respect to steam pipes and return pipes such as those which are shown on the photographs, Plaintiff's Exhibits 1 and 2?*

A. *Yes, I am familiar with that.*

Q. *Now, sir, what was the custom and usage in 19___ in the City of New York with respect to return pipes such as are shown in Plaintiff's Exhibits 1 and 2?*
Defendant's Attorney: Objected to as being incompetent, immaterial.
The Court: I will take it. Overruled.

A. *The custom and usage is that return pipes are not permitted to be exposed. We put lining on them and cover them or box them in.*

Q. *Now, when you cover them, what is the usage with respect to the type of covering employed?*

A. *Asbestos, different kinds of felt.*

Q. *Insulation, is that right?*

A. *That's right.*

Q. *You also said that they can be boxed in. What does that mean?*

A. *Well, it depends on the size of the pipe.*

Q. *I am talking about a pipe this size (indicating).*

A. *You box it in, put on a four-inch boxing so it is all covered.*

§ 5:11   Knowledge of Collateral Details

That a witness has knowledge of a fact may often be demonstrated by having him testify regarding incidental details which are peripheral to the subject under inquiry. When a witness asserts that he has personal knowledge of a certain subject, it is logical to assume that he would know the details of that subject and of other closely related subjects. *Such detailed knowledge, especially of matters not known to the general public, will go far in persuading the jury that the witness knows whereof he speaks.* For example, if the question is the identity and relationship of a claimant to an uncle who left an estate, his assertion that he knows that he is a nephew of the deceased would be greatly strengthened if he also had knowledge of the details of his alleged uncle's life, family, habits, mannerisms, etc. Particularly is this true when such data, while seemingly unimportant, is of a nature that would not be known unless the witness was indeed related to the decedent.[35]

§ 5:12 Facts Judicially Noticed

It is not necessary to offer evidence of certain facts which are judicially noticed.[36] The term "judicial notice" is very elastic and embraces an endless variety of facts including matters of law; records of court proceedings; political, historical and geographical matters; the course of nature; matters of art and science; and various aspects of human, animal, and vegetable life which are generally known.

While it may save expense, the reliance on judicial notice is not always most effective and persuasive. There is an advantage in calling living witnesses and producing exhibits to establish facts which, while they may be judicially noticed, are not known to the jury. Proof of these matters beyond any doubt, by unimpeachable witnesses and unquestionably accurate books and records, will add to the impression of reliability of the entire case.

In the event it is decided to request the court to take judicial notice, the attorney should be sure that he has complied with any statutory requirement or rule requiring notice to his adversary;[37] and that he can call the court's attention to the place where the fact or law may be found which is to be judicially noticed.[38] Better still, he should have with him in court, the encyclopedia, almanac, dictionary, law book, medical book, public map, paper or record, table, etc., with a marker at the page where the pertinent data is set forth. A fact will not be judicially noticed merely because it can be ascertained by reference to such a document or publication but it will help.

ILLUSTRATIVE THREAD OF TESTIMONY

Calling on the Court to Judicially Notice A Fact

Attorney: I respectfully ask Your Honor to take judicial notice that the sun set on November 20th of last year at ___ P.M. and I have here and submit the World Almanac, to refresh Your Honor's recollection of that fact.

§ 5:13 How to Negate Knowledge

The objective in calling a witness may be to have him negate rather than assert his personal knowledge. He may want to deny knowledge of a given fact for either of two reasons, (a) to create an inference that a certain fact did not exist or a certain act did not occur, else he surely would have known of it or, (b) that he had no notice or knowledge of a certain fact which concededly did exist or event which did occur.

To illustrate the first, a witness who mailed a letter wishes to establish that it was not returned to him by the post office (therefore presumably it was delivered to the addressee). To do this, after testifying to the details of the mailing and that there was a return address on the envelope, he might show that it was his duty to receive and open all the incoming mail, that any letter returned would come to his attention, and that, in fact, he has no knowledge of it ever having been returned.[39]

Another illustration might be that of a defendant in a personal injury action who denies any notice or knowledge on his part of the existence of a defect or dangerous condition so that he may not be charged with fault in failing to correct it. The denial of knowledge by such a witness may be strengthened by other testimony indicating the likelihood that the denial is true as, that the witness had no opportunity to know the fact or that he knew other contrary facts. For example, a denial of any knowledge that a device was dangerous would be re-enforced by testimony of its prior extensive use without accident.

ILLUSTRATIVE THREAD OF TESTIMONY

No Knowledge of any Prior Accident [40]

Q. *How long have you been employed by the defendant?*
A. *Twenty years.*

Q. *Do you remember when the slide in question was installed?*
A. *I do.*

Q. *How long was it in operation before the accident?*
A. *Ten years.*

Q. *How many people do you estimate, go on that device during the year?*
A. *About 40,000.*

Q. *During the time that you have been connected with the defendant, have you of your own knowledge, known of any other similar accident which happened upon this device at any time?*
A. *No, sir, I have not.*

Illustrative of the second objective might be the testimony of the plaintiff in a personal injury action who may want to prove that he had no knowledge and was unaware of the danger which confronted him and was, therefore, free from contributory negligence.

ILLUSTRATIVE THREAD OF TESTIMONY

No Knowledge of Defect Because of Shadow [41]

Q. *Before you fell, at the point where you fell, what, if anything did you notice about the sidewalk?*

A. *There was a shadow across the sidewalk.*

Q. *And what caused the shadow, if you know?*

A. *The tree at the curb.*

Q. *Where did the shadow extend?*

A. *All the way across the sidewalk.*

Q. *Now, did you see anything in the shadow up to the time of the accident?*

A. *No.*

Q. *What was the first thing that called your attention to the presence of anything there?*

A. *When I tripped and fell, I looked down and saw the rock there.*

Q. *Had you any knowledge whatsoever as to the presence of a rock there before you fell?*

A. *No, absolutely not.*

Chapter Five

FOOTNOTES

[1] Dennis v. Prisock (Miss. 1969), 221 So. 2d 706.
[2] Tenta v. Guarly (Ind. App. 1966), 221 N.E. 2d 577.
[3] Dennis v. Prisock.
[4] Wilkins v. Hester (Ga. App. 1969), 167 S.E. 2d 167.

[5] United States v. Ventresca (1965), 85 S.Ct. 741, 751.

[6] See Section 12.05, "Background and Antecedents Indicative of Credibility."

[7] *Ibid.*

[8] *Wigmore on Evidence,* (3d ed.), Section 1395 *et. seq.*

[9] In the novel *Buried Alive* by Arnold Bennett (George H. Doran Company, New York), the entire plot hinges upon the development of this simple question and answer:

"Q. Your name is Priam Farll? . . .

"A. It is, said Priam. . . ."

The records of the trial of any contested claim of kinship will reveal to what great lengths one may go to corroborate identity. In *The Recluse of Herald Square* (1964, The Macmillan Company, N.Y.), by Surrogate Joseph A. Cox, the author tells of the difficulties in establing the true identity of Ida Wood to the discomfiture of more than a thousand false claimants who had woven a fantastic cocoon of lies, forgeries, and subterfuges.

[10] See Section 17.06, "The Witness' Age."

See also Section 19.09, "Age, Sex, Intelligence."

[11] See Section 6.02, "Incompetent Testimony: One's Own Age."

[12] See Section 12.10, "A Child's Competency to Take an Oath."

[13] See next section.

[14] Waters v. Commonwealth (1939), 276 Ky. 315, 124 S.W. 2d 97.

[15] See Section 19.14, "Lack of Interest or Attention."

[16] Ernest R. Hilgard, *Introduction to Psychology* (New York, Harcourt, Brace and Company, Inc.,), 301–02.

[17] People v. Rector (1838), 19 Wend. (N.Y.) 569.

[18] Slocovich v. Orient Mutual Insurance Co. (1888), 108 N.Y. 56, 141 N.E. 802.

[19] Counihan v. J. H. Webelovsky's Sons, Inc. (1957), 5 App. Div. 2d 80, 168 N.Y.S. 2d 829; but the court may curtail an unduly protracted qualification of an expert witness.

[20] Louis E. Schwartz, *Trial of Accident Cases,* 3rd ed. (New York, Matthew Bender, 1968), Section 1316.

George W. Lacey, *Scientific Automobile Accident Reconstruction* (New York, Matthew Bender, 1966), pp. 15–20, qualifying an accidentologist.

[21] Fox v. Allstate Insurance Co. (Utah 1969), 453 P. 2d 701.

[22] See Section 6.07, "Character Evidence in a Civil Trial."

[23] *In re* Monaghan (Vt. 1966), 222 A. 2d 665.

Wigmore on Evidence, 3rd Ed., Section 920.

[24]*Ibid.,* Section 928.

[25] Sherrill v. Phillips (Tex. Civ. App. 1966), 405 S.W. 2d 627.

See also Proposed Rules of Evidence for the United States District Courts and Magistrates, Rule 4–05, which permits proof of character by testimony as to reputation or in the form of an opinion or by specific instances of conduct.

[26] Francis X. Busch, *Trial Procedures Materials* (Indianapolis, The Bobbs-Merrill Co. Inc., 1961), pp. 341–348.

State v. Hauptmann (1935), 115 N.J.L. 412, 180 A. 809; examination by Attorney General Wilentz.

[27] Jacobson Electric Co. v. Rome Fastener Corp. (Conn. 1968), 238 A. 2d 415.

[28] McGee v. Adams Paper & Twine Co. (1966), 271 N.Y.S. 2d 698.

McCarthy v. Kroger Co. (D.C. Pa. 1966), 260 F. Supp. 384.

[29] Frankel v. Styer (3d Cir. [Pa.] 1967), 386 F. 2d 151.

[30] Saviola v. Sears, Roebuck & Co. (Ill. App. 1967), 232 N.E. 2d 4.

[31] See Section 10.10, "Proving Whether Something Was Mailed."

[32] Olson v. Hardware Mutual Fire Insurance Co. (Wis. 1968), 156 N.W. 2d 429; it must be shown that the custom and practice was followed in each case. See also, *Wigmore on Evidence*, (3rd ed) Section 95.

[33] Thomas v. Busch (1956), 1 N.Y. 2d 702, 134 N.E. 2d 71.

[34] See Section 5.06, "The Expert's Background and Qualifications."

[35] See Section 17.13, "Exposing Inability to Recall Collateral Details." See also Section 19.31, "Cross-Examination as to Details."

[36] *Wigmore on Evidence*, (3rd ed) Section 2565, *et seq.*

Schwartz, *Trial of Accident Cases*, Section 908, *et seq.*

[37] The Uniform Judicial Notice of Foreign Law Statute has been enacted in many states. See *Wigmore on Evidence*, (3rd ed) Section 2573.

[38] Turnage v. Gibson (1947), 211 Ark. 268, 200 S.W. 2d 92.

[39] See Section 10.10, "Proving Whether Something Was Mailed."

[40] Schwartz, *Trial of Accident Cases*, Section 6210.

[41] *Ibid.*, Section 5306.

OBJECTIONS TO PROOF
BASED ON PERSONAL KNOWLEDGE

TABLE OF CONTENTS

OBJECTIONS TO PROOF
BASED ON
PERSONAL KNOWLEDGE

Not everything that a witness knows may be testified to. He may not testify to anything at all unless he is competent to take an oath. Nor is it enough that the witness himself is competent if the testimony is incompetent and improper; based on hearsay; merely a conclusion on his part; irrelevant to any issue in case; or immaterial and prejudicial. It may be difficult to recognize that a given question calls for such improper testimony in time to prevent the harmful answer. The illustrations and discussions which follow should facilitate timely objections.

§ 6:01   Incompetent Witness

The plaintiff was a young child who was called as a witness in his own behalf and was asked by the court:

Q. *How old are you?*
A. *I am eight years old.*

Q. *What grade are you in?*
A. *The third grade.*

Q. *Do you remember how you got hurt?*
A. *Yes.*

Q. *That was three years ago, do you know how old you were then?*
A. *I was five.*

Q. *Do you go to Sunday School?*
A. *No.*

Q. *Do you know what it means to take an oath?*
A. *No.*

Q. *Do you know what would happen to you if you told a lie?*
A. *No, what would happen?*

Opposing Counsel: I object to the witness' being sworn.

A witness may not be sworn unless he is competent to take an oath.[1] At common law, the child would be presumed to be competent if he was 14 years of age,[2] a lesser age may be fixed by statute.[3] When the child is under age, he must be examined as to his competency.[4] This is usually done by the court, who must then decide, *in his discretion,* whether the child is competent. Inasmuch as this child does not know what it means to take an oath and has no conception of the punishment for false testimony, the court would be justified in refusing to administer the oath.[5] An unsworn statement may not be the basis for a judgment.[6]

Should the attorney, when preparing for trial, find that a witness who is a young child is not aware of the nature of an oath, he should then insist that the child's parents or a clergyman teach the child regarding the obligation to tell the truth. In one case when it appeared at the trial that the child was ignorant of the nature of an oath, the attorney asked for an adjournment for the purpose of having the witness receive instruction from a priest, and, on the adjourned day, he was re-examined by the court and found to be ready to take an oath.[7]

Where there are no other witnesses to the occurrence and the testimony of the child is the only evidence available, that fact should be made known to the court before the child is presented. The court should stretch a point under such circumstances. The refusal to allow a child to be sworn with the result that his action was dismissed has been considered to be an abuse of discretion.[8]

The competency of the witness is determined as of the time he is to testify and not as of the time of the occurrence.[9] The important consideration is not the child's knowledge of theology. In determining the child's competency, the court is not limited solely to the age or his appreciation of the nature of an oath, but should also consider his capacity to be a witness. This means that the child may be sworn if the court finds that, at the time of the occurrence, he had the mental capacity to receive an accurate impression of the occurrence, that his memory is sufficient to retain a recollection, a present capacity to express in words his recollection, and he can understand and answer simple questions about the event.[10]

Even if the child cannot possibly be sworn, it is still possible to make use of the child on the issue of damages by using the child as an exhibit to demonstrate his injuries. He need not be sworn for such a purpose.[11]

In a criminal case involving child abuse, statutes often permit the child's unsworn statement to be received, provided there be some slight corroboration.[12]

§ 6:02   Incompetent Testimony

One's Own Age

The defendant was charged with statutory rape of complainant, a female under the age of consent. The complainant took the stand, was sworn, and asked by the District Attorney:

Q. *Do you remember the ___ day of _____ 19__ (date of alleged rape)?*
A. *I do.*

Q. *Did you see the defendant on that day?*
A. *I did.*

Q. *What was your age on that day?*

Defense Attorney: I object.

No one remembers being born, so the witness' knowledge of the date of his own birth must necessarily be based upon what the witness had been told by others and is, therefore, hearsay. In a criminal case where the essential element of the alleged crime would depend entirely upon the proof of age, as that the complainant was under the age of consent on the day of the rape, this must be established beyond a reasonable doubt and may not be based upon hearsay.[13]

In a case where the age of the witness is not a vital factor, the witness will be permitted to testify as to his own age as this is considered in the nature of evidence of pedigree which is an exception to the hearsay rule.[14] However, in a statutory rape case, where age is an essential element of the crime, the complainant's age may be established by producing a certified birth certificate or other authenticated records or documents[15] or by the testimony of her mother or father or anyone who has personal knowledge that she was born on a given date.[16]

§ 6:03   Use of Medical Treatise on Direct Examination

A physician testifying on behalf of plaintiff in a personal injury action was asked, on direct examination by Plaintiff's Attorney:

Q. *Do you know Dr. Charles L. Dana as a medical writer?*
A. *Yes, sir.*

Q. *Are his writings on nervous diseases accepted by the profession as authoritative?*
A. *They are.*

Q. *Have you read his recent book on Traumatic Neurosis?*
A. *I have.*

Q. *Does this statement from Dr. Dana's book on Traumatic Neurosis, which I shall read to you, agree with your own understanding of the subject?*

Defendant's Attorney: I object.

The plaintiff's doctor is attempting to bolster his testimony by showing that another eminent authority has written something which is in accord with the witness' testimony. A medical book may not be read on direct examination to corroborate the expert's opinion. The statements contained in the book are not under oath nor is there any opportunity to cross-examine the author, therefore, they are hearsay.[17]

Some courts will take *judicial notice* of the contents of recognized scientific treatises[18] or permit them to be read into evidence on direct examination.[19] Local cases and statutes should be checked.

The plaintiff will be allowed to introduce the contents of treatises and periodicals when offered for the purpose of showing that the defendant reasonably should have known certain facts therein set forth. For example, in an action against a drug company for injuries allegedly resulting from the use of a certain drug, articles in medical journals were properly admitted, even though hearsay, for the limited purpose of showing that the drug company reasonably should have known of the existence and nature of the ill effects of using the drug.[20]

While scientific treatises cannot be used on direct examination, they may be used in cross-examining opposing experts to test their learning.[21]

§ 6:04   Another Person's Knowledge

Plaintiff sought to hold the defendant liable for negligent entrustment of his automobile in that he had loaned his automobile to the driver although he knew that the driver was incompetent and reckless. The plaintiff was testifying and was asked by Plaintiff's Attorney:

Q.   *Is the defendant Smith (owner of automobile) a neighbor of yours?*
A.   *He is.*

Q.   *And is the codefendant, Jones, who was driving Smith's automobile, also a neighbor?*
A.   *He is.*

Q.   *How long have you known them both?*
A.   *I know them for ten years that I have been living on that street.*

Q.   *Did you have personal knowledge of Jones' driving experience?*
A.   *I did.*

Q.   *Did the defendant Smith know that Jones had been arrested for reckless driving prior to the day he loaned him his automobile?*

Defendant's Attorney: I object.

A witness may testify as to his own knowledge of facts which are relevant, but for him to say that another person possessed certain knowledge is a mere conclusion and of no probative value.[22] The plaintiff in this type of case is usually required to produce evidence of actual knowledge by the owner Smith of the incompetence or recklessness of the driver Jones. In an action of this type, for negligent entrustment, facts such as prior arrests of the driver may be shown but only if they were known to the automobile owner. The theory is that if the owner knew of such facts he should not have loaned his automobile to one whom he had reason to believe was an incompetent driver. The plaintiff's conclusory statement that the defendant had such knowledge is inadmissible[23] but plaintiff may show actual knowledge on the part of the owner[24] and he may be allowed to prove circumstances which would raise a question of fact as to whether the defendant did have personal knowledge.[25]

§ 6:05   Oral Testimony of Ownership

Action to recover for personal injuries sustained by plaintiff while walking down the stairs of the premises where he resided. The defense was a general denial. Plaintiff was testifying in his own behalf and was asked by Plaintiff's Attorney:

Q. *Where do you reside?*
A. *At 100 Main Street.*

Q. *Do you recall the ____ day of _____, the day you were injured?*
A. *I do.*

Q. *Tell us what happened.*
A. *I was going down the stairs leading to the ground floor when my foot got caught and I fell.*

Q. *How long have you lived at 100 Main Street?*
A. *Five years.*

Q. *Who owns the premises, if you know?*

Defendant's Attorney: I object.

The ownership of the land was an element of the case which had to be established by the plaintiff by competent evidence. The question is objectionable as it calls for the opinion and oral testimony of the witness as to the ownership of the land.[26] Even the owner himself, it has been held, may not testify that he is the owner, where that is a material issue, because such testimony amounts to merely a conclusion as to the meaning of facts or documents not in evidence.[27] Title to land may not be proved by oral testimony.[28]

The proper way to prove title to land when that is at issue is to produce the deed or a duly certified copy thereof. The defendant having put in a general denial, this should have alerted the plaintiff's attorney who could have taken steps to examine the defendant before trial or to obtain an admission of ownership.[29]

Proof of the allegation of ownership is not always essential. Liability for negligence will be imposed upon a defendant who was in control of the premises[30] or who created the dangerous condition even though he is not the owner.[31] Possession, operation, dominion, or control may be established in various ways by direct or circumstantial evidence. For example, proof that the defendant acted in a certain manner may indicate that he was in control as by collecting rents,[32] making repairs,[33] taking out insurance on the property,[34] or otherwise exercising dominion.

With respect to ownership of chattels, the rule is different and any witness who has seen manifestations of ownership may testify directly as to ownership [34a] and, of course, the owner himself could do so.[35]

§ 6:06 Contents of a Writing

In an action for breach of contract the plaintiff was asked by Plaintiff's Attorney:

Q. After those conversations with the defendant, was a writing drawn up and signed by both of you?

A. Yes.

Q. Do you know what that writing contained?

A. I do.

Q. Will you tell the court and jury what was stated in that writing?

Defendant's Attorney: I object.

Whenever a party seeks to prove the contents of a writing, he must produce the original writing.[36] This is required by the best evidence rule which has been applied with respect to the proof of a contract,[37] or other instrument,[38] construction plans,[39] letters,[40] photographs,[41] x-rays,[42] writing assignments,[43] checks and stubs,[44] a mere memorandum on a slip of paper,[45] or a card bearing an address and telephone number.[46]

A witness may testify to the contents of a writing which is not produced provided its absence is properly accounted for. This may be by proof that it was lost and could not be found after diligent search,[47] or was in the possession of the adverse party who refuses to produce it after getting a notice to produce or after being served with a subpoena *duces tecum*.[48]

It is unnecessary to produce the writing when a party seeks to prove an existing collateral fact, even though it is evidenced by a writing as, for example, the fact of birth, marriage, citizenship, etc.[49] Testimony at a prior trial [50] or a confession [51] may be proved without producing the written transcript, unless it was reduced to writing and subscribed by the witness.[52] Where the writing is of minor importance, collateral to the issue and no useful purpose would be served in requiring its production, it need not be produced.[53] A mere label or tag attached to an object which only serves to identify it need not be produced [54] and if the writing is inscribed on something which makes it impossible or inconvenient to be brought into court, as, for example, the wall of a building, its production will be excused.[55]

§ 6:07   Irrelevant Testimony: Character Evidence in a Civil Trial

In a civil action the defendant calls a "character" witness who is asked by Defendant's Attorney:

Q. *Do you know the defendant?*
A. *I do.*

Q. *How long do you know him?*
A. *Ten years.*

Q. *How did you come to know him?*
A. *He is my employee.*

Q. *How often have you seen him and spoken to him during that time?*
A. *I see him every day, he is directly under my supervision.*

Q. *What do you personally know about him as to his honesty and trustworthiness?*

Plaintiff's Counsel: I object.

This testimony, being offered in a civil trial, is objectionable because in a civil case, the character of the parties is not ordinarily at issue and is irrelevant.[56] Thus, in an action for breach of contract, the only question would be whether the defendant performed his obligation, and it would make no diffference whether or not he was of good character.[57] In an action based on negligence, the issue is whether the party exercised due care on that particular occasion and not whether he was usually careful. Evidence of reputation for care, lack of care, or proneness to accident is inadmissible on the issue of negligence.[58]

Generally, evidence of a person's character or a trait of his character is not admissible for the purpose of proving that at a given time he acted in conformity therewith.[59] It is felt that character evidence is of slight probative value and tends to distract the jury from the main question of what actually happened on the particular occasion. "It subtly permits them to reward the good man and to punish the bad man because of their respective characters despite what the evidence in the case shows actually happened." [60] Exceptions are made in criminal cases.[61]

Character evidence will be relevant in a civil case where it is directly in issue, as for example, in an action for defamation,[62] or malicious prosecution,[63] or for negligent entrustment of a motor vehicle to an incompetent driver,[64] or in an action for wrongful death on the issue of the value of decedent's life.[65]

In criminal cases, the accused is permitted to introduce evidence of his good character, which may then be rebutted by the prosecution for the purpose of raising an inference that he would not be likely to commit the offense charged.[66] Such evidence may create a reasonable doubt of guilt.[67] The defendant, in a criminal case, may give evidence of the bad reputation of the victim of the alleged crime and that this had come to his knowledge in support of defendant's claim that he acted in self-defense.[68] In a criminal case, evidence of the character of a witness may be offered to attack or support his credibility.[69]

When character evidence is admissible, what is received is not evidence of character but rather evidence of reputation. The proof consists of testimony of the witness that he knew people who lived in the community in which the person in question resided and that he knew the person's reputation among people with whom he associated.[70] A good reputation may also be shown by negative evidence as by the testimony of a witness to the effect that he has lived in the same community as the defendant for a length of time and has never heard anything said against him.[71]

The prior habit of care of a plaintiff has been allowed when the plaintiff is unable to testify because of a Dead Man's Statute [72] and possibly when the action is for the death of decedent when there are no eyewitnesses.[73]

While evidence of a general disposition of carefulness or recklessness of a party or of prior similar acts indicating such a disposition will not be admissible in civil actions,[74] if the evidence is offered concerning the habit of a *third person,* knowledge of which is sought to be charged against a party to the action, such evidence is admissible. For example, if the action is brought against an employer because of the negligence of an employee, it may be possible to obtain punative damages on proving that the employee was incompetent and nevertheless retained by him in his employ.[75] In such an action, the plaintiff may show the specific prior acts of incompetence on the part of the employee as well as the fact that this was known to the employer.[76] Some cases hold that actual knowledge is necessary,[77] but others hold that it is enough to show that such prior acts of incompetence were generally known in the community.[78]

Evidence of a custom or usage in a trade or profession is also admissible,[79] but only if it is the general practice or usage in the trade, not what was done in one specific instance.[80]

§ 6:08   Evidence of One's Good Conduct

A witness in a civil case was asked on direct examination:

Q. *Did you receive an honorable discharge from the Army?*
Opposing Counsel: I object as being irrelevant and immaterial.

The general rule is that, unless character is directly at issue,[81] direct examination as to specific acts indicating good character are not admissible.[82] The rationale is that it will be assumed that the witness is a person of good character and that, unless and until that is challenged, all evidence on that score is held to be irrelevant.[83] Similarly, in a civil case the war record or patriotism of a witness is irrelevant unless it has first been challenged.[84]

§ 6:09   Wealth or Poverty

Plaintiff sues to recover a debt allegedly owed by defendant. The defense is that the debt was paid. Defendant, testifying in his own behalf was asked by Defendant's Attorney:

Q. *Did you borrow the sum of $1000 from the plaintiff?*
A. *I did.*

Q. *Do you now owe him any money?*
A. *I do not, the money was repaid by me on November 12th.*

Q. *What was your net worth on November 12th?*

Plaintiff's Attorney: I object.

The subject of the wealth or poverty of a party is generally inadmissible and irrelevant and immaterial.[85] It may be prejudicial if the testimony is designed to create sympathy or favor because rich and poor should stand equally before a bar of justice and, where the purpose of the testimony is to create sympathy for one or prejudice against the other party, it is clearly improper.[86] Thus, in a personal injury action, the fact that the defendant was wealthy [87] or insured [88] or that the plaintiff was obliged to work because her husband was disabled [89] would be equally improper and reversible error.

In the problem set forth, the testimony is offered, not out of any improper motive to create prejudice, but to give rise to an inference that the defendant, having the means to pay the debt, did pay it. However, the testimony would be rejected as irrelevant because "experience is not sufficiently uniform to raise a presumption that one who has the means of paying a debt will actually pay it,"[90] especially where there has been no attempt by the adverse party to show that he (defendant) was, in fact, unable to pay.[91]

If the evidence offered was that defendant did *not* have enough money with which to pay the debt, that would be received as raising an inference that the debt was *not* paid.[92]

Proof of a party's wealth or poverty is admissible whenever it is relevant to an issue as, for example, in an action for defamation it has a bearing upon the damages to be assessed.[93] In an action to recover for brokerage commissions where it must appear that the alleged prospective purchaser was not only ready and willing but also *able* to purchase, this makes the finances of the purchaser a material fact to be established.[94]

§ 6:10   Number of Children and Marital Status

Plaintiff is testifying in a personal injury action and is asked by his attorney:

Q. *State how many children you have and give us their ages and names.*

Defendant's Attorney: I object.

Questions asked of the plaintiff in a personal injury suit as to the number of his children are deemed immaterial and prejudicial because they tend to arouse sympathy in his favor.[95]

The facts regarding marital status and number of children will be received if directly pertinent to the issue as, where there is a claim by a young person of loss of sex power,[96] or with respect to a claim for the loss of consortium of a wife, where the value of her services may depend upon the size of the family of which she took care.[97]

§ 6:11   Prejudicial Testimony

Defendant in a personal injury action was being cross-examined when he was asked by Plaintiff's Attorney:

Q. *Are you covered by liability insurance?*

Defendant's Attorney: I object and move for a mistrial.

Any reference to the fact that the defendant would be indemnified by an insurance company is usually condemned as being prejudicial and likely to improperly influence the jury.[98]

The existence of insurance may be shown if presented as being relevant to the issues. For example, the fact that the defendant took out an insurance policy would be relevant and proper where defendant denied control of a certain building, and this evidence would be received on the limited issue of his control. It may also be relevant as proof of agency, bias or prejudice of a witness.[99]

Chapter Six

FOOTNOTES

[1] Olshandsky v. Prensky (1918), 185 App. Div. 469, 172 N.Y.S. 856.

Rosche v. McCoy (1959), 397 Pa. 615, 156 A. 2d 307.

John Henry Wigmore, *Evidence* 3rd ed. (Boston, Little, Brown and Company, 1940), Section 505.

[2] People v. Sims (Ill. App. 1969), 251 N.E. 2d 795.

[3] N.Y., Crim. Pro. L. § 60.20 (2), 12 years.

[4] Olshandsky v. Prensky.

Wigmore on Evidence, 3rd ed. Section 505.

[5] Rittenhouse v. North Hempstead (1960), 11 App. Div. 2d 957, 205 N.Y.S. 2d 564.

State v. Sanchez (1961), 11 Utah 2d 429, 361 P. 2d 174.

Musil v. Barron Electric Co-op. (1961), 13 Wis. 2d 342, 108 N.W.2d 652.

[6] Razaukas v. New York Dugan Bros. (1942), 263 App. Div. 1002, 33 N.Y.S. 2d 411, aff'd. 289 N.Y. 592, 43 N.E. 2d 722.

[7] Comm. v. Tatisos (1921), 238 Mass. 322, 130 N.E. 495.

Wigmore on Evidence (3d ed.), Section 1821.

[8] State v. Allen (Wash. 1967), 424 P. 2d 1021.

[9] Sommers v. Deepdale Gardens Third Corp. (1958), 178 N.Y. 2d 516.

[10] Wheeler v. United States (1895), 159 U.S. 523, 524, 40 L. Ed. 244, 16 Sup. Ct. Rep. 93.

State v. Manlove (1968), 79 N.M. 189, 441 P. 2d 229.

See also Section 12.10, "A Child's Competency to Take an Oath."

[11] Yellow Cab Co. v. Henderson (Md. 1944) 39A. 2d 546.

[12] N.Y. Crim. Pro. L. § 60.20 (2) (3).

[13] People v. Lammes (1924) 208 App. Div. 533, 203 N.Y.S. 736.

[14] Antelope v. United States (10th Cir. 1950), 185 F. 2d 174, 175.

West Main v. New York State Liquor Authority (4th Dept. 1955), 285 App. Div. 756, 141 N.Y.S. Section d 46; adopted, illegitimate child, liquor violation.

People v. Mishlanie (1960), 24 Misc. 2d 277, 204 N.Y.S. 2d 450.

Wigmore on Evidence, 3rd ed. Section 667.

[15] Wistrand v. People (1904), 213 Ill. 72, 72 N.E. 748.

Beglin v. Metropolitan Life Insurance Co. (1903), 173 N.Y. 374, 66 N.E. 102.

[16] People v. Lammes, *supra.*

[17] Rice v. Clement (Fla. App. 1966), 184 So. 2d 678.

Carr v. Ingle (Okla. 1964), 395 P. 2d 650.

[18] Lewandowski v. Preferred Risk Mutual Insurance Co. (1966), 33 Wis. 2d 69, 146 N.W. 505.

Wigmore on Evidence, 3rd ed. Section 2580, Note 1.

[19] Permitted in Alabama, Massachusetts, Nevada, Pennsylvania, Wisconsin, and possibly Wyoming. See *Wigmore on Evidence,* 3rd ed. Sections 665b and 1693.

See also Note 84, ALR 2d 1338.

[20] Kershaw v. Sterling Drug Inc. (5th Cir. [Miss.] 1969), 415 F. 2d 1009.

[21] See Section 18.16, "Revealing That Expert's Opinions Are Contrary to Scientific Authorities."

[22] Saunders v. Vikers (Ga. App. 1967), 116 Ga. App. 733, 158 S.E. 2d 324.

[23] *Ibid.*

[24] Harris v. Smith (Ga. App. 1969), 167 S.E. 2d 198.

[25] Guedon v. Rooney (1939), 160 Or. 621, 87 P. 2d 209, 120 ALR 1298. See also Note 120 ALR 1313–1315.

Wigmore on Evidence, 3rd ed. Sections 249, 250.

[26] Hodge v. Ellis (Tex. Civ. App. 1954), 268 S.W. 2d 275.

Wigmore on Evidence, 3rd ed., Section 1960, Note 2.

The question "How often do you go to James Brown's camp?" would be improper because it embodies within itself the assumption that James Brown is the owner. State v. Oliver (Me. 1967), 225 A. 2d 398.

[27] Little v. Georgia Power Co. (Ga. 1949), 52 S.E. 2d 322, 324.

[28] State *ex rel.* Walton v. Superior Court for Snohomish County (1943), 18 Wash. 810, 140 P. 2d 554.

Wigmore on Evidence, 3rd ed., Section 1960, Note 2.

Ibid., Section 1246.

[29] Louis E. Schwartz, *Trial of Accident Cases,* 3rd ed. (New York, Matthew Bender, 1968), Section 5255.

[30] Lipsitz v. Schecter (1966), 377 Mich. 685, 142 N.W. 2d 1.

Cullings v. Goetz (1961), 256 N.Y. 287, 176 N.E. 398.

[31] Webster v. Triple Cities Const. Co. (1939). 258 App. Div. 760, 14 N.Y.S. 2d 771.

[32] Jewell v. Price (1934), 12 N.J. Misc. 737, 174 A. 518.

[33] Virzi v. Kings County Lighting Co. (1938), 255 App. Div. 889, 8 N.Y.S. 2d 239.

[34] Pagano v. Leisner (1955), 5 Ill. App. 2d 223, 125 N.E. 301.

[34a] Strickland Transportation Co. v. Ingram (Tex. Civ. App. 1966), 403 S.W. 2d 192.

[35] General Motors Acceptance Corp. v. Elder (1960), 24 Ill. App. 2d 55, 163 N.E. 2d 7.

Pichler v. Reese (1902), 171 N.Y. 577, 64 N.E. 441.

[36] Herzig v. Swift & Co. (2nd Cir. [N.Y.] 1945), 146 F. 2d 444.

Butler v. Mail & Express Publishing Co. (1902), 171 N.Y. 208, 211, 63 N.E. 951.

[37] Mahaney v. Carr (1903), 175 N.Y. 454, 67 N.E. 903.

[38] Wiggins v. Stapleton Baptist Church (Ala. 1968), 210 So. 2d 814.

[39] Continental Casualty Co. v. Wilson-Avery, Inc. (Ga. App. 1967), 156 S.E. 2d 152.

[40] Griffin v. H. L. Peterson Co. (Tex. Civ. App. 1968), 427 S.W. 2d 140; even if letters contained warranties, statements as to contents of letters by party claiming breach of warranty would not be admissible in evidence over objection that letters themselves constituted the best evidence of their own contents.

[41] People v. Doggett (1948), 83 Cal. App. 2d 405, 188 P. 2d 792.

[42] Daniels v. Iowa City (1921), 191 Iowa 811.

Cellamare v. Third Avenue Transit Corp. (1948), 273 App. Div. 2d 260, 77 N.Y.S. 2d 9.

Patrick v. Tilman & Matkin (1955), 154 Okla. 232, 7 P. 2d 414.

[43] Schack v. Wormser (1920), 185 N.Y.S. 580.

[44] Matter of Carrington (1914), 163 App. Div. 544, 148 N.Y.S. 952.

[45] Taft v. Little (1904), 178 N.Y. 127, 70 N.E. 211.

[46] Young v. People (1906), 221 Ill. 51, 77 N.E. 536.

[47] Kearney v. Mayor of New York (1883), 92 N.Y. 617.

[48] Mather v. Eureka Mower Co. (1890), 118 N.Y. 629, 23 N.E. 993.

In a criminal case, secondary evidence of the contents of any writing which appears prima facie to be in the possession of the accused, may be given and no notice to produce is necessary. People v. Gibson (1916), 218 N.Y. 70, 112 N.E. 730.

[49] Commonwealth v. Dill (1892), 156 Mass. 226, 30 N.E. 1016.

[50] People v. Colon (1953), 281 App. Div. 354, 119 N.Y.S. 2d 503.

[51] People v. Giro (1910), 197 N.Y. 152, 90 N.E. 432.

[52] Kain v. Larkin (1892), 131 N.Y. 300, 30 N.E. 105.

People v. Apicello (1937), 275 N.Y. 222, 9 N.E. 2d 844, 12 ALR 40 (dying declaration).

Wigmore on Evidence, (3rd ed) Section 1450.

[53] *Ibid.,* Section 1253.

[54] Wright v. State (1898), 88 Md. 436, 41 A. 795.

Carroll v. Gimbel Brothers, New York (1921), 195 App. Div. 444, 186 N.Y.S. 737.

[55] Kansas Pacific Railway Co. v. Miller, 2 Colo. 442

[56] Beach v. Richtmyer (1949), 275 App. Div. 466, 90 N.Y.S. 2d 332.

Greenberg v. Aetna Insurance Co. (Pa. 1967), 235 A. 2d 582.

[57] *Wigmore on Evidence,* (3rd ed.) Sections 64, 65.

[58] Thornburg v. Perleberg (N.D. 1968), 158 N.W. 2d 188.

James and Dickinson, "Accident Proneness and Accident Law," 63 *Harvard Law Review,* 1950, 791–94.

[59] Proposed Rules of Evidence for the United States District Courts and Magistrates, Rule 4-04.

[60] *Ibid.*

California Law Revision Commission Rep. Rec. & Studies (1964), p. 615.

[61] See Note 66 *et seq.,* this section.

[62] *Wigmore on Evidence,* (3rd ed.) Sections 66 and 70.

[63] Hart v. McLaughlin (1900), 51 App. Div. 411, 413, 64 N.Y.S. 827.

[64] See Section 103, "Another Person's Knowledge."

[65] Gamble v. Hill (Va. 1967), 156 S.E. 2d 888.

[66] People v. Van Gaasbeck (1907), 189 N.Y. 408, 82 N.E. 718.

Proposed Rules of Evidence for the United States District Courts and Magistrates, Rule 4-04 (a) (1).

[67] People v. Trimarchi (1921), 231 N.Y. 263, 131 N.E. 910.

[68] People v. Rodawald (1904), 177 N.Y. 408, 70 N.E. 1.

Proposed Rules of Evidence for the United States District Courts and Magistrates, Rule 4-04 (a) (2).

[69] Charles T. McCormick, *Handbook of the Law of Evidence* (St. Paul, Minn., West Publishing Co., 1954), Sections 155–61.

Proposed Rules of Evidence for the United States District Courts and Magistrates, Rule 4-04 (a) (3).

[70] United States v. Battaglia (7th Cir. [Ill.] 1968), 394 F. 2d 304.

State v. Woods (Mo. 1968), 428 S.W. 2d 521.

People v. Van Gaasbeck.

[71] People v. Van Gaasbeck.

[72] McElroy v. Force (Ill. 1967), 232 N.E. 708.

[73] Gibson v. Casein Manufacturing Co. (1913), 157 App. Div. 46, 141 N.Y.S. 887.

Petricevich v. Salmon River Canal Co. (Idaho 1969), 452 P. 362.

[74] Granadier v. Surface Transportation Corp. (1946), 271 App. Div. 460, 66 N.Y.S. 2d 130.

[75] Cleghorn v. The New York Central & Hudson River Railroad Company, (1874), 56 N.Y. 44.

[76] Park v. New York Central & Hudson Railroad Co. (1898), 155 N.Y. 215, 49 N.E. 674.

[77] See Section 13.01, "Witness Incompetent to Testify as to State of Mind of Another."

[78] McCarthy v. Ritch (1901), 50 App. Div. 145, 69 N.Y.S. 129.

[79] See Section 5.10, "Knowledge of Custom or Usage."

[80] Garthe v. Ruppert (1934), 264 N.Y. 290, 190 N.E. 643.

Marolia v. American Family Mutual Insurance Co. (1968), 38 Wis. 2d 539, 157 N.W. 2d 674.

[81] Stafford v. Morning Journal Assoc. (1894), 142 N.Y. 598, 37 N.E. 625; answer denied plaintiff's allegation of good reputation.

[82] Kesten v. Forbest (1948), 273 App. Div. 648, 78 N.Y.S. 2d 769.

Thus the fact that a witness for the defense testified "I have served as a foreman of the grand jury in my county" was held to be irrelevant and properly excluded. Smith v. State of Georgia (1918), 147 Ga. 689, 95 S.E. 281, ALR 490.

[83] *Wigmore on Evidence,* (3rd ed) Section 64.

[84] State v. Taylor (1922), 293 Mo. 210, 238 S.W. 489.

[85] Love v. Wolf (Cal. 1964), 38 Cal. Rptr. 183.

[86] *Wigmore on Evidence,* (3rd ed) Sections 224, 251–7.

[87] *Ibid.,* Section 154.

[88] See Section 6.05, Note 34.

[89] Giles v. Yellow Cab Co. (Ohio App. 1964), 1 Ohio App. 2d 404, 205 N.E. 2d 86.

[90] Atwood v. Scott, 99 Mass. 177, 178.

[91] Dick v. Marvin (1907), 188 N.Y. 426, 81 N.E. 162.
Wigmore on Evidence, (3rd ed) Section 89, Note 4.

[92] Pontius v. People (1880), 82 N.Y. 339, 350.

[93] Darling v. Mansfield (1923), 222 Mich. 278, 192 N.W. 595.
Bahrey v. Poniatishin (1921), 95 N.J.L. 128, 112 A. 481.
Hindle v. Commercial Travelers Loan & Homestead Ass'n. (1939), 298 Ill. App. 628, 19 N.E. 2d 101.

[94] Rosenblatt v. Bergen (1922), 202 App. Div. 200, 195 N.Y.S. 276, mod. 237 N.Y. 8, 142 N.E. 361.

[95] Donze v. Swofford (Mo. App. 1963), 368 S.W. 2d 917; a verdict for plaintiff was reversed simply because he had testified to the names, number, and ages of his children.

Such testimony as to family status has been allowed in one case wherein the court said, "The plaintiff was permitted to testify as to how many children he had; this was admissible within the discretion of the trial judge, in order to enable the jury to get in a general way what sort of man is on the witness stand." Cushing v. Jolles (1935), 292 Mass. 72, 197 N.E. 466. This ruling was severely criticized by Professor Wigmore, *Wigmore on Evidence,* (3rd ed.) Section 1104, Note 3.

cf. Daniel v. Banning (Mo. 1959), 329 S.W. 2d 647; the mere reference to the fact that plaintiff had two children, under the facts and circumstances of the case, was held error, but one which did not require a reversal of the judgment.

See Richard H. Rovere, *Howe & Hummel: Their True and Scandalous History* (New York, Paperback Library, Inc., 1963), pp. 65–57, for an entertaining account of how the infamous Howe, of the firm of Howe & Hummel, imposed upon juries by arranging that a pretty wife and fond children would be in the courtroom even when the defendant was single and childless.

[96] Hedge v. Midwest Contractors Equipment Co. (1964), 53 Ill. App. 2d 365, 202 N.E. 2d 869.
Simpson v. The Foundation Co. (1911), 201 N.Y. 479, 95 N.E. 101.
Daniels v. Banning (Mo. 1959), 329 S.W. 2d 647.

[97] Armstrong Furniture Co. v. Nickle (1961), 105 Ga. App. 61, 123 S.E. 2d 330.

[98] Love v. Wolf (1964), 226 Cal. App. 2d 378, 38 Cal. Rptr. 183.
Chess v. Wallis (1918), 134 Ark. 136, 203 S.W. 274; (except when punitive damages may be awarded).
Leotta v. Plessinger (1960), 8 N.Y. 2d 449, 461, 462, 171 N.E. 2d 454.
Oltarsh v. Aetna (1965), 15 N.Y. 2d 111, 256 N.Y.S. 2d 577, 204 N.E. 2d 622.
Trimble v. Merloe (1964), 413 Pa. 408, 197 A. 2d 457.
Herstein v. Kember (1936), 19 Tenn. App. 681, 94 S.W. 2d 76.

[99] Barnett v. Butler (Fla. App. 1959), 112 So. 2d 907.
Pagano v. Leisner (1955), 5 Ill. App. 2d 223, 125 N.E. 2d 301.
Cesarino v. Filiberto (1939), 257 App. Div. 241, 12 N.Y.S. 2d 912.
Jerdal v. Sinclair (Wash. 1939), 342 P. 2d 585.

THE TEN FACTORS
OF PERCEPTION

TABLE OF CONTENTS

THE TEN FACTORS
OF PERCEPTION

When a witness is to testify as to his Perceptions, particularly as to what he saw or heard, there are psychological ways in which to enhance the weight of such testimony by questions designed to demonstrate the witness' perceptive powers and the surrounding circumstances which favor perception. These are explored and exemplified in this chapter.

Q. WHAT, IF ANYTHING, DID YOU SEE (HEAR, TOUCH, TASTE, SMELL)?

§ 7:01 Perceptions Are Not the Equivalent of Facts

The word "perception" is used to connote awareness through any one of the five senses. We speak of five senses, i.e., sight, hearing, touch, taste, and smell, although there are more.[1] Each of the senses has its individual characteristics and will be dealt with in turn in this chapter. The *Generic Question* for this category is *Q. What, if anything, did you see (hear, touch, taste, smell)?* The phrase "if anything," is included in the *Generic Question* to avoid the objection that it is leading and suggestive.[2]

The testimony of a witness as to what he perceived is generally treated in law as a statement of fact for which no preliminary foundation need be laid. Such testimony seems to be factual when, actually, it includes the witness' conclusions and interpretations. When a witness is testifying to something he perceived, he is testifying only to the images or impressions caught by his eye or ear or nerve endings and conveyed as sensations through the nerves to his brain, where they are assembled and interpreted.[3] These interpretations are personal. *Two individuals, while honestly attempting to testify as to their perceptions of the same object or event, may yet differ materially.* Sight is only a sensation or impression which may present itself to many minds in many different aspects, and can be easily affected by many external and internal factors.

§ 7:02   Enhancing the Weight of Testimony as to Perceptions

In determining what additional facts are to be elicited from the witness in order to add to the weight of his testimony, or what arguments may be advanced in summation to persuade a jury of the likelihood that the witness did, in fact, perceive that which he claims to have observed, the following should be considered:

- The perceptive powers of the witness.
- The surrounding circumstances favoring perception.[4]
- The details observed.[5]

Similar considerations are applicable when the perception is by means of the sense of hearing, touch, taste, or smell.[6]

§ 7:03   The Perceptive Powers of the Witness: Sight

The power of perception varies greatly among individuals, and the sensations are affected by the personal history, mentality, and faculties of the one who perceives and his interpretation of the external event perceived.[7] When a witness is called for the purpose of testifying as to his observations, preliminary questions regarding his perceptive powers which would enhance the value of his testimony may be suggested by the following check list:

1. *His Good Eyesight.* A person with good eyesight will, of course, be more likely to observe correctly.[8]
2. *Good Health.* A person in good health is likely to observe better than one in poor health.[9]
3. *Lack of Fatigue or Pain.* All faculties are more alert when one is not tired, fatigued, or in pain.[10]
4. *Age.* Children are very observant of details but their attention is extremely mobile, their conceptions of magnitude, space, beauty, distance, etc. are quite different than those of an adult. An adult sees an infinite variety of things that are meaningless to a child.[11]
5. *Knowledge, Familiarity, and Intelligence.* Perception is augmented by knowledge, familiarity, and appreciation of what is observed. Facts which are imperfectly understood will be imperfectly observed. Attention and intelligence go hand in hand.[12]
6. *Interest and Motivation.* The witness who has the greater interest in observing an occurrence is to be believed in preference to one

who had a lesser interest or was wholly indifferent. Such interest may be the result of his vocation, duty, or other motivation.[13]

7. *Attention, Lack of Distraction.* One who is attentive and not distracted or preoccupied is the better observer.[14]

8. *Expectation.* An occurrence which was expected or which the witness was "set" to observe will be seen with greater detail than one which is sudden and unexpected.[15]

9. *Special Reason for Scrutiny.* A witness who can mention special circumstances which would be likely to arouse his attention is more impressive than one who merely states the facts observed.[16]

10. *State of Mind.* The state of mind, attitude, prejudice, or bias of the witness at the moment when he made his observations has a great deal to do with what he observed as well as what he later reports.[17]

§ 7:04 Surrounding Circumstances Favorable to Perception

The weight of the witness' testimony as to what he observed may be increased by having him describe the favorable surrounding circumstances such as the following:

1. *Favorable Position.* The witness should fix his position with relation to what was observed and, obviously, the nearer he was to the object, the more likely it is that the object was seen clearly.[18]

2. *View Unobstructed.* If there was nothing between the witness and the thing perceived, that fact should be brought out. On the other hand, if there were other objects, it should be made clear that these objects did not obstruct the view. The mere fact that there are some obstructions would not mean, however, that a witness' testimony must be discarded.[19]

3. *Opportunity to Observe.* The ability to perceive details depends in part upon the opportunity which the witness had to observe while he was in a position to do so. A careful observation is likely to be more accurate than a fleeting impression.[20] The fact that the witness had only a momentary opportunity to observe does not make the testimony inadmissible but does affect its weight and credibility.[21]

4. *Motion and Change.* The clarity and accuracy of observation may be affected by the circumstances that either the witness, object, or both were stationary or in motion. Observations from a stationary point of view are more dependable than from a moving vehicle.[22]

5. *Illumination and Visibility.* The accuracy of observations are dependent upon the degree of illumination, the intensity of the light and the distinctness and sharpness of the outline of the object.[23]

6. *Atmospheric Conditions.* A clear atmosphere adds to the distinctness of outline and helps in the identification of objects.[24]

7. *Contrast to Background.* The fact that there was a contrast between
the object observed and its background will greatly aid visibility.[25]

§ 7:05   The Details Observed

The best proof of good perception is the ability to testify as to many
details of what was seen. Such details should include any special markings
or signs which would indicate close observation. *Testimony describing the
details of the thing observed, its size, shape, color, and other attributes, will,
in itself, make it appear likely that it was indeed perceived.* Visibility of an
object depends in part upon its size, color, and shape. A large object attracts
attention better than a small one.[26] Naturally, the larger the object, the
better and further away it can be seen with clarity. Its color will take on
meaning, particularly in relation to the background and surrounding condition of light and darkness.[27] If the witness can describe some details which
would differentiate the person or object observed from other persons or objects, this would not only tend to establish the fact that he observed it, but
also would establish its identity.[28]

§ 7:06   Proving an Occurrence by the Observations of Eyewitnesses

Testimony as to what the witness saw is the most common method used
to prove the actions of others. The question, "What took place?" or, "What
occurred?" is but another form of *Q. What, if anything, did you see?* The
observations of eyewitnesses are often decisive in determining what took
place. The eyewitnesses appearing for each of the contesting parties may all
seem to be truthful, and yet the testimony of the witnesses for one party
may be diametrically opposite to that of the witnesses for the other. The
jury will likely be persuaded to accept the testimony of one set of witnesses
and reject that of the others on the basis of which witnesses are more likely
to have observed correctly. *It is not enough, therefore, to have each witness
state what he saw. Rather he should be questioned with a view to establishing as many of the items as has been set forth in the preceding sections as
possible which will add to the weight of his testimony.* Such facts would
emphasize (a) the perceptive powers of the witness, (b) the surrounding circumstances which favored perception, and (c) the details which he observed.

By way of illustration, an eyewitness to an automobile collision might
be asked questions similar to those which are set forth in the following
example.

ILLUSTRATIVE THREAD OF TESTIMONY

Observations of an Automobile Collision

Recollection: Introductory

Q. *Do you recall the ___ day of _____, 19__, the date when plaintiff was injured?*

A. *I do.*

(a) Perceptive Powers of Witness:

Q. *What is your occupation?*

A. _____.

Q. *Is your eyesight good?*

A. *It is.*

(b) Surrounding Circumstances Favorable to Perception:

Q. *Where were you at or about __ o'clock on that day?*

A. *I was on Main Street near First street.*

Q. *What, if anything, were you doing at that place?*

A. *I was walking.*

Q. *On what street were you walking?*

A. *On Main Street.*

Q. *Were you walking alone or with someone?*

A. *I was walking all alone.*

Q. *In what direction were you walking?*

A. *I was walking toward First Street.*

Q. *On which side of the street were you walking?*

A. *On my right hand side.*

Q. *How far were you from the corner of First Street when you saw something occur?*

A. *About 50 feet.*

Q. *Which way were you looking?*
A. *I was looking ahead of me.*

Q. *Was there anything between you and the automobile which would obstruct your view?*
A. *No.*

Q. *What was the condition of the weather?*
A. *It was clear.*

Q. *Was the street dry?*
A. *Yes.*

(c) Details Observed:

Q. *Did you notice what kind of pavement was laid on Main Street and First Street?*
A. *Yes, it was asphalt pavement.*

Q. *Describe the condition of the pavement as you saw it?*
A. *It was smooth.*

Q. *Is Main Street a wide or narrow street?*
A. *It is a wide street.*

Q. *Wider than First Street?*
A. *Yes, about twice as wide.*

Q. *Is there a traffic light at that corner of First Street and Main Street?*
A. *No.*

Q. *At that time when the accident happened, did you see automobiles on Main Street?*
A. *There were a few cars on Main Street approaching the corner of First Street.*

Q. *Did you notice whether there were any cars parked on Main Street near the sidewalk on which you were walking?*
A. *There were no cars parked there.*

Q. *Did you see the occurrence involved in this law suit?*
A. *I did.*

Q. *What called your attention to the occurrence?*
A. *I heard a screech of brakes.*

Q. *Tell the Court and jury what you saw at that time and place.*
A. *(Witness relates his observations as to the movements of vehicles and persons in detail).*

§ 7:07   Identification of Persons Based on Observations

There is no rule of law which requires an identification to be positive beyond any shadow of doubt—even in a criminal case.[29] However, a mere vague impression, or a scanty one as to the identity of a defendant such as that the defendant "looked like" the murderer, or that the eyes of the defendant were similar to those of a man who looked at her through a window cannot sustain a criminal conviction.[30] Testimony as to personal identity is proverbially fallacious.[31] Furthermore, it is very difficult to describe a person so as to convey a correct image or to point out precisely on what factors the recognition was based. Ordinarily, the jury must accept the conclusion of the witness as to identity and has little or nothing with which to test its accuracy. The commonplace description consisting of the height, weight, color of hair, and manner of dress is applicable to so many people that it means little. *If, however, the witness can show that he made careful observations and testifies as to certain marks, scars, peculiarities in look, dress,[32] and mannerisms[33] of the individual he observed, such details will go a long way in persuading the jury that anyone having such marks or peculiarities is indeed the person who was observed by the witness.*

A good illustration of this is given by Busch[34] in a direct examination of a bank teller who identified the defendant as the person who passed a forged check. He testified that he had asked the person who presented the check to endorse it in his presence; that he had ample opportunity to notice the right hand of the man as he was writing, that the hand was unusually thin, and that he had a number of small brown spots or blotches in the flesh on the back of it.

Details are most important. Each mark or circumstance may be commonplace, but, in combination, may make it improbable that they all exist in more than one object. Each added circumstance makes it less likely that there is more than one object they would fit. When we achieve a combination of marks which could not conceivably coexist in more than one single object, we may be certain that any two objects having such combination of marks must be identical i.e., must be one and the same.[35]

The cumulative effect of every distinctive feature which differentiates the particular person from man in general increases in a geometrical ratio. Conversely, every distinctive feature testified to by the witness and possessed by the person being identified makes it immeasureably less likely that the witness is in error in his identification. The law of probability operates so that what might be a mere coincidence, with each additional point of similarity, becomes so much more probable and turns into certainty.

Attempts have been made in criminal trials to have mathematicians testify as experts as to the mathematical odds that the identification was correct. Such testimony is, however, inadmissible because of inadequate evidentiary foundation and also because no mathematical formula could ever establish beyond a reasonable doubt that the prosecution's witnesses correctly observed and accurately described the distinctive features which were employed to link the defendants to the crime.[36] The fact that mathematical formulas are inadmissible does not diminish the persuasive effect of testimony pointing out peculiar details observed which are possessed by the person being identified.

Familiarity with the One Identified

A witness may not be able to describe a single peculiar feature different from that of any other man and yet be able to identify him with confidence. "We may recognize a person, and be able to testify as to his identity with confidence, without being able to describe a single peculiar feature different from that of every other man."[37]

The important thing is to show that the witness was familiar with the person in question. The greater the familiarity, the more likely that the identification was correct. Familiarity produces that kind of knowledge that acts instantaneously, by an immediate and single process of recognition. There is little likelihood of mistaking the identity of a close acquaintance, or friend,[38] although such mistakes do occur.[39] On the other hand, the uncorroborated testimony of a witness professing to identify a person whom he had never seen but once, several years before the occasion in question, would not suffice.[40] Certainly a conviction based upon the uncorroborated testimony of a witness who saw the defendant only once and who was not positive of his identification would not be sustained.[41]

After the witness has testified as to the circumstances indicating that he should be able to recognize a person, he may be asked to point him out if he is in the courtroom.

ILLUSTRATIVE THREAD OF TESTIMONY

Identification of Accused

Q. *Do you see that man in the courtroom now?*

A. *Yes, sir.*

Q. *Will you point him out?*

A. *There he is, sitting in the third chair on the side of the table across from where you are (indicating the defendant).*

Q. *Are you positive that is the man you have described?*

A. *Positively.*

The mere fact that persons are related to one another means little with respect to identification. What is more important is how often they see each other. If a child has been separated from its parents at birth, its mother or father would not be able to identify it years later, because what is needed is opportunity for observation and not mere instinct.[42]

ILLUSTRATIVE THREAD OF TESTIMONY

Identification of Corpus Delicti

By the District Attorney:

Q. *Do you know John Jones?*

A. *I do.*

Q. *Are you related to him?*

A. *Yes.*

Q. *What is your relationship?*

A. *I was his brother.*

Q. *Did you live with him in the same household?*

A. *I did.*

Q. *On the ___ day of _____, 19__, did you have occasion to view a body at the City Morgue?*

A. *I did.*

Q. *Could you identify that body?*

A. *Yes, I could.*

Q. *When had you seen him last before that date?*

A. *The day before.*

Q. Who was it?

A. It was my brother, John Jones.

If the witness knew the person in question by name, he may testify that he saw Mr. So and So (naming him) at a certain time and place. Identity of name is *prima facie* evidence of identity of person.[43] However, the mere fact that the defendant's name agrees with the appellation used by the witness is not always sufficient in a criminal case unless fortified by circumstances or corroborated by other facts.[44] It is not enough identification should the witness refuse to identify the defendant.[45]

If the witness has seen the person only once or infrequently and some time has elapsed since then, the matter of the witness' memory assumes great significance.[46]

Human memory being what it is, identification of an accused shortly after the crime, or, at least at a time nearer the crime than the trial, is likely to carry more weight than an identification at a much later time.[47] This gives rise to an interesting question as to whether the witness who identifies the defendant in court may testify to the fact that he had previously identified the defendant, or whether this will be disallowed as a prior consistent statement and hearsay. Such testimony may be made admissible by statute and, if so, such prior identification constitutes substantive proof.[48] Even when permitted, only the identifying witness may himself testify to his prior identification.[49] The testimony of another witness to the fact that he was present and saw such prior identification will not be received.[50] Nor is evidence that the witness had previously identified a photograph of the accused at a police station admissible; the identification must have been of the accused in person.[51] A composite picture may not be used[52] unless the credibility of the witness is under violent attack or there is a claim that this testimony is a recent fabrication.[53] However, photographs may be used at the trial for identification of persons, and a witness, in determining whether a picture resembles the original, need not have special skill or knowledge of the photographic art.[54]

§ 7:08 Negative Evidence: Failure to See

At times it is necessary to use negative evidence to prove that the witness did *not* see a certain object or condition. A witness who is shown to have been in a position to see or hear what occurred may testify not only to what he saw and heard but also to what he did not see and did not hear.[55]

There may be one of two objectives of such testimony: (a) to give rise to an inference that the object was not seen because it was not there, or (b) that it was there, but for some reason, was not seen by the witness.

To accomplish the first objective, the witness' testimony will follow the suggestions in the previous sections to indicate that the object was clearly within the range of his vision and that if the object or condition was, in fact, present, it would have been seen by him. For example, the witness could testify that, although his eyesight was good, and he could plainly see the automobile in the dark, he did not observe any lights on it. Although this is a negative impression, there arises a rational inference that such lights were not seen because they were not lit.[56]

At other times, the object or condition was unquestionably present, but the witness denies having seen it. The objective then is to persuade the jury to accept his denial. For example, in a personal injury action, a person has the duty of avoiding a visible and apparent danger.[57] In order to forestall a charge of contributory negligence, it will be necessary to establish that the plaintiff did not see the danger either because it was not visible to him, or, if visible, that there existed certain facts or circumstances which excuse his failure to observe it. In such event, instead of eliciting testimony which would tend to establish that the witness should have seen the object or condition, facts pointing in the opposite direction would be emphasized. For example, testimony such as his poor health or eyesight, his unfamiliarity with the surroundings, that he had no opportunity to observe or was in such a position where he had no view, or only an obstructed view, that the background, visibility, and atmospheric conditions were not propitious, that his attention was distracted, that he was laboring under some stress of circumstances or other facts might explain his failure to see.[58]

ILLUSTRATIVE THREAD OF TESTIMONY

Defect Not Seen Because Attention Was Distracted

Q. *Now, as you approached Spring Street was your attention attracted to anything?*

A. *It was.*

Q. *What attracted your attention?*

A. *The shoes in the window.*

Q. *When you say, "in the window," what window do you mean?*

A. *The Acme Shoe Store.*

Q. *Did you continue to look at the shoes in the window?*

A. *I did.*

Q. *Tell us what you were doing as you looked at the shoes?*

A. *I turned at an angle and went to look in the window to see the shoes when my foot caught in a hole.*

At times a negative identification may be required, i.e., that the witness saw a person whom he did not know but that he can state that it was *not* one of the parties to the action, as for example, that the intruder was not the defendant.

In an action for divorce it was necessary to establish that the woman with whom the defendant was living was *not* the plaintiff's wife.

By Plaintiff's Attorney:

Q. *What is your occupation?*
A. *I am a doorman at 300 East 50th Street.*

Q. *Do you know Mr. M_____, the defendant?*
A. *I do.*

Q. *How do you know him?*
A. *He lives at 300 East 50th Street for the past two years.*

Q. *Did Mr. M_____ live at those premises alone or with someone else?*
A. *He lived there with a woman.*

Q. *Describe the woman.*
A. *(Witness describes her).*

Q. *Was that woman known as Mrs. M_____?*
A. *Yes.*

Q. *Have you seen this woman with whom he lived there on many occasions?*
A. *Yes, sir.*

> *Plaintiff's Attorney: Will the plaintiff please rise.*
> *(Plaintiff stands up.)*

Q. *Look at this lady and tell us is this the lady with whom he has been living at that address?*
A. *No, sir.*

§ 7:09   The Witness' Hearing

Most of what has been written with respect to Sight applies with equal force to Hearing and to the other senses. As with Sight, the testimony of a witness stating what he heard appears to be factual yet it includes his conclusions and interpretations. In determining what additional facts are to be elicited from the witness in order to add to the persuasiveness of his testimony as to what he heard, you should consider:

- The hearing ability of the witness.
- Surrounding circumstances favoring hearing.
- Detailed description of what was heard.

§ 7:10   The Hearing Ability of the Witness

The value of testimony of a witness to the fact that he heard certain sounds depends as much upon his faculties as upon his credibility.[59] Thus, a deaf man who swears that he heard a certain sound will not stand before the jury on an equal footing with another witness who has good hearing.[60]

§ 7:11   Surrounding Circumstances Favoring Hearing

There is no rule of law requiring any foundation to be laid for testimony as to what was heard (except in instances of impeachment), it being left to the cross-examiner to delve into the surrounding circumstances if he so desires.[61] However, it is desirable to elicit any favorable circumstances, such as the following:

1. *Time of Day.* Obviously, sound will be conveyed more easily and perfectly in the stillness of the night or early morning, whereas it may be deadened or overpowered by other noises during business hours.[62]

2. *Favorable Atmospheric Conditions.* Calm weather is more conducive to hearing than is stormy, windy weather.[63] A fog makes it more difficult to locate the direction from which sounds emanate.[64]

3. *Position and Opportunity to Hear.* It should appear that the witness was so situated with relation to the place where the sound emanated that he would be able to hear clearly and distinctly.[65]

4. *Lack of Competitive Sounds.* Sounds are more likely to be heard where there are no competitive sounds or where the competitive sounds are of less intensity or interest.[66]

§ 7:12   Detailed Description of What Was Heard

The likelihood that a certain sound was heard will also be affected by:

1. *Its Type and Intensity.* Whether high or low; loud or soft; sudden or steady.[67]

2. *How It Was Produced.* The human voice is weak compared with the noise of machinery. The sound of a siren is more penetrating and carries further than an automobile horn. A passenger car will not make as much noise as a truck or trailer.[68] It is a matter of common knowledge that a train of cars drawn at a rate of 50 miles an hour makes a great noise.[69]

3. *Repetition.* Repetition aids hearing. "From a distance the crack of a rifle is not so likely to be heard as the repeated rattle of a machine gun. A weak stimulus frequently repeated may be as effective as a strong one presented once." [70]

4. *Novelty, Strikingness.* Something which is novel will create a greater stimulus to perception than what is commonplace.[71] On the other hand, words spoken in a language with which the witness was very familiar would be understood even when spoken in low tones and far off.[72]

§ 7:13   Declarations or Conversations Heard

If the witness is to testify as to a declaration or conversation he overheard or participated in, he should testify as to

- the date, time and place
- the identity of the speaker or speakers
- indicate that he was in a position to hear
- the fact that he did hear what was said
- who else was present
- the words or substance of what was said
- what, if anything, was done pursuant to the conversation. Such an action might constitute an important corroborating circumstance.[73]

It is preferable that the witness relate the exact words heard by him, although this too is not essential for admissibility, and the substance of the conversation will be received.[74] The witness should not, however, give his conclusions of what was said as by using such a term as "they agreed" instead of relating the words which constituted the agreement.

ILLUSTRATIVE THREAD OF TESTIMONY

A Conversation Between the Parties Heard by the Witness

Q. *Do you recall the 10th day of February of last year?*
A. *I do.*

Q.   *Where were you at about 2:30 P.M. of that day?*
A.   *I was in the office.*

Q.   *What were you doing at the time?*
A.   *I was called in to take dictation.*

Q.   *What, if anything, fixes the occurrence in your mind?*
A.   *A note in the office diary and a memorandum I made.*

Q.   *Have you refreshed your recollection by looking at the diary and memorandum?*
A.   *Yes.*

Q.   *Do you know the defendant, Mr. Jones?*
A.   *I do.*

Q.   *Who was in the room at the time?*
A.   *My employer, Mr. Smith, the defendant, Mr. Jones, and myself.*

Q.   *Where were you all?*
A.   *Mr. Smith was seated behind his desk, Mr. Jones sat on the side of the desk, and I sat directly opposite Mr. Smith.*

Q.   *Was there anyone else present at that time?*
A.   *No.*

Q.   *Was that a quiet or a noisy office?*
A.   *It was quiet.*

Q.   *Did you hear the conversation between Mr. Jones and Mr. Smith?*
A.   *I did.*

Q.   *Tell us in words or substance what Mr. Jones said to Mr. Smith and what Mr. Smith said to Mr. Jones.*
A.   *Mr. Jones said (quoting his words), then Mr. Smith said (quoting his words).*

Q.   *What, if anything, did you do after the conversation?*

A.   I went to my desk and made a memorandum of the conversation and opened a file.

§ 7:14   Identification of Person Through Hearing

Identification might be made by a witness who heard the person in question where that person has a voice which is known to him or which was of a distinctive character.[75] Although, like the features of the human face, there is a general resemblance in the voices of all mankind, there are marked differences which indicate its possessor very clearly. Recently, it has been demonstrated scientifically that every voice is peculiar and different than every other voice in the same way that fingerprints are distinctive.[76] The degree of certainty of identification by the voice does not depend upon the ability of the witness to describe its peculiarities.[77]

The fact that the witness did not know the person and never heard the voice before is not conclusive. An identification can be made based upon hearing the voice *subsequent* to the event.[78] However, identification of the voice of an unseen speaker by a witness who had slight acquaintance with the tones of his voice would not be entitled to much consideration.[79]

§ 7:15   Telephone Conversations

When the witness is to testify as to what he heard on the telephone, the voice must first be identified before the conversation will be received, for otherwise it would be hearsay, as an anonymous telephone call is not admissible in evidence.[80] There are various ways in which the identification can be accomplished. The witness may have recognized the voice from prior personal talks with the speaker.[81] The witness may testify that, while he had never spoken to the person on the telephone before, he did speak to him subsequently and so can now identify the voice.[82] The identity may also be established by circumstantial evidence as, that the conversation itself revealed that the caller was familiar with the subject matter which would not be known to another,[83] or that later the caller did something pursuant to the telephone conversation.[84] If the witness initiated the telephone call to an established place of business by calling a listed number, a presumption of identity may arise and overcome the problem of identity.[85]

ILLUSTRATIVE THREAD OF TESTIMONY

Telephone Conversation: Recognition of Voice

The plaintiff is testifying as to an alleged conversation had with the defendant who telephoned him:

Q. *On or about the 10th day of January of last year, did you receive a telephone call pertaining to the property in question? Please answer yes or no.*

A. *Yes, I did.*

Q. *Did you place the call or was it made to you?*

A. *The call was made to my office.*

Q. *Had you ever spoken to Mr. Miller, the defendant, prior to January 10th?*

A. *Yes, sir, I have.*

Q. *How many times have you spoken to him since that date?*

A. *At least a dozen times.*

Q. *How did you speak to him, was it face to face or on the telephone?*

A. *I have spoken to him both face to face and on the telephone.*

Q. *Getting back to the telephone call on January 10th, can you recall the voice on the telephone?*

A. *I can.*

Q. *Do you know whose voice you heard on the telephone on that day?*

A. *I do.*

Q. *Whose voice did you hear on the telephone on that day?*

A. *I heard the voice of Mr. Miller, the defendant.*

Q. *Did the party calling say who he was?*

A. *He did.*

Q. *Who did he say he was?*

A. *He said, "This is Mr. Miller calling."*

Q. *Now, will you tell us, in words or substance, the conversation, what Mr. Miller said to you on the telephone on January 10th and what you said to him.*

A. *(The plaintiff relates the conversation.)*

§ 7:16   Avoiding the Hearsay Rule

Whenever it is desired to have a witness testify as to any statement or declaration made by another which he heard, it is necessary to consider whether the testimony will be objectionable as hearsay being a declaration made out of court by one who is not a witness under oath and subject to cross-examination. There are many situations in which the hearsay objection can be circumvented.

- By offering it as an admission by a party.[86]
- By offering it, not as proof of the truth of the matter asserted but merely as evidence that the statement was made.[87]
- By showing that the declarant is unavailable and that there is an assurance of truthworthiness of the testimony.[88]

§ 7:17   Using Admissions by a Party

Admissions by a party-opponent are excluded from the category of hearsay and no assurance of trustworthiness is required.[89] Any declaration which a party made which is contrary to the position taken by him at the trial is an admission.[90] The declaration, to constitute an admission, need not be based upon his personal knowledge, it being sufficient that the party adopted or believed it, and it may be in the form of an opinion.[91]

ILLUSTRATIVE THREAD OF TESTIMONY

Admission Made by Defendant

Q. *Did you speak to the defendant after the accident?*
A. *I did.*

Q. *Where did you speak to him?*
A. *He came over to my automobile.*

Q. *When was that?*
A. *A minute or two after it happened.*

Q. *What, if anything, did he say to you?*
A. *He said, "I am so sorry but my brakes did not hold."*

§ 7:18 Admissions and Confessions in a Criminal Case

Constitutional guarantees against self-incrimination require that before any confession or admissions made by a defendant charged with crime be received, it must first appear that the statement was made voluntarily, without duress, and after the required warnings were given.[92]

§ 7:19 Admissions by Agents Authorized to Speak for Party

Before a witness will be permitted to testify as to a statement made by a servant or agent of a party, it is generally required that it be shown that he was authorized by the party to make the statement for him. It is not enough merely that the declarant was a servant or agent of the party. Thus, in many jurisdictions, admissions made after an accident by defendant's agent or servant who drove the automobile will not be received as admissions which are binding on the master. It is held, in those jurisdictions, that authority to drive does not confer authority to make admissions to bind the employer or the automobile owner.[93] The modern trend, however, is to receive the declarations of the servant or agent provided only that they pertain to the subject matter of the agency.[94] The proposed Federal Rule would permit "(iii) a statement by a person authorized by him to make a statement concerning the subject, or (iv) a statement by his agent or servant concerning a matter within the scope of his agency or employment, made before the termination of the relationship."[95]

§ 7:20 Plea of Guilty

A plea of guilty to a criminal charge is admissible as an admission in a later civil action growing out of the same offense insofar as it amounts to an admission of facts material in the civil trial.[96] Such a plea is to be considered by the jury as any other declaration against interest, but it does not remove the issue of liability from its consideration.[97] The plea may be explained.[98]

ILLUSTRATIVE THREAD OF TESTIMONY

Police Officer Heard Defendant Plead Guilty [99]

Q. *Officer, after you got the identification of the owner of the tractor-trailer, did you take him somewhere?*
Defendant's Attorney: Just a moment. I object to that on the ground it is incompetent, irrelevant and immaterial, Your Honor.

Plaintiff's Attorney: I will withdraw it.

Q. *Did you go somewhere with Mr. C_____, the operator of the tractor-trailer?*

A. *I did.*

Q. *Tell us where you went with him.*

A. *We went before _____, Justice of the Peace of _____ Township.*
    Defendant's Attorney: I object.

Plaintiff's Attorney: This is introductory and I offer it subject to connection.

The Court: Overruled. I will take it subject to connection.

Q. *What did the Justice of the Peace, in your presence, say to Mr. C_____*
    and what did Mr. C_____ say to the Justice of the Peace?

A. *The Justice of the Peace told Mr. C_____ that he was being charged*
    with failing to yield the right of way driving from a private drive on-
    to a public highway. He further asked him how he wished to plead,
    guilty or not guilty? And Mr. C_____ stated, "I'm guilty."

Defendant's Attorney: On behalf of defendant company, I object and
move to strike it out as not binding.

The Court: Sustained as to defendant _____ Company. I will take it
only as against defendant C_____.

§ 7:21 Offer Not as Proof of Truth of the Matter Asserted

Frequently, declarations which would ordinarily be excluded as hearsay or self-serving are received on the theory that they are not offered as proof of the matter asserted, but merely as evidence of the fact that the statement was made. Illustrations of this are:

- Declarations as to a Mental, Emotional, or Physical Condition of the declarant.[100]
- Prior Inconsistent Statement made by a Witness.[101]
- Prior Consistent Statement to Rehabilitate.[102]
- A Verbal Act or Verbal Part of an Act.[103]
- Excited Utterances or Spontaneous Declarations (Res Gestae).[104]

§ 7:22 Declarations as to Mental, Emotional or Physical Condition of Declarant

The testimony of a witness as to what he heard another say is often inadmissible as being hearsay or self-serving. However, such testimony may be received in some jurisdictions when it is offered, not to prove the truth of the assertion, but only as circumstantial evidence of the declarant's then existing state of mind, emotion, sensation, or physical condition. Such declarations may be received as evidence of the declarant's intent, plan, motive, design, mental feeling, pain, and bodily health.[105]

Thus, a physician who rendered medical treatment will be permitted to testify to statements by the patient as to his present condition, if made for the purpose of diagnosis and treatment in view of the patient's strong motivation to be truthful.[106] Some jurisdictions extend this to statements of past conditions and medical history[107] and some extend it to pertinent statements as to the cause of his condition.[108] But, generally, narratives of past occurrences bearing on fault are not permitted even when made to a treating doctor.[109]

Generally, a physician who was consulted only for the purpose of enabling him to testify may not state the patient's complaints and symptoms.[110] In some jurisdictions such statements will be allowed, not as substantive evidence, but only as indicating the basis of his diagnosis.[111] The modern tendency is to permit the statements.[112]

ILLUSTRATIVE THREAD OF TESTIMONY

History Given by Patient to Doctor[113]

The physician was first qualified and then asked:

Q. *Did you examine the plaintiff?*
A. *I did.*

Q. *When did you first see him?*
A. *On _____, 19__.*

Q. *Where did you see him?*
A. *At his home.*

Q. *Did you see him for the purpose of treating him for his injuries?*
A. *Yes, I did.*

Q.   Did you obtain a history from him before you examined him?
A.   I did.

Q.   Please tell us the history he gave you?
A.   [Witness states history]

*Q.   Did you obtain and make note of his present complaints which he made
      at the time of your first examination?*
A.   I did.

Q.   Please state what his complaints were.

§ 7:23   Effective Use of a Prior Inconsistent Statement
Made by a Witness

A prior inconsistent statement made by a witness is not the same as an admission by a party. Before a witness will be permitted to testify as to a prior inconsistent statement of another witness, a foundation must be laid, i.e., the witness who is to be impeached must first be warned by being asked whether at a stated time and place he made the statement to a certain named person.[114] It is only if the witness denies making the statement[115] or states that he does not recall making it,[116] or refuses to either admit or deny having made such statement or gives indirect or evasive answers[117] that the impeaching witness can testify to the prior inconsistent statement. *The questions which may then be put to the impeaching witness follow a fixed pattern and the declaration inquired about must be the same one which had been denied.*[118] Leading questions are proper for this purpose.[119] The contradictory statement is generally received only to impeach credibility[120] and not as substantive evidence of the truth thereof.[121] The recent trend, however, is to receive it as substantive evidence.[122]

ILLUSTRATIVE THREAD OF TESTIMONY

Proof of Prior Inconsistent Statement

The witness who is to be impeached must have first been warned as a foundation for the impeaching testimony which follows.[123]

Q.   What is your occupation?
A.   Investigator.

*Q.   Did you at my request go to interview Mrs. White who has testified
      here on behalf of the plaintiff?*
A.   I did.

Q. *When did you interview her?*

A. *On January 16th of this year.*

Q. *Where did you see her?*

A. *At her home.*

Q. *Did she at that time and place say to you, in words or substance, that the defendant's truck got to the corner first, but that the plaintiff, Mrs. Kaye, tried to beat him across?*

§ 7:24   Prior Consistent Statement to Rehabilitate

Prior consistent statements are generally inadmissible. The mere fact that a witness said the same thing before trial as at the trial does not add to its weight or credibility.[124] Where, however, a witness has been attacked on cross-examination to imply that his testimony was a recent fabrication, then, in the discretion of the court, it may be shown that the witness had, prior to the trial and when there was no motive to fabricate, made statements similar to his testimony at the trial.[125]

§ 7:25   A Verbal Act or Verbal Part of an Act

There are declarations made which are not assertions, but rather circumstantial evidence of a fact; for example, to show the state of mind of a third person or that he had knowledge of a certain fact.[126] Sometimes the words spoken constitute a verbal act or a verbal part of an act rather than an assertion. For example, a witness may testify that he saw the police officer put his hand on the plaintiff's shoulder and say, "You are under arrest." The words are not hearsay, they are part of the act and serve to explain it.[127] Or, a witness will be permitted to testify that he heard the plaintiff, or someone else, complain of a defective condition to the defendant owner or his agent when such a statement constitutes the verbal act of giving notice of a defective condition.[128] The evidence bears on whether notice of a defect was given and not whether the defect did in fact exist.[129]

ILLUSTRATIVE THREAD OF TESTIMONY

Oral Notice of Defect Heard by Witness

Q. *Do you know the defendant, Mr. R_____?*

A. *I do.*

Q. *Do you recall accompanying the plaintiff's son to Mr. R_____'s apartment in March?*

A. *I do.*

Q. *Can you fix the date and time?*

A. *It was the first week of March at about 4 o'clock in the afternoon.*

Q. *Did you hear a conversation between the plaintiff's son and defendant at that time and place?*

A. *I did.*

Q. *Who else, if anyone, was present?*

A. *Just the three of us.*

Q. *Where was the conversation held?*

A. *At the door leading into Mr. R_____'s apartment. Mr. R_____ came to the door and opened it.*

Q. *What, if anything, did you hear the plaintiff's son say to the defendant?*

A. *He said, "I have your rent for my apartment. I would like you to fix the pads on the stairs leading down from my apartment; they are loose."*

Q. *What, if anything, did Mr. R_____ say?*

A. *Mr. R_____ said, "Let us go look at them."*

Q. *What, if anything, took place after that?*

A. *We all went to the stairs and the plaintiff pointed out the loose pads.*

Q. *What, if anything, did Mr. R_____ say then?*

A. *He said, "The superintendent will take care of this. I'll tell him about it."*

§ 7:26   Excited Utterances or Spontaneous Declarations (Res Gestae)

Testimony by a witness that he heard some other person make a certain statement may avoid the hearsay rule if the statement can be shown to come within the excited or instinctive utterance rule, i.e., if it was a spontaneous declaration or part of the *res gestae*. Spontaneous utterances are such as are prompted by the exciting event without time to reflect.[130] In theory, *res gestae* is not the witness speaking, but the transaction voicing itself, and the voicing must have occurred in such circumstances as to raise a presumption that the utterances constituting the voice are spontaneous utterances arising out of the transaction.[131]

In order to assure the admissibility of the declaration, the following must appear:

1. The identity of the declarant as a participant or eyewitness. The declaration made by an unidentified person should be excluded.[132]

2. The event must be a startling or shocking one as, for example, an accident.[133]

3. The speaker, it must appear, was under the stress of nervous shock or excitement produced by the act in issue at the moment he made the declaration.[134]

4. The declaration must be concomitant with and so intimately connected with the occurrence in point of time as to be regarded as a part of it.[135] Usually it is required that it be made either immediately before[136] or immediately after the event[137] with no time in which to reflect, or in any event, while the nervous excitement still dominates the mind of the declarant.[138]

5. Generally, the declaration must relate to and illuminate the circumstances of the occurrence.[139]

§ 7:27   Declarant Unavailable, Assurance of Trustworthiness

Some declarations which are clearly hearsay are, nevertheless, received because of necessity due to the fact that the declarant is not available. Even then it is also required that the circumstances surrounding the statement are such as to give some assurance of trustworthiness.

Unavailability as a witness has been defined[140] to include situations in which the declarant is:

- Exempted by ruling of the judge on the ground of privilege from testifying concerning the subject matter of his statement;[141] or

- Persistent in refusing to testify despite an order of the judge to do so;[142] or

- Unable to be present or to testify at a hearing because of death or then–existing physical or mental illness or infirmity.[143]

- Absent from the hearing and beyond the jurisdiction of the court to compel appearance and the proponent of his statement has exercised reasonable diligence but has been unable to procure his attendance.[144] Mere absence from the jurisdiction is not sufficient unless the witness is a non-resident.[145] Of course, if a party arranges with the witness to stay away or prevents him from attending or testifying, this is not considered unavailability.[146]

ILLUSTRATIVE THREAD OF TESTIMONY

Unavailability of Witness—Deceased

Plaintiff's Attorney:

Q. *What is your occupation?*
A. *I am a process server.*

Q. *Did you, at my request, go to the home of John Johnson last Wednesday?*
A. *I did.*

Q. *What was your purpose in going there?*
A. *I had a subpoena which you gave me to serve upon him.*

Q. *I show you this paper and ask you what it is?*
A. *That is the subpoena.*
   Plaintiff's Attorney: I offer it in evidence (Marked Plaintiff's Exhibit 9).

Q. *Where did you go with that subpoena?*
A. *To 150 East 96th Street.*

Q. *Tell us what happened when you got there?*
A. *I found the name John Johnson listed for Apartment 3C. I pushed the button and went up. A woman came to the door and asked me what I wanted. I told her I wanted to see Mr. Johnson. She told me he had died a month ago and she started to cry. I told her I was sorry to hear that and left.*

Plaintiff's Attorney: I offer in evidence a certified death certificate attesting to the death of John Johnson (Marked Plaintiff's Exhibit 10 in evidence).

Where a witness is unavailable, there is an assurance of trustworthiness in the following types of declarations:

- Former testimony of unavailable witness.[147]
- Declarations as to Pedigree.[148]
- Declarations Against Interest.[149]
- Dying Declarations.[150]

§ 7:28   Former Testimony of Unavailable Witness

When it appears that a witness who has previously testified is not available, his prior testimony may, in a proper case, become admissible. What is a proper case requires a study of the statutes of the jurisdiction.[151] Thus, it may be required that, in addition to the unavailability of the witness, it appear that the parties in the subsequent trial be substantially the same as the parties in the former trial,[152] and that the questions at issue or the subject matter in the subsequent suit be substantially the same as in the former.[153] Another prerequisite may be that the testimony was taken in an action or proceeding where the parties against whom it is offered had both the right and the opportunity to cross-examine the witness as to the statement offered.[154] It need not appear that he had actually been cross-examined so long as the opportunity had been afforded to do so.[155]

Anyone who heard the former testimony, whether stenographer, attorney, judge, juror, or witness, may prove the former testimony.[156] His memory may be refreshed by notes or other memoranda of the former testimony [157] or, if a proper foundation be laid, such notes may be introduced into evidence as a memorandum of a past recollection recorded.[158] The testimony need not be recounted in the precise words of the witness, the substance being sufficient.[159]

Whenever former testimony is offered in a subsequent trial it is considered as if given for the first time by the witness on the stand [160] and is subject to all objections irrespective of what objections were or were not made at the prior trial.[161]

§ 7:29   Declarations as to Pedigree

In cases involving proof of such matters as family relationship, descent, marriage, birth of children, legitimacy or illegitimacy, death, etc., whenever pedigree is directly at issue, declarations made respecting such matters may be received in a proper case as exceptions to the hearsay rule.

There is authority for the statement that pedigree declarations will be received only if the declarant is unavailable by reason of his death.[162] This is doubtful, however, and the general rule is that the unavailability may also be because of the fact that the declarant was incompetent or beyond the jurisdiction of the court.[163] Indeed, in the proposed Rules of Evidence for the United States District Courts and Magistrates, this is placed amongst those hearsay exceptions where the availability of declarant is immaterial.[164]

In addition to proof of the unavailability of the witness it must also appear:

1. That the declarant was related by blood or affinity to the family concerning which he speaks.[165] Such relationship can not be established

by the statement of the declarant, but must be shown by evidence independent of the declaration itself.[166] Slight proof may be enough, but some proof of relationship or intimate association with the family must be there.[167]

2. The pedigree declaration must have been made before the controversy in question originated.[168]

3. Pedigree must be directly at issue and not merely incidental.[169]

The declaration may be oral or written and take any form; or pedigree may be shown by hearsay evidence of long-continued conduct or general reputation in the family.[170] The declarant need not have spoken from personal knowledge.[171]

§ 7:30   Declaration Against Interest

It may happen that some one has made a statement which would be helpful to the case but that this person is unavailable at the trial. It may be possible to get such a declaration into evidence as an exception to the hearsay rule. Of course, if such a statement was made by a party to the action, it would be admissible as an admission even though he has since died or become incompetent to testify.[172] What we are now considering is a declaration by one who is *not* a party to the action. Such declarations are termed declarations against interest.

Declarations against interest are only admissible when:

- The declarant is unavailable. Admissions are received against a party even though he is present at the trial, whereas if the declaration was made by one not a party or in privity with a party, it is not admissible unless the declarant is unavailable at the time.[173] Generally, it is required that the declarant be dead,[174] but there are instances when the declaration was admitted when the declarant was incompetent, absent from the jurisdiction, or otherwise unavailable.[175]

- The declaration was against the declarant's interest at the time it was made (not necessarily at the time of trial). The general rule is that the declaration must have been against the declarant's pecuniary or proprietary interest,[176] but the modern tendency is to include any statement which so tends to subject the declarant to civil or criminal liability or to make him an object of hatred, ridicule, or social disapproval, that a reasonable man in his position would not have made the statement unless he believed it to be true.[177]

- The declaration was with respect to a fact within the declarant's own knowledge.[178]

- The declarant had no motive to misrepresent the facts.[179]

Declarations against interest may be oral or written [180] and may include incidental facts not against interest which are also admissible.[181]

ILLUSTRATIVE THREAD OF TESTIMONY

Oral Declaration Against Interest

The plaintiff, a ditchdigger, sued the manufacturer of a steam shovel which injured him, allegedly because it was defective. The shovel itself was owned and operated by one John Peters who has since died. A witness was called and asked by the Defendant's Attorney:

Q. *What is your occupation?*
A. *Investigator.*

Q. *Did you try to subpoena John Peters to court?*
A. *He is dead. He died on January 6th.*

Q. *Had you spoken to Mr. Peters after the accident and before his death?*
A. *I did, the day after the accident.*

Q. *Where did you speak to him?*
A. *At his home.*

Q. *Who was present?*
A. *His wife.*

Q. *What, if anything, did Mr. Peters say with reference to the shovel?*
A. *I asked him if there was any defect in the steam shovel. He said, "No, there was nothing wrong with the machine. It was a good machine."*

Such declarations, being against the proprietary interest of John Peters as it exculpates the shovel manufacturer and indicates his own negligence, have been considered a declaration against his interest and admissible.[182]

§ 7:31 Dying Declarations

A statement made by a declarant while believing that his death was imminent may be received in a proper case as a dying declaration hearsay exception.[183] Dying declarations are only admissible when:

- Offered in a prosecution for criminal homicide [184] or in such other types of cases as allowed by statute or decisions in the particular jurisdiction. Thus the area has been expanded to include abortions [185] and even to include civil cases.[186]

- The declarant was in extremis [187] although death need not immediately follow the declaration.[188]

- The declarant was under a sense of impending death without hope of recovery.[189]

- The declaration is made by the victim and relates to acts which resulted in the declarant's condition. A narrative of past occurrences will be excluded.[190]

- The declaration must constitute statements of fact and not a mere expression of belief or suspicion.[191] It may be in the form of a shorthand rendition of the fact.[192]

There is no fixed form which dying declarations must follow.[193] Printed forms have been disapproved.[194] Oral testimony may be received and if reduced to writing, there is a conflict of authority whether the best evidence rule applies.[195] When the victim is unable to speak, he may make a dying declaration by means of nodding his head and pointing.[196]

§ 7:32 Failure to Hear

At times, the witness' testimony negates hearing as, that he did not hear a signal or warning, or did not hear a person make a certain statement. The purpose of such testimony is to have the jury infer that the signal was not heard because it was not given, or the declaration was not heard because the statement was not made. In order to justify such an inference, it should appear that the witness' hearing was good, that he was listening, that he was in a position to hear if there had been a sound, and that there was nothing else to prevent his having heard it.[197] A witness will be permitted to express an opinion that, from the place where he was located, he could have heard the bell or whistle of a train if it had sounded, but that he did not hear it.[198] Every person is a competent judge of his capacity to hear.[199] In order that such testimony have any probative weight, however, it must appear that the witness was in a position to hear and that he was listening, and that he would have heard it if there was such a sound.[200] It is not enough that he simply "did not recall" hearing it.[201]

As between a witness who testifies affirmatively and one who is negative, the rule of credibility has been stated as follows: "Whenever it can be perceived that a positive witness is guilty of perjury unless his statement is true, while a negative witness may be honestly mistaken, the issue must be found in favor of the former if both witnesses are of equal credibility, according to one of the strongest rules for weighing evidence." [202]

In the following illustration it was desired to impress upon the jury the fact that a signal was not heard by a witness for the reason that there was none given. The testimony establishes that the witness was in a position to hear, was listening for the signal, that there was nothing to interfere with his hearing ability, and that he would have heard the signal had it been sounded.

ILLUSTRATIVE THREAD OF TESTIMONY

Witness Did Not Hear Train Whistle

Q. *Do you recall February 15th of this year?*
A. *I do.*

Q. *Where were you at about three o'clock on that day?*
A. *I was on the Jamaica Station of the Long Island Railroad.*

Q. *What were you doing there?*
A. *I was waiting for the train to New York.*

Q. *When was the train scheduled to arrive?*
A. *At 2:55.*

Q. *Was the train late that day?*
A. *It was.*

Q. *Had you even taken that train before?*
A. *Yes, I take it to go home at the same time every weekday.*

Q. *Were you familiar with the locality east of the station?*
A. *Yes, I know it very well.*

Q. *Is the track headed in a westerly direction straight or curved as it approached the station?*
A. *It is a curve.*

Q. *Is there a grade crossing the train must pass before reaching the station?*
A. *Yes, about 200 feet to the west.*

Q. *What were you doing at 3 P.M. that day?*
A. *I was waiting and listening for the train.*

Q. *Were you customarily on the station every weekday before the train arrived?*

A. *Yes.*

Q. *And was it customary for you to wait and listen for the train?*
A. *Yes.*

Q. *And on those days when you were there, would you see or did you hear the 2:55 first?*
A. *I would hear it.*

Q. *What, if anything, would you hear?*
A. *I would hear its whistle as it approached the crossing to the west before it came into sight.*

Q. *On February 15th at about 3 P.M. what was the weather condition?*
A. *It was clear.*

Q. *Any wind?*
A. *No.*

Q. *At that time, were you listening for the train whistle?*
A. *I was.*

Q. *Did you hear the train whistle that day?*
A. *No.*

Q. *Would you have heard it if the whistle had been sounded?*
A. *I would.*

§ 7:33   Silence as an Admission

The failure to speak when there was a duty to do so may be received in a civil case as an admission by silence. Where a statement is made to another person in the presence of a party to the action, be it civil or criminal, containing an assertion of fact which, if true, the party would, under all the circumstances, naturally be expected to deny, his failure to speak is circumstantial evidence that he believed the statement to be true, and his conduct is thus received against him as an admission of such belief.[203] It is doubtful whether this would apply today in a criminal case in view of the recent interpretations of the Constitutional guarantees against self-incrimination.[204] In any event, before silence will constitute an admission, (a) the statement must have been made in the person's presence and hearing, (b) when the person was capable of understanding it, (c) when the truth of the facts stated were within his own knowledge, (d) when he was in such a situation that he was at liberty to make a reply, and (e) when there was a duty to reply or when the statement was made under such circumstances and by such persons as naturally to call for a reply if he did not intend to admit it.[205]

§ 7:34   Touch

The sense of touch gives the impression of contact with external material objects or their impact upon the body and conveys the knowledge of their existence or properties to the brain. It is one of the ways in which one perceives or feels.

The sense of touch includes sensations not only of touch, but also of pain, temperature, pressure, muscle, and position. These sensations are received by the nerve endings and transmitted through the nerve trunks to the brain which receives and interprets the stimuli.[206] The sensation may be only a part of the person's awareness. For example, one may be aware not only of a sensation of coldness, but of the coldness of ice. This is a perception rather than a nerve sensation.[207]

§ 7:35   Details of Perceptions by Touch

It is not always easy to describe the details of the witness' awareness of his contact with external objects and their impact upon his body. It is more difficult to describe one's impressions of what one has touched or felt, for example, than to describe what one has seen or heard. Resort must be made to analogy.[208] The description of the nature of the object which he felt is usually a matter of sight rather than touch.[209] The effect of the contact, such as pain, is a matter of state of mind.[210] In most instances, the testimony is a combination of what was seen and felt.

In the following illustration, the plaintiff, who had slipped and fallen on a slimy, wet substance on the floor, described it by how it felt to the touch of her fingers while on the floor, and by its appearance when she got up from the floor. Having fallen into an area of this substance extending two feet on every side, it would be expected that her clothes would be soiled by it and so she corroborated her testimony by a description of the stains she observed on her clothes. The clothes might be produced in substantiation.

ILLUSTRATIVE THREAD OF TESTIMONY

Condition of Floor by Sight and Touch [211]

Q. *Tell us what you did and what you observed as you went into this room.*

A. *I went in and walked a few feet when my foot shot out from under me. I tried to catch myself but failed and went down with a crash. I tried to help myself up. I put my hand out but it slipped in slimy wetness.*

Q. *Where did you put your hand?*

A. *On the floor.*

Q. *What did you feel?*

A. *My hand slipped into what felt like slimy wetness.*

Q. *Did you notice at that time how big an area had the slimy wetness on it?*

A. *As I was getting up I could not notice, but when I stood up I could see this area about me.*

Q. *How much of the floor could you see in that condition?*

A. *About two feet on all sides of me.*

Q. *Did you observe its color?*

A. *Yes. It was yellowish. It seemed darker around the outside. In the center it was yellow.*

Q. *Can you describe the feel of that substance?*

A. *It was slick, slimy, and slippery.*

Q. *After you got up, what if anything, did you notice about your clothing?*

A. *My clothes were soiled and wet from about my knees down as well as the bottom of my jacket.*

ILLUSTRATIVE THREAD OF TESTIMONY

An Assault

Q. *Do you recall the morning of March 31st of this year, about 1:30 A.M.?*

A. *I do.*

Q. *Where were you then?*

A. *I was on 200th Street, between Jerome Avenue and the Grand Concourse.*

Q. *What, if anything, did you see at that time?*

A. *As I was walking on 200th Street going toward the Grand Concourse, I looked down the street and I saw no one.*

Q. *What did you observe after that?*

A. *As I approached the bakery shop, I saw two fellows come from a doorway.*

Q. *Describe these two men you saw.*

A. *One was tall and thin, the other was short and stocky.*

Q. *What, if anything, did [you see] these men do?*

A. *They got me between them and they viciously attacked me.*
Defense Counsel: I move to strike it out.

The Court: Strike out the word "viciously." What did they do?

The Witness: The tall one grabbed me in front and held me around my arms and waist.

Q. *And where was the other one?*

A. *The short one was behind me. I couldn't see but I felt hands in my pocket and I felt my wallet being removed and I was hollering and screaming and they started beating me.*

Q. *Which of the men hit you?*

A. *They both hit me.*

Q. *With what did they hit you?*

A. *With their fists and then I fell to the pavement and I felt being stomped on and kicked.*

§ 7:36 Taste

Our senses of taste and smell constitute a most astonishing chemical laboratory. In a fraction of a second, they can identify the chemical structure of compounds it would take a chemist days to analyze by the usual laboratory methods.

Taste and smell go together. With food, for instance, you cannot really taste something if you have lost your sense of smell.[212]

Taste is not too often of legal importance. The description of taste is quite difficult. The ordinarily descriptive words are sweet, sour, bitter, salty. These carry a good and easily understood meaning, but such terms as "stinging," "metallic," "burning," etc., are more questionable.[213]

The fact that food is not fit to eat can be established by plaintiff's testimony that it tasted bad, since nonexpert opinion testimony is admissible where sensory perception is the subject matter of the testimony.[214]

§ 7:37 Smell

The sensation of smell is far more sensitive than taste and may be stimulated at a greater distance. It has been demonstrated that a single sniff of an odoriferous substance "contains many millions of molecules. When the molecules arrive at the olfactory hairs and cells in the upper part of the nose, they must produce a reaction in the cells, giving rise to electrical impulses which are transmitted to the olfactory lobe of the brain."[215]

Testimony as to smell is of comparatively little practical importance. It must be confirmed by the proof of the other senses or by other proof, else it has little value. For example, the perception of flavor depends on both taste and smell.[216]

Some people do have peculiar odors and might be recognized or identified by such odor or the odor of the clothes they are wearing.[217]

Chapter Seven

FOOTNOTES

[1] That there are other than five senses—for example, a muscle sense and a kinesthetic or movement-perceiving sense, the equilibrium sense—see Ross Stagner and T. F. Karwoski, *Psychology* (N.Y., McGraw-Hill Book Co. Inc., 1952), pp. 148–49, and Edward B. Titchener, *A Beginner's Psychology* (The Macmillan Company, 1916) pp. 43–47.

[2] See Section 2.03, "Ambiguity and Confusion Avoided by the Use of Generic Questions."

[3] Samuel Brock, *Injuries of the Brain and Spinal Cord* (New York, Springer Publishing Company, Inc., 4th ed., 1960) p. 119.

Louis E. Schwartz, *Trial of Accident Cases,* 3rd ed. (New York, Matthew Bender, 1968), Section 1476.

[4] See Section 7.04. "Surrounding Circumstances Favorable to Perception."

[5] See Section 7.05. "The Details Observed."

[6] See as to hearing, Section 7.12; touch, Section 7.34; taste, Section 7.36; smell, Section 7.37.

[7] Francis L. Wellman, *Art of Cross-Examination* (4th ed., New York, The MacMillan Company, 1936) pp. 157–58. "*The unconscious sense impressions*—sight, sound, or touch—would be the same to every human mind; but once you awaken the mind to consciousness, then the original impression takes on all the color of motive, past experience, and character of the individual mind that receives it. The sensation by itself will be always the same. The variance arises when the sensation is *interpreted* by the *individual* and becomes a *perception* of his own mind." (Welman's italics.)

See also Section 19.06, "Exposing the limitations of the Perceptive Powers of the Witness."

[8] See Section 19.10, "Revealing Impaired Eyesight."

[9] Section 19.08, "State of Health and Faculties."

[10] *Ibid.*

[11] Section 19.09, "Age, Sex, Intelligence."

[12] See Section 19.16, "Novelty or Familiarity with What Was Seen or Heard."

[13] See Section 19.14, "Lack of Interest or Attention." Section 19.15, "When to Cross-Examine as to Special Interest."

[14] *Ibid.*

See also Section 19.20, "Prior Activity as Diverting Attention."

[15] See Section 19.17, "The Occurrence Was Unexpected."

[16] See Section 19.15, "When to Cross-Examine as to Special Interest."

[17] See Section 19.32, "The Insidious Effects of Bias."

[18] See Section 19.19, "The Witness' Position," *et seq*.

[19] *Ibid*.

[20] See Section 19.26, "Lack of Opportunity to Perceive."

[21] Conway v. Tamborini (Ill. App. 1966), 215 N.E. 2d 303; estimate of speed based on momentary observation.

[22] See Section 19.25, "Motion and Change."

[23] See Section 19.27, "Illumination and Atmospheric Conditions," *et seq*.

[24] *Ibid*.

[25] See Section 19.28, "Contrast to Background."

[26] "Size. A large advertisement attracts attention better than a small one. A recent report shows that advertisers are coming to make more and more use of the full-page advertisement in attracting the reader's attention." Floyd L. Ruch, *Psychology and Life* (Chicago; Scott, Foresman & Co., 1953), Section 238.

[27] See Section 19.27, "Illumination and Atmospheric Conditions." Section 19.28, "Contrast to Background; Sudden Change in Illumination."

[28] See Section 7.07, "Identification of Persons Based on Observations."

[29] People v. Spinello (1951), 303 N.Y. 193, 203, 101 N.E. 2d 457, 462.

[30] People v. Klavna (1926), 241 N.Y. 481, 150 N.E. 523.

[31] James, *Psychology, The Briefer Course,* p. 190.

[32] Alford v. State (1904), 47 Fla. 1, 36 So. 436; peculiar foot prints.

People v. Van Wormer (1903), 175 N.Y. 188, 67 N.E. 299; shoes which fit footprints in the snow.

[33] State v. Lucas (1881), 57 Iowa 502, 10 N.W. 868; peculiar shrugging of the shoulders.

Trulock v. State (1902), 70 Ark. 558, 69 S.W. 677; mode of walking.

[34] Francis X. Busch, *Trial Procedure Materials* (Indianapolis, The Bobbs-Merrill Company, Inc., 1961) pp. 195–197.

[35] *Wigmore on Evidence,* 3rd ed. Sections 411, 414.

[36] People v. Collins (Cal. 1968), 66 Cal. Rptr. 497, 438 P. 2d 33; after a mugging, a witness saw a woman, her dark blonde ponytail flying, run out of an alley, enter a yellow automobile driven by a male Negro, wearing a moustache and beard, and speed away.

[37] De Witt v. Barley, 13 Barb (N.Y.) 550, 554.

[38] Cunningham v. Burdell (4 Brad. (N.Y.) 343, 473, 474.

Charles C. Moore, *A Treatise on Facts* (Northport, L.I., Edward Thompson Co. 1908), Section 1221.

[39] *Ibid*.

[40] *Ibid*.

Reid v. Reid, 17 N.J. Eq. 101.

[41] People v. Mullen (1906), 49 Misc. 289, 99 N.Y.S. 227.

Moore, op. cit., Section 1224.

[42] *In re* Sheehan (Pa. 1891), 20 A. 1003, 1009.

Lee Sing Far v. United States (1899), 94 F. 834, 837.

Moore, *op. cit.*, Section 1230.

[43] *In re* Orange (1936), 272 N.Y. 61, 4 N.E. 2d 417.

[44] People v. Reese (1932), 258 N.Y. 89, 179 N.E. 305, 79 A.L.R. 1329.

People v. Rubin (1941), 286 N.Y. 56, 35 N.E. 2d 649.

[45] People v. Sellinger (1934), 265 N.Y. 149, 191 N.E. 868.

[46] See Section 17.04, "Time Erases Memory."

[47] *New York Law and Proof* (New York, Matthew Bender & Co., Inc.), Section 151, Note 4.

People v. Spinello.

[48] People v. Spinello.

See Section 8.08, "Prior Identification."

[49] People v. Carter (1963), 19 App. Div. 2d 662, 241 N.Y.S. 2d 447.

People v. Smalls (1964), 22 App. Div. 2d 778, 253 N.Y.S. 2d 1009.

[50] People v. Trowbridge (1953), 305 N.Y. 471, 113 N.E. 2d 841.

[51] People v. Cioffi (1963), 19 App. Div. 2d 577, 240 N.Y.S. 2d 188; this is an attack upon defendant's character.

People v. Chandler (1963), 19 App. Div. 2d 577, 240 N.Y.S. 2d 188.

[52] People v. Jennings (1965), 23 App. Div. 2d 621, 257 N.Y.S. 2d 456.

[53] People v. Coffee (1962), 13 App. Div. 410, 217 N.Y.S. 2d 176; aff'd. 11 N.Y. 2d 142, 182 N.E. 2d 92.

[54] Bender's *New York Law and Proof*, p. 934, *et seq.*

A portrait or a miniature painted from life and proved to resemble the person may be used to identify him. Moore, *op. cit.*, Section 1217, Note 59.

[55] Wilson v. Hartford Accident & Indemnity Co. (1967), 272 N.C. 138, 158 S.E. 2d 1.

[56] Murphy v. Adams (1923), 99 Conn. 632, 122 A. 398.

[57] Schwartz, *Trial of Accident Cases*, Section 408 Note 36; Section 568 Note 5.

[58] Collins v. City of Janesville (1903), 117 Wis. 415, 425, 94 N.W. 309, 313.

Schwartz, *op. cit.*, Section 5308.

[59] Halcomb v. Halcomb (1859), 28 Conn. 177, 181; "the force of all human testimony depends as much upon the ability of the witness to observe the facts correctly as upon his disposition to describe them honestly."

[60] Grabill v. Ren (1903), 110 Ill. App. 587, 590.

[61] Shallenberger v. Duncan (Cal. App. 1966), 53 Cal. Rptr. 77.

[62] Atlantic Coast Line Railroad v. Miller (1907), 53 Fla. 246, 44 So. 247.

Davidson v. Lake Shore etc. Railway Co. (1897), 179 Pa. St. 227, 36 A. 291.

[63] See Section 19.29, "Effect of Atmospheric Conditions on Hearing."

[64] *Ibid.*

[65] *Ibid.*

[66] Davidson v. Lake Shore etc. Railway Co.; supra, the noise of a passing train on one railroad track would naturally drown that of a remoter train upon another track.

See also Section 19.30, "Competitive Sounds."

[67] *Ibid.*

[68] Schwartz, *Trial of Accident Cases*, Section 794 D.

[69] Chicago etc. Railroad Co. v. Andrews (8th Cir. [Iowa] 1904), 130 F. 65, 71.

[70] Ruch, *Psychology and Life* (4th ed), p. 239.

[71] See Section 19.16, "Novelty or Familiarity."

[72] James, *Psychology, The Briefer Course*, p. 190.

[73] See Section 7.15, note 84.

[74] Lugo v. United States (9th Cir. [Cal.] 1967), 370 F. 2d 992.

Wright v. State (Wis. 1970), 175 N.W. 2d 646, when an eyewitness is asked what a particular defendant said, the required answer is what the defendant then said in the exact language he used at the time.

[75] Pilcher v. United States (1902), 113 F. 248, 250; the identification was insufficient in this case.

[76] People v. King (1968) 266 Cal. App. 2d 437, 72 Cal. Rptr. 478.

State v. Hedman, (1971) 289 Minn. 548, 185 N.W. 2d 273.

State v. Cary, (1968) 99 N.J. Super. 323, 239 A. 2d 680.

[77] Commonwealth v. Williams (1870), 105 Mass. 62, 67.

[78] People v. Strollo (1908), 191 N.Y. 42 and see next section.

[79] Brown v. Brown (1901), 63 N.J. Equity, 348, 357, 50 A. 608, 611.

Ramsay v. Ryerson (1889), 40 F. 739, 744;

Moore, *op. cit.*, Section 1225.

[80] Richard v. M.V.A.I.C. (1965), 23 App. Div. 2d 922, 258 N.Y.S. 2d 970.

Richards v. Lake Hills (1964), 15 Utah 2d 150, 389 P. 2d 66.

[81] Weinstein v. Ohio Bottle Gas Co. (Ohio 1959), 160 N.E. 2d 436.

[82] Walker Discount Corp. v. Sapin (1965), 48 Misc. 2d 277, 264 N.Y.S. 2d 841.

People v. Dunbar Contracting Co. (1915), 215 N.Y. 416, 109 N.E. 554.

[83] Liberty Mutual Insurance Co. v. Preston (Tex. Civ. App. 1966), 399 S.W. 2d 367, ref. n.r.e.

[84] Ottida Inc. v. Harriman National Bank and Trust Co. (1940), 260 App. Div. 1008, 24 N.Y.S. Supp. 2d 63.

[85] Lynn v. Farm Bureau Mutual Automobile Insurance Co. (4th Cir. [N.C.] 1959), 264 F. 2d 921;

See also Section 10.15, "A Technique to Prove Notice by Telephone."

[86] See Section 7.17, Using Admissions by a Party," *et seq.*

[87] See Section 7.21, "Offer Not as Proof of the Matter Asserted," *et seq.*

[88] See Section 7.27, "Declarant Unavailable, Assurance of Trustworthiness," *et seq.*

[89] *Wigmore on Evidence,* (3rd ed) Section 1048.

[90] Reed v. McCord (1899), 160 N.Y. 330, 341, 54 N.E. 737.

[91] *Ibid.*

Davidson v. Long Island Home (1935), 243 App. Div. 791, 278 N.Y.S. 167.

[92] See Section 9.02, "No Miranda Warning"; Section 10.13, "Verbal Acts: Miranda Warnings."

[93] Northern Oil Co. v. Socony Mobil Oil Co. (2d Cir. [Vt.] 1965), 347 F. 2d 81, 85.

[94] Grayson v. Williams (10th Cir. [Wyo.] 1958), 256 F. 2d 61.

KLM v. Tuller (3rd Cir. [D.C.] 1961), 292 F. 2d 775, 784.

Martin v. Savage Truck Line, Inc. (3rd Cir. [D.C.] 1954), 121 F. Supp. 417.

[95] Proposed Rules of Evidence for the United States District Courts and Magistrates, Rule 8-01 (c) (3).

[96] Leavitt v. Gillaspie (Alaska 1968), 443 P 2d 61.

Cherry v. Vinson (1968), 244 Ark. 742, 427 S.W. 2d 17;

Morris's Case (Mass. 1968), 238 N.E. 2d 35.

[97] Nichols v. Blake (Mo. 1967), 418 S.W. 2d 188.

[98] Ando v. Woodberry (1960), 8 N.Y. 2d 165, 168 N.E. 2d 520.

[99] Schwartz, *Trial of Accident Cases*, Section 812.

[100] See next section.

[101] See Section 7.23, "Prior Inconsistent Statement Made by a Witness."

[102] See Section 7.24, "Prior Consistent Statement to Rehabilitate."

[103] See Section 7.25, "A Verbal Act or Verbal Part of an Act."

[104] See Section 7.26, "Excited Utterances or Spontaneous Declarations (Res Gestae)."

[105] Proposed Rules of Evidence for the United States District Courts and Magistrates, Rule 8-03: "(3) THEN EXISTING MENTAL, EMOTIONAL OR PHYSICAL CONDITION. A statement of the declarant's then existing state of mind, emotion, sensation, or physical condition (such as intent, plan, motive, design, mental feeling, pain and bodily health), but not including memory or belief to prove the fact remembered or believed unless it relates to the execution, revocation, identification, or terms of declarant's will."

[106] *Ibid*, Rule 8–03 (4): "(4) STATEMENTS FOR PURPOSE OF MEDICAL DIAGNOSIS OR TREATMENT. Statements made for purposes of medical diagnosis or treatment and describing medical history, or past or present symptoms, pain, or sensations, or the inception or general character of the cause or external source thereof insofar as reasonably pertinent to diagnosis or treatment."

Korleski v. Needham (1966), 77 Ill. App. 2d 328, 222 N.E. 2d 334;

Regan v. National Postal Transportation Ass'n. (1967), 53 Misc. 2d 901, 280 N.Y.S. 2d 319.

[107] *Wigmore on Evidence*, (3rd ed) Section 1722.

Meaney v. United States (2d Cir. [N.Y.] 1940), 112 F. 2d 538, 130 A.L.R. 973.

[108] Shell Oil Co. v. Industrial Commn. (1954), 2 Ill. 2d 590, 119 N.E. 2d 224.

[109] Pinter v. Parsekian (1966), 92 N.J. Super 392, 223 A. 2d 635.

Pacific Finance Corp. v. Rucker (Tex. Civ. App. 1965), 392 S.W. 554;

Schoenrock v. City of Sisseton (S.D. 1960), 103 N.W. 2d 649. .

[110] Lessin v. Direct Delivery Service (1960), 10 App. Div. 2d 624, 196 N.Y.S. 2d 751.

[111] Gentry v. Watkins-Carolina Trucking Co. (1967), 249 S.C. 316, 154 S.E. 2d 112.

[112] See Proposed Rules of Evidence for the United States District Courts and Magistrates, Rule 8-03 (4).

[113] Schwartz, *op. cit.*, Sections 1184, 1185, 1703.

[114] *Wigmore on Evidence,* (3rd ed) Section 105.
Mindlin v. Dorfman (1921) 197 App. Div. 770, 189 N.Y.S. 265.

[115] Commonwealth v. Binenstock (1948), 358 Pa. 644, 57 A. 2d 884.

[116] McGehee v. Perkins (1948), 188 Va. 116, 49 N.E. 2d 304. *Contra* Anthony v. Hobbie (1948), Cal. App. 2d 798, 193 P. 2d 748.

[117] Blackford v. Kaplan (1939), 135 Ohio St. 268, 20 N.E. 2d 522.

[118] *Wigmore on Evidence,* 3rd ed. Section 1029.

[119] *Ibid.,* Section 779.

[120] Roge v. Valentine (1939), 280 N.Y. 268, 20 N.E. 2d 751.
Wigmore on Evidence, 3rd ed. Section 1018.

[121] People v. Johnson (1968), 68 Cal. Rptr. 599, 441 P. 2d 111.

[122] Proposed Rules of Evidence for United States District Courts and Magistrates, Rule 8-01 (c) (2) (i).

[123] *Wigmore on Evidence* (3d ed.) Section 2184 b.

[124] Schoppel v. United States (4th Cir. [Va.] 1959), 270 F. 2d 413.

[125] Affronti v. United States (8th Cir. [Mo.] 1944), 145 F. 2d 3.
Wigmore on Evidence, (3rd ed) Section 1126.

[126] Hagerty v. Radle (1949), 228 Minn. 487, 37 N.W. 2d 819;
Wigmore on Evidence, (3rd ed) Section 252, Note 2.

[127] *Wigmore on Evidence,* (3rd ed) Section 1772 *et seq.*

[128] Dowling v. L. H. Shattuck, Inc. (1941), 91 N.H. 234, 17 A. 2d 529.

[129] Schwartz, *op. cit.,* Section 6042.

[130] Sawyer v. Miseli (D.C. 1959), 156 A. 2d 141.

[131] Ray v. Gage (Tex. Civ. App. 1954), 269 S.W. 2d 411.

[132] Koeneman v. Aldridge (1954), 125 Ind. App. 176, 122 N.E. 2d 345.

[133] Swensson v. New York Albany Dispatch Co. (1956), 309 N.Y. 497, 131 N.E. 2d 902.

[134] Hamilton v. Huebner (1945), 146 Neb. 320, 19 N.W. 2d 552, 558.

[135] Arenson v. Skouras Theatres Corp. (1943), 130 N.J.L. 347, 32 A. 2d 858.
cf. Sawyer v. Miseli (D.C. 1959), 156 A. 2d 141.

[136] Swensson v. New York Albany Dispatch Co., supra.

[137] Melville v. Greyhound Corp. (1954), 99 Ohio App. 411, 133 N.E. 2d 436.

[138] Williams v. Martin (1956), 226 Ark. 431, 290 S.W. 2d 442; declaration made several minutes after the event was not part of *res gestae.*

[139] Beebe v. Kleidon (1954), 242 Minn. 521, 65 N.W. 2d 614.

[140] Proposed Rules of Evidence for the United States District Courts and Magistrates, Rule 8-01, (d).
N.Y.CPLR, Rule 4517.
Wigmore on Evidence, (3rd ed.) Sections 1401–18.

[141] The claim of privilege must be made, and a ruling by the judge is required.
Wyatt v. State (1950), 35 Ala. App. 147, 46 So. 2d 837.
State v. Stewart (1911), 86 Kan. 404, 116 P. 489.

[142] Johnson v. People (1963), 152 Colo. 586, 384 P. 2d 454.

People v. Pickett (1954), 339 Mich 294, 63 N.W. 2d 681, 45 A.L.R. 2d 1341. *Contra,* Pleau v. State (1949), 255 Wis. 362, 38 N.W. 2d 496.

[143] *Wigman on Evidence,* (3rd ed) Sections 1403 and 1406.

[144] Barber v. Page (1968), 390 U.S. 719;

Wigmore on Evidence, (3rd ed) Section 1404.

[145] Fink v. 37 West 36th Street Co. (1935), 244 App. Div. 622, 280 N.Y.S. 269.

[146] Fried v. New York, New Haven & Hartford Railroad Co. (1917), 178 App. Div. 309, 165 N.Y.S. 495, 497, 498, aff'd. 230 N.Y. 619, 130 N.E. 917.

[147] See next section.

[148] See Section 7.29, "Declaration as to Pedigree."

[149] See Section 7.30, "Declaration Against Interest."

[150] See Section 7.31, "Dying Declarations."

[151] *Wigmore on Evidence,* (3rd ed) Section 1413.

N.Y.CPLR Rule 4517.

N.Y. Crim. Pro. Law, Sections 670.10, 670.20.

[152] Martin v. Cope (1863), 28 N.Y. 180.

Shaw v. New York Electric Railroad (1904), 187 N.Y. 186, 79 N.E. 984. See 142 ALR 673.

[153] Hassett v. Rathbone (1923), 204 App. Div. 229, 198 N.Y.S. 381.

See Boschi v. City of New York (1946), 187 Misc. 875, 65 N.Y.S. 2d 425.

[154] Turner v. Sunshine Taxi Corp. (1945), 269 App. Div. 997, 58 N.Y.S. 2d 422.

Young v. Valentine (1904), 177 N.Y. 347, 357, 69 N.E. 643, 646.

[155] Wyatt v. State (1950), supra.

Bradley v. Mirick (1883), 91 N.Y. 293.

Wigmore on Evidence, (3rd ed) Section 1371.

[156] People v. Downs (1952), 114 Cal. App. 2d 758, 251 P. 2d 369.

McRorie v. Monroe (1911), 203 N.Y. 426, 96 N.E. 724.

People v. Colon (1953), 281 App. Div. 354, 119 N.Y.S. 2d 503.

Wigmore on Evidence, (3rd ed) Section 1330.

[157] Trimmer v. Trimmer (1882), 90 N.Y. 676.

[158] *Ibid.*

McIntyre v. N. Y. Central Railroad Co. (1867), 37 N.Y. 287.

[159] *Ibid.*

Hayes v. Pitts-Kimball Co. (1903), 183 Mass. 262, 67 N.E. 249.

[160] Murphy v. McMahon (1917), 179 App. Div. 837, 167 N.Y.S. 270, 272.

[161] *Ibid.*

Pratt, Hurst & Co. Ltd. v. Tailer (1909), 135 App. Div. 1, 119 N.Y.S. 803.

Wallach v. The Manhattan Railway Company, et al. (1905), 105 App. Div. 422; if the qualifications of an expert were not objected to at the prior trial, the objection cannot be raised at a subsequent trial.

[162] Aalholm v. People (1914), 211 N.Y. 406, 105 N.E. 647.

Wigmore on Evidence, (3rd ed) Section 1605.

[163] Young v. Shulenberg (1901), 165 N.Y. 385, 59 N.E. 135;

In re Strong's Estate (1938), 168 Misc. 716, 6 N.Y.S. 2d 300, aff'd. 256 App. Div. 971, 11 N.Y.S. 2d 225.

[104] Proposed Rules of Evidence for the United States District Courts and Magistrates, Rule 8-03(.19).

[105] Aalholm v. People, *supra.*

In re Wendel's Estate (1933), 146 Misc. 260, 262 N.Y.S. 41.

[106] Aalholm v. People, *supra.*

[107] Young v. Shulenberg, *supra.*

Fulkerson v. Holmes (1886), 117 U.S. 389, 6 S Ct. 780, 29 L. Ed. 915.

Wigmore on Evidence, (3rd ed) Section 1487.

[108] Aalholm v. People.

[109] Eisenlord v. Clum (1891), 126 N.Y. 552, 566, 27 N.E. 1024.

[170] Farmers' Loan & Trust Co. v. Wagstaff (1921), 194 App. Div. 757, 185 N.Y.S. 8.

Jacobs v. Fowler (1909), 135 App. (Div. 713, 119 N.Y.S. 647.

Wigmore on Evidence, (3rd ed) Section 1480 *et seq.*

[171] Eisenlord v. Clum.

Wigmore on Evidence, (3rd ed) Section 1486.

[172] See Section 137, "Using Admissions by a Party."

[173] MacDonald v. Protestant Episcopal Church (1967), 150 Mont. 332, 435 P. 2d 369.

Livingston v. Arnoux (1874), 56 N.Y. 507.

Lyon v. Ricker (1894), 141 N.Y. 225, 36 N.E. 189.

[174] Lyon v. Ricker.

Tompkins v. Fonda Glove Lining Co. (1907), 188 N.Y. 261, 80 N.E. 933.

[175] Weber v. Chicago R.I. & P. Ry. Co. (1915), 175 Iowa 358, 151 N.W. 852.

Sutter v. Easterly (1945), 354 Mo. 282, 189 S.W. 2d 284, 162 A.L.R. 437.

[176] Kittredge v. Grannis (1926), 244 N.Y. 168, 155 N.E. 88.

People v. Storrs (1912), 207 N.Y. 147, 100 N.E. 730.

Hileman v. Northwest Engineering Co. (6th Cir. 1965), 346 F. 2d 668.

Donnelly v. United States (1913), 228 U.S. 243.

[177] People v. Spriggs (1964), 36 Cal. Rptr. 841, 389 P. 2d 377.

Sutter v. Easterly (1945), 354 Mo. 282, 189 S.W. 2d 284.

Proposed Rules of Evidence for the United States District Courts and Magistrates, Rule 8-04 (b) (4).

[178] Clark & Jones, Inc. v. American Mutual Liability Insurance Co. (E.D. Tenn. 1953), 112 F. Supp. 889.

Dempsey v. Meighen (1958), 251 Minn. 562, 90 N.W. 2d 178.

[179] Hoge v. Lee (1922), 184 N.C. 44, 113 S.E. 776.

Halvorsen v. Moon & Kerr Lumber Co. (1902), 87 Minn. 18, 91 N.W. 28.

Wigmore on Evidence, (3rd ed) Sections 1483, 1484.

[180] *Ibid.,* Section 1469.

[181] Livingston v. Arnoux (1874), 56 N.Y. 507.

Wigmore on Evidence, (3rd ed) Section 1465.

[182] Hileman v. Northwest Engineering Co. *supra.*

Wigmore on Evidence, (3rd ed.) Section 1461

[183] Proposed Rules of Evidence for the United States District Courts and Magistrates, Rule 8-04 (b) (3).

Wigmore on Evidence, (3rd ed) Sections 1430–52.

[184] Waldele v. New York Central and Hudson Railroad Co. (1884), 95 N.Y. 274.

Stevens v. Stevens (1959), 355 Mich. 363, 94 N.W. 2d 858.

[185] *Wigmore on Evidence,* (3rd ed) Section 1432.

[186] Thurston v. Fritz (1914), 91 Kan. 468, 138 P. 625. *Contra* Blair v. Rogers (1939), 185 Okla. 63, 89 P. 2d 928.

[187] People v. Chase (1894), 79 Hun. 296, 29 N.Y.S. 376, aff'd. 143 N.Y. 669, 39 N.E. 21.

State v. Ensley (1947), 228 N.C. 271, 45 S.E. 2d 357.

[188] Batten v. Commonwealth (1949), 190 Va. 235, 56 S.E. 2d 231.

[189] People v. Allen (1949), 300 N. Y. 222, 227-228, 90 N.E. 2d 48.

Shepard v. United States (1933), 290 U.S. 96, 100, 78 L. Ed. 196, 54 S. Ct. Rep. 22.

[190] People v. Smith (1902), 172 N.Y. 210, 64 N.E. 814.

People v. Morse (1909), 196 N.Y. 306, 89 N.E. 816.

[191] People v. Shaw (1875), 63 N.Y. 36.

[192] People v. Haber (1927), 221 App. Div. 150, 223 N.Y.S. 133; "He murdered me" accepted.

Shepard v. United States.

[193] Shepard v. United States.

People v. Bartelini (1947), 285 N.Y. 433, 35 N.E. 2d 29, 167 A.L.R. 139.

[194] People v. Sarzano (1914), 212 N.Y. 231, 106 N.E. 87.

[195] *Wigmore on Evidence,* (3rd ed) Section 1450.

People v. Apicello (1937), 275 N.Y. 222, 228, 9 N.E. 2d 844.

[196] People v. Madas (1911), 201 N.Y. 349, 94 N.E. 857.

[197] Anthony v. New York Central Railroad Co. (1965), 61 Ill. App. 2d 466, 209 N.E. 2d 686.

Wilson v. Hartford Accident and Indemnity Co. (N.C. 1967), 158 S.E. 2d 1.

Schwartz, *Trial of Accident Cases,* Section 741.

[198] Chicago and N. W. Ry. Co. v. Golay (10th Cir. [Wyo.] 1946), 155 F. 2d 842.

Latourelle v. New York Central R.R. Co. (1950), 301 N.Y. 103, 92 N.E. 2d 911.

[199] Heafner v. Columbus and G.R. Co. (1939), 185 Miss. 773, 190 So. 1.

[200] Cope et ux v. Southern Pac. Co. (1947), 66 Ariz. 197, 185 P. 2d 772.

Dohar v. Boston & M.R.R. (1949), 95 N.H. 464, 66 A. 2d 707, 710.

[201] Dixon v. Texas & P. Ry. Co. (Tex. Civ. App. 1942), 164 S.W. 2d 252.

[202] Draper v. Baker, 61 Wis. 450.

Moore, on Facts, Sections 735, 1335, 1339, 1351.

Latourville v. New York Central Railroad Co. (1950), 301 N.Y. 103, 92 N.E. 2d 911; negative testimony may support a verdict despite affirmative testimony to the contrary.

[203] Mooney v. Underwriters at Lloyd's, London (Ill. 1965), 213 N.E. 2d 283.

People v. Weinstein (Ill. App. 1965), 213 N.E. 2d 115.

Barens v. State (1967), 1 Md. App. 123, 227 A. 2d 763.

Wigmore on Evidence, (3rd ed) Sections 1071, 1072

[204] Kelley v. United States (1956), 99 D. C. App. 13, 236 F. 2d 746.

[205] Knox Lime Co. v. Maine State Highway Co. (Me. 1967), 230 A. 2d 814.

[206] I. S. Wechsler, A Textbook of Clinical Neurology (7th ed 1952) (W. B. Saunders Co.), pp. 41–43.

Schwartz, *Trial of Accident Cases,* Section 1352.

[207] Warner Brown and Howard C. Gilhousen, *College Psychology* (Prentice-Hall, 1949), p. 285.

[208] See Section 12.17, "Vivid Description of Subjective Feelings."

[209] See Section 19.12, "That Witness Relied on Only One of the Senses."

[210] See Section 12.17, ˙Vivid Description of Subjective Feelings."

[211] Schwartz, *Trial of Accident Cases,* Section 5365.

[212] A. J. Haagen-Smit, "Smell and Taste," *Scientific American,* Vol. 187, No. 3 (March 1952).

[213] Wigmore, *Principles of Judicial Proof,* (Boston, Little Brown and Company 1931) Section 170.

[214] Martel v. Duff-Mott Corp. (Mich. App. 1968), 166 N.W. 2d 541.

[215] A. J. Haagen-Smit, *op. cit.*

[216] *Ibid.*

[217] Moore *on Facts.* Sections 717 and 718.

OBJECTIONS TO PROOF
BASED ON SIGHT

TABLE OF CONTENTS

OBJECTIONS TO PROOF BASED ON SIGHT

While listening to a witness testify as to something he saw, opposing counsel should be alert to object should the witness be incompetent to testify (because he is an interested witness, or not qualified to interpret what he saw or because he would be revealing a privileged communication). If he is testifying as to the contents of a document, then an objection should be made unless the writing itself is produced. Then again, the witness may have seen something which public policy prevents him from disclosing (such as subsequent repairs) or the evidence may be too remote, irrelevant, or unduly prejudicial to your client. This chapter discusses and gives illustrations of all of these objections.

§ 8:01   Incompetent Witness: Interested Party

In an action against a decedent's estate brought by a passenger who had been riding in an automobile which was driven by the decedent, the plaintiff was asked by Plaintiff's Attorney:

Q.   Before you got to the place where the accident occurred, where did you go with decedent?
A.   The Tourist's Cafe.

Q.   What did you see him do at the cafe?
A.   We were drinking together.

Defendant's Attorney: I object and move to strike out the answer.

At common law, a witness was incompetent to testify on many grounds. These have been described as "the five I's"—interest, insanity, infancy, infidelity, and infamy.[1] Most, if not all, of these grounds have been abrogated. In some jurisdictions, traces of the common law disqualification still survive in that parties and interested persons are disqualified from testifying against the estate of a deceased person. This is usually accomplished by means of the so-called "Dead Man's Act" which is justified on the theory that where death has closed the lips of one of the parties, the law will close those of his opponents.[2]

Whether or not the objection will be sustained depends upon the existence and wording of a Dead Man's Statute and whether the proffered testimony violates such enactment.[3] Where the statute prohibits an interested witness from testifying as to a "personal transaction" with the decedent, the objection might be sustained on the theory that drinking together constitutes such a personal transaction.[4] The statute which governs is that of the *lex fori,* where the action is tried.[5]

The objection might be overruled under the following circumstances:

(a) The common law disqualification against the testimony of an interested witness has been abrogated. This has been done in most jurisdictions and by the proposed Rules of Evidence for the United States District Courts and Magistrates.[6]

(b) Even where there is a Dead Man's Statute, it may be so worded as not to include the decedent's actions but only personal conversations.[7] For example, the statute may, by its terms, permit an interested witness to testify as to the facts of the accident itself as observed by him, for such testimony does not constitute a personal transaction with the decedent.[8]

(c) The witness may not be considered as being an interested party within the meaning of the statute. For example, an agent or employee of a party is not an interested party for this purpose;[9] the spouse or relative of a party is not an interested party;[10] a nominal party such as a guardian *ad litem*[11] will not be incompetent unless, in addition, he has an adverse interest in the event. To be "interested in the event" means one who will either gain or lose by direct legal operation of the judgment to be obtained in the very action about which he is called to testify.[12]

(d) The witness may be incompetent insofar as concerns the action against a deceased driver but be a competent witness against other surviving parties.[13]

(e) The witness, although interested, will be permitted to testify *against his own interest.*[14]

(f) Where the disqualification has been waived, which may occur in many ways besides failing to object to the testimony,[15] as where the personal representative opens the door (1) by his own testimony as to the prohibited transaction or communication;[16] (2) by calling the adverse party as his own witness to testify as to the personal transaction;[17] (3) by reading into the record the testimony or deposition of the disqualified witness; [18] (4) by introducing other similar evidence on behalf of the estate as to the personal transaction.[19]

§ 8:02 Privilege of Spouse

In a criminal trial, a witness was called and asked by the District Attorney:

Q. *Are you related to the defendant?*
A. *Yes, I am his wife.*

> *Defense Attorney: I object to the witness testifying.*

At common law, a husband or wife in a criminal case was incompetent to testify either for the state or for the defense.[20] With the disappearance of the disqualification of parties and interested persons, spousal incompetency has virtually disappeared in both civil and criminal actions by reason of statutory enactments as well as by the process of court decision.[21] Even though a spouse is competent to testify, in many jurisdictions and under the proposed rules of evidence for the United States courts, an accused in a criminal proceeding has the privilege to prevent his spouse from testifying against him.[22] A few jurisdictions recognize a privilege on the part of the witness not to testify against his or her spouse.[23]

Generally, there are exceptions to such privilege and one spouse is permitted to testify against the other under certain circumstances, as (a) when one spouse is charged with a crime against the person or property of the other or of a child of either,[24] (b) as to matters occurring prior to the marriage, thus eliminating the possibility of suppressing testimony by marrying the witness; [25] (c) in proceedings in which a spouse is charged with importing an alien for prostitution [26] or violations of the Mann Act.[27]

Generally, one spouse is not prohibited from testifying in favor of the other, for example as an alibi witness.[28] There is nothing preventing a witness from testifying as to the actions of the accused's spouse in a proceeding against him.[29]

Even though the spouse may testify, there may be a privilege against disclosure of confidential communications between the spouses or of information learned by virtue of the existence of the relationship.[30] Local statutes must be consulted as to all these matters.

§ 8:03 Confidential Communication Between Spouses

The defendant was charged with larceny of goods from a department store where he was employed. The District Attorney called defendant's wife as the People's witness, and she was asked by the District Attorney:

Q. *Were you ever in the bedroom when your husband came home from work?*

A. *I was.*

Q. *Did you ever see him secrete packages under the bed?*

Defendant's Attorney: I object.

Even jurisdictions which permit one spouse to testify against the other may recognize the privilege against disclosures of confidential communications between spouses. These matters are largely governed by statute and such privilege has virtually disappeared in both civil and criminal actions.

In the illustration above, the question Q. *Did you ever see him secrete packages under the bed?* is leading and suggestive, but aside from this, the objection is that it calls upon the wife to disclose a confidential communication arising by reason of the marital relationship. This objection will be sustained in those jurisdictions which recognize the privilege against disclosure of confidential communications between husband and wife and extend it to include information learned by virtue of the relationship.[31]

Even where such a privilege is recognized, if the wife happened to see something which her husband was trying to hide from her, it would not be privileged. Thus, if the questions sought to elicit that the wife had, unknown to her husband, observed him digging a hole in the back yard in which he buried some object, this would not be privileged because the husband was not relying upon the marital relationship at the time.[32] And, where the wife returned home unexpectedly and allegedly discovered her husband committing acts of sodomy with their child, she was competent to testify against her husband at his prosecution, since the alleged acts were not disclosed to her by reason of the marital relationship.[33]

§ 8:04 Physician-Patient Privilege

The defendant was charged with drunken driving in which both he and another motorist were injured. A physician was called by the State and asked by the District Attorney:

Q. *Are you a physician duly licensed by this State?*

A. *I am.*

Q. *Did you examine and treat the defendant on the ____ day of _____ for injuries arising out of an automobile collision which had occurred on that day?*

A. *I did.*

Q. *Where did you first see him?*

A. *In the hospital emergency room where he had been brought by am-bulance.*

Q. *Tell us what you observed on making a physical examination of the defendant?*

Defense Attorney: I object.

Whether the objection will be sustained will depend upon whether or not, under the Rules of Evidence of the jurisdiction wherein the case is tried, the testimony of the physician would be privileged. The common law recognized no general physician-patient privilege[34] but many states have created it by statute.[35]

Where the privilege exists, what a physician sees by looking at his patient is as privileged as what he hears.[36]

The proposed Rules of Evidence for the United States District Courts and Magistrates contain no provision for a general physician-patient privilege except as between a psychotherapist and patient.[37] Even where the privilege exists, there are so many exceptions that there is little left of the rule. Unless otherwise provided, the privilege is extended only to a physician or others specifically mentioned in the statute;[38] the relationship must be that of physician and patient;[39] if the doctor did not examine the person for diagnosis or treatment, it is not within the privilege rule.[40] Thus the privilege does not cover an autopsy[41] and would not extend to an examination by a court-appointed physician.[42] The privilege may not be applicable in criminal prosecutions[43] or in malpractice[44] or personal injury actions where the physical condition is put in issue,[45] nor where reports are required by law.[46] The mere fact of medical consultation or of the date thereof is not privileged.[47] The physician may disclose information which was plain to the observation of anyone and not acquired in a professional capacity.[48]

§ 8:05 Witness Not Qualified

During the direct examination of a physician called by the plaintiff in a personal injury action, he was asked by Plaintiff's Attorney:

Q. *Are you a duly licensed physician of the State?*

A. *I am.*

Q. *Doctor, look at this x-ray, Plaintiff's Exhibit 1, and tell us what it shows.*

Defendant's Attorney: I object.

Although the witness is asked merely to state what he sees on an x-ray plate, more than mere perception is involved because the reading and interpretation of an x-ray requires a specialized knowledge not possessed by every doctor. The mere fact that the witness is a licensed physician is not sufficient to qualify him to read x-rays, and the objection should be sustained unless he establishes his knowledge and experience in that respect to the satisfaction of the trial court.[49]

The testimony of the witness to the fact that he has experience in reading and using x-rays in his practice is generally sufficient and the weight of his testimony will be for the jury.

The general rule is that a physician who is licensed to practice medicine is *prima facie* qualified to express any medical opinion.[50]

§ 8:06   Evidence Incompetent Because of Best Evidence Rule

The plaintiff's medical witness in a personal injury action was asked by Plaintiff's Attorney:

Q. Doctor, are you experienced in reading x-ray plates?
A. I am.

Q. How many x-rays have you read?
A. I have read thousands of them.

Q. Did you examine the x-rays which were taken at the hospital?
A. Yes, sir.

Q. Now, Doctor, tell us what the x-rays disclosed.

Defendant's Attorney: I object.

Although the doctor is qualified, he should not be permitted to answer the question because he is being asked for the contents of a document not in evidence.[51] The requirement that the original writing be produced, or its absence accounted for, originally applied only to writings, but present day techniques have broadened the rule to include not only what has been set down by handwriting but also to what is recorded by typewriting, printing, photostating, photographing, x-rays, motion pictures, mechanical or electronic recording, magnetic impulse, computer, or other form of data compilation.[52] The x-rays should, therefore, be produced and authenticated before any testimony as to their contents will be received.[53]

This requirement will be waived should it appear that the x-ray or other document is only collateral and not closely related to a controlling issue, or where it appears that the original was lost or destroyed or not available by any judicial process or the original is in the possession of the opponent who refuses to produce it after being put on notice, or if it is impossible to produce it for any other reasons.[54]

§ 8:07   Hearsay: Learned Treatise Not in Evidence

In an action for personal injuries, the plaintiff's doctor was asked, on direct examination by Plaintiff's Attorney:

Q.   *Doctor, have you read Professor Wechsler's book on Neurology?*
A.   *I have.*

Q.   *What does Professor Wechsler say about this condition?*

Defendant's Attorney: I object.

Hearsay is generally thought of as something one has heard. However, it may also refer to something one has read, in this case a learned medical treatise. By the great weight of authority, even if the book itself had been shown to be authoritative and offered into evidence as part of the direct examination of the witness, it would not be admissible.[55] Here it is not the book, but the witness' recollection of its contents which is called for. This is obviously hearsay, as it calls for the statement of the author who is not in court, nor under oath, and not subject to cross-examination[56] and might violate the best evidence rule and constitute testimony as to the contents of a document not in evidence.[57]

In a few jurisdictions, authoritative learned treatises are received in evidence as part of the direct examination of an expert.[58] The proposed rules for the United States Courts would permit such use when an expert witness is on the stand and relies on the treatise and is available to explain and assist in the application of the treatise if desired.[59] Of course, such treatises could be used on cross-examination to test the learning of the witness.[60]

§ 8:08   Prior Identification

In a criminal case, the complainant identified the accused in court. Thereafter a police officer was called by the People and asked by the District Attorney:

Q. Were you present at the police station, together with the complainant, when the defendant was brought in?

A. I was.

Q. What, if anything, did you see the complainant do?

A. I saw her point to the defendant and say, "That's the man."

Defense Attorney: I object and move to strike out the answer.

The People are endeavoring to bolster the complainant's identification by calling a police officer to swear that he saw the complainant identify the same person upon a previous occasion. There is a difference of authority as to whether prior out-of-court identifications are admissible or violate either the hearsay rule or the right of confrontation because the prior identification was not made under oath, subject to immediate cross-examination.[61] If the witness testifying was the identifier, then his testimony would be merely a prior consistent statement which is generally not allowed.[62] When the testimony is given by a third person who witnessed the prior identification, it is hearsay.[63] "The reasons for this rule are well understood. One of the most stubborn problems in the administration of the criminal law is to establish identity by the testimony of witnesses to whom an accused was previously unknown, from quick observation under stress or when, as here, there was no particular reason to note the person's identity. Where the *opportunity for observation* is limited and the opportunity and *ability of the witness to identify the defendant is questionable,* it is all too easy to bolster such testimony by calling a succession of witnesses who swear that they saw and heard him identify the same person upon previous occasions. This tends to give the idea to a jury that there is an impressive amount of testimony to identification when such is really not the fact. As for previous identification from photographs, not only is it readily possible to distort pictures as affecting identity, but also where the identification is from photographs in the *rogues' gallery* (even though the name or number on the pictures has been exscinded) the inference to the jury is obvious that the person has been in trouble with the law before. Such an inference is accentuated where the defendant fails to take the witness stand." [64]

Some courts permit evidence of recent identification [65] and statute and rules may allow it.[66]

§ 8:09   Evidence Against Public Policy

The plaintiff sued to recover for personal injuries he sustained allegedly due to a defective step in a stairway. While testifying on direct examination he was asked by Plaintiff's Attorney:

Q. *Did you see the janitor two weeks after your accident?*
A. *I did.*

Q. *What, if anything, did you see the janitor do with respect to repairing that step?*

Defendant's Attorney: I object.

The question calls for evidence of subsequent repairs which is excluded as a matter of public policy as not constituting an admission of fault.[67] The rationale is not to discourage people from taking steps in furtherance of added safety. It is thought that if such evidence were admitted, it might deter owners of property from making repairs lest that be construed as an admission of liability. The objection would, therefore, be sustained if the evidence is offered as proof of negligence or culpable conduct.[68]

Evidence of subsequent remedial measures would be received, however, for other purposes or on other theories as, for example, to establish ownership or control where the defendant has denied it,[69] or to show that changes and safeguards were feasible[70] and for impeachment.[71]

§ 8:10   Objecting to Evidence Which is Irrelevant or Remote

The plaintiff claimed that a hallway was in darkness and no artificial lights were lit at 9:30 P.M., the time when he was injured. Defendant called a witness who was asked on direct examination by Defendant's Attorney:

Q. *Were you in the premises at 7 P.M. on the day in question?*
A. *I was.*

Q. *What, if anything, did you observe as to the artificial lights in the hall-way at that time?*

Plaintiff's Attorney: I object.

The objection should be sustained because lights can be turned on and off and changed in a moment, and whether the lights were lit at 7 P.M. is too remote to the issue as to whether they were lit at 9:30 P.M. in the absence of proof that the condition remained the same in the interim. If the question was asked whether the lights were lit a few hours *after* the accident, the ruling would be similar.[72] What is so remote as to be irrelevant, speculative, or conjectural is for the court to decide.[73]

§ 8:11 Objecting to What Is Immaterial or Prejudicial

The issue was whether the defendant was intoxicated at the time of the accident. A witness was called and asked by Plaintiff's Attorney:

Q. *Did you see the defendant's car right after the accident?*
A. *I did.*

Q. *What, if anything, did you see on the road near the door of his car?*
A. *I saw an empty whiskey bottle.*

Defense Attorney:I object and move to strike the answer.

The objection should be sustained and the answer stricken as being immaterial and prejudicial, the whiskey bottle not having been shown to have been in defendant's possession.[74] Evidence that a whiskey bottle was found *inside* the defendant's automobile [75] might be received on the issue of negligence in driving, there being a close connection between intoxication and negligence.[76]

Chapter Eight

FOOTNOTES

[1] Chandler v. Gately (Ga. App. 1968), 167 S.E. 2d 697.
Slovenko, "Witnesses, Psychiatry and the Credibility of Testimony," 19 *Fla. L. Rev.* 1, 3 (1966).
[2] *In re* Erdmann's Estate (1950), 198 Misc. 1087, 98 N.Y.S. 2d 111.
[3] Brautigan v. Hoffman (Mo. App. 1969), 444 S.W. 2d 528.
Wigmore on Evidence, (3rd ed), statutes in all jurisdictions collated in Section 488; as to disqualification by reason of survivor's interest, see Wigmore, Sections 577, 578.
[4] Trombly v. Deso (1932), 235 App. Div. 151, 256 N.Y.S. 225.
See Note 7, this section.
[5] United States Mortgage & Trust Co. v. Ruggles (1932), 258 N.Y. 32, 40, 179 N.E. 250, 252, 79 A.L.R. 802.
Restatement Conflicts of Laws, Section 597.

[6] See Proposed Rules of Evidence for the United States District Courts and Magistrates, Rule 6.01.

Wayne Law Review, Vol. 15, No. 3 (1969), p. 1250, Note 89.

[7] Spafford v. Hahn (1966), 274 Minn. 180, 143 N.W. 2d 81.

[8] McCarthy v. Woolston (1924), 210 App. Div. 152, 205 N.Y.S. 507.

[9] Sheets v. Davenport (1967), 181 Neb. 621, 150 N.W. 2d 224.

Morrison v. Walker Bank & Trust Co. (1961), 11 Utah 2d 416, 360 P. 2d 1015.

[10] Gushurst v. Benham (Colo. 1966), 417 P. 2d 777.

Gladman v. Carns (1964), 9 Ohio App. 2d 135, 223 N.E. 2d 378.

[11] Duncan v. Clarke (1955), 308 N.Y. 282, 125 N.E. 2d 569.

[12] Baumel v. Travelers Insurance Co. (D.C.N.Y. 1959), 179 F. Supp. 88.

[13] Busser v. Nohle (1959), 22 Ill. App. 2d 433, 161 N.E. 2d 150.

Scott v. State (1967), 27 App. Div. 2d 961, 279 N.Y.S. 2d 314.

[14] Matter of Fitzpatrick (1929), 252 N.Y. 121, 169 N.E. 110.

[15] Black Mountain Corp. v. Jones (1940), 283 Ky. 707, 142 S.W. 2d 973.

[16] Schmidt v. Jennings (1960), 359 Mich. 376, 102 N.W. 2d 589.

[17] *In re* Berardini (1934), 263 N.Y. 627, 189 N.E. 730.

[18] Baumel v. Travelers Insurance Co.

[19] Pearce v. Barham (N.C. 1966), 149 S.E. 2d 22.

[20] State v. Alford (N.C. 1968), 161 S.E. 2d 575.

[21] Funk v. United States (1933), 290 U.S. 371.

Ross v. State (Fla. App. 1967), 202 So. 2d 582.

Proposed Rules of Evidence for the United States District Courts and Magistrates, Rule 5-05.

[22] State v. Hand (1968), 101 N.J. Super 43, 242 A. 2d 888.

Hawkins v. United States (1958), 358 U.S. 74.

[23] Funk v. United States.

Wyatt v. United States (1960), 362 U.S. 525.

Proposed Rules of Evidence for the United States District Courts and Magistrates, Rule 5-05.

[24] People v. Brown (Cal. App. 1968), 68 Cal Rptr. 657.

Grulkey v. United States (8th Cir. [Iowa] 1968), 394 F. 2d 244.

Proposed Rules of Evidence for the United States District Courts and Magistrates, Rule 5-05 (b).

Wigmore on Evidence, (3rd ed.) Section 2239.

[25] Proposed Rules of Evidence for the United States District Courts and Magistrates, Rule 5-05 (b).

[26] 8 U.S.C. Section 1328.

[27] Hawkins v. United States.

Proposed Rules of Evidence for the United States District Courts and Magistrates, Rule 5-05 (b) (3).

[28] State v. Sprouse (1968), 13 Ohio App. 2d 170, 234 N.E. 2d 922.

Ferrell v. State (Tex. Cr. App. 1968), 429 S.W. 2d 901.

[29] Boyd v. State (Miss. 1967), 204 So. 2d 165.

[30] See next section.

[31] Funk v. United States.

People v. Daghita (1949), 299 N.Y. 194, 199, 86 N.E. 2d 172.

[32] People v. Dudley (1968), 29 App. Div. 2d 232, 287 N.Y.S. 2d 443.

[33] People v. Fuentes (1966), 51 Misc. 2d 354, 273 N.Y.S. 2d 321.

[34] Chamberlayne, *Modern Law of Evidence,* Section 3701.

Wigmore on Evidence, (3rd ed.) Section 2380.

[35] Carlton v. Superior, Court (Cal. App. 1968), 67 Cal. Rptr. 568.

Grattan v. Metropolitan Life Insurance Co. (1883), 92 N.Y. 274, 286.

N.Y. CPLR, Section 4504.

[36] Grattan v. Metropolitan Life Insurance Co.

[37] Proposed Rules of Evidence for the United States District Courts and Magistrates, Rule 5-04.

[38] Elliott v. Watkins Trucking Co. (7th Cir. [Ind.] 1969), 406 F. 2d 90 (Indiana Law).

[39] Fisher v. Fisher (1892), 129 N.Y. 654, 29 N.E. 951.

[40] State v. Kuljis (Wash. 1967), 422 P. 2d 480.

[41] *Wigmore on Evidence,* (3rd ed) Section 2382, Note 11.

[42] People v. English (1964), 31 Ill. 2d 301, 201 N.E. 2d 455.

[43] If statute so provides: Commonwealth v. Sykes (1946), 353 Pa. 392, 45 A. 2d 43.

[44] Beckwell v. Hosier (1894), 10 Ind. App. 5, 37 N.E. 580.

Cramer v. Hunt (1900), 154 Mo. 112, 55 S.W. 258.

[45] Randa v. Bear (1957), 50 Wash. 415, 312 P. 2d 640.

[46] State v. Antill (1964), 176 Ohio St. 61, 197 N.E. 2d 548.

[47] *Wigmore on Evidence,* (3rd ed) Section 2384.

[48] *Ibid.* Where a physician took off an injured person's shoes and socks to test the soles of his feet, and a packet of heroin fell out, which he turned over to the police, this was not a disclosure of information acquired in a professional capacity.

People v. Capra (1966), 17 N.Y. 2d 670, 269 N.Y.S. 2d 451, 216 N.E. 2d 610.

[49] Liles v. Hannah Pickett Mills Inc. (N.C.) 150 S.E. 363; sufficiency of the witness' qualifications is for the court's discretion.

[50] Chicago v. McNally (1907), 227 Ill. 14, 81 N.E. 23.

Seawall v. Brame (1963), 258 N.C. 666, 129 S.E. 2d 283.

[51] Gay v. United States (7th Cir. 1941), 118 F. 2d 160, 162.

Richter v. Trailways of New England, Inc. (1967), 28 App. Div. 2d 737, 282 N.Y.S. 2d 148.

Simon v. Hendricks (Okla. 1958), 330 P. 2d 186, 188.

Wigmore on Evidence, (3rd ed) Section 795, Note 3.

[52] Proposed Rules of Evidence for the United States District Courts and Magistrates, Rule 10-01 (a) (b).

[53] State Highway Department v. Alexander (Ga. 1966), 149 S.E. 2d 788; may not question a witness regarding a plat not in evidence.

Sullivan v. Minneapolis St. P. & St. M.R. Co. (1927), 55 N.D. 353, 213 N.W. 841.

[54] Proposed Rules of Evidence for the United States District Courts and Magistrates, Rule 10-04 (d);

Wigmore on Evidence, (3rd ed) Sections 1179 to 1183.

See also Section 6.06, "Contents of a Writing."

[55] Ross v. Gardner (6th Cir. [Ky.], 1966), 365 F. 2d 554.

Sayers v. Gardner (6th Cir. [Ky.] 1967), 380 F. 2d 940.

Colwell v. Gardner (6th Cir. [Ky.] 1967), 386 F. 2d 56.

[56] Pahl v. Troy City Railway Co. (1903), 81 App. Div. 308, 310, 81 N.Y.S. 46.

Hallworth v. Republic Steel Corp. (1950), 153 Ohio St. 349, 91 N.E. 2d 690, 693.

Wigmore on Evidence, (3rd ed) Section 1690.

[57] See Section 6.06, "Contents of a Writing."

[58] City of Dothan v. Hardy (1939), 237 Ala. 603, 188 So. 264.

Lewandowski v. Preferred Rick Mutual Insurance Co. (1966), 33 Wis. 2d 69, 146 N.W. 2d 50.

Wigmore on Evidence, (3rd ed) Section 1692.

[59] Proposed Rules of Evidence for the United States District Courts and Magistrates, Rule 8-03 (a) (b) (18).

[60] See Section 18.16, "Revealing That Expert's Opinions Are Contrary to Scientific Authorities."

[61] 71 ALR 2d 449.

[62] Rogers v. State (1908), 88 Ark. 451, 115 S.W. 156.

Crawford v. Nilan (1943), 249 N.Y. 444, 46 N.E. 2d 512.

[63] People v. Moore (1966), 26 App. Div. 2d 954, 275 N.Y.S. 2d 66.

People v. Trowbridge (1953), 305 N.Y. 471, 113 N.E. 2d 841.

People v. Cioffi (1956), 1 N.Y. 2d 70, 150 N.Y.S. 2d 192, 133 N.E. 2d 703.

People v. Herrmann (1961), 9 N.Y. 2d 665, 212 N.Y.S. 2d 77, 173 N.E. 2d 52.

[64] Van Voorhis J., in People v. Caserta (1966), 19 N.Y. 2d 18, 224 N.E. 2d 82, 277 N.Y.S. 2d 647.

People v. Hagedorny (1947), 272 App. Div. 830, 70 N.Y.S. 2d 511.

Gilbert v. California (1967), 388 U.S. 263, 272 n 3.

[65] People v. Gould (1960), 54 Cal. 2d 621, 354 P. 2d 865.

Jady v. State (1958), 218 Md. 168, 146 A. 2d 29.

State v. Simmons (1963), 63 Wash. 2d 16, 385 P. 2d 389.

[66] N.Y. CPL, Sections 60.25 and 60.30; only the person who made the previous identification may testify to it—not any other witness who observed him make the identification.

Proposed Rules of Evidence for the United States District Courts and Magistrates, Rule 8-01 (c) (i) (iii).

[67] Proposed Rules of Evidence, *Ibid.,* Rule 4-07.

Morse v. Minneapolis & St. Louis Railway Co. (1883), 30 Minn. 465, 16 N.W. 358.

[68] Columbia and Puget Sound Railroad Co. v. Hawthorne (1892), 144 U.S. 202, 208, 36 L.Ed. 405, 12 Sup. Ct. Rep. 591.

Wigmore on Evidence, (3rd ed) Section 283.

[69] Haffey v. Lemieux (Conn. 1966), 224 A. 2d 551.

Antonsen v. Bay Ridge Savings Bank (1944), 292 N.Y. 143, 54 N.E. 2d 338.

Powers v. J. B. Michael & Co. (6th Cir. [Tenn.] 1964), 329 F. 2d 674.

[70] Boeing Airplane Co. v. Brown (9th Cir. [D.C.] 1961), 291 F. 2d 310.

[71] *Wigmore on Evidence,* (3rd ed) Section 283.

Annot. 64 ALR 2d 1296.

[72] Stokes v. Old Colony Trust Co. (Mass. 1968), 242 N.E. 2d 853.

Majors v. Mirsky (1947), 272 App. Div. 764, 70 N.Y.S. 2d 570.

[73] *Wigmore on Evidence,* (3rd ed) Sections 28 and 29.

[74] Wurtzman v. Kalinowski (1931), 233 App. Div. 187, 251 N.Y.S. 328.

Cf. McKenzie v. Ruggles Construction Co. (1930), 129 Kan. 759, 284 P. 407; whiskey bottle found near automobile admitted where doctor and nurse testified that the driver was intoxicated

[75] Davis v. Rodney (Ala. 1949), 8 So. 2d 867.

[76] State v. Himmelmann (Mo. 1966), 399 S.W. 2d 58.

OBJECTING TO QUESTIONS DEALING WITH HEARING

TABLE OF CONTENTS

OBJECTING TO QUESTIONS DEALING WITH HEARING

There are more possible grounds for objecting to questions as to what the witness heard, than as to any other testimony. The law may prevent the disclosure of a conversation by making it privileged, or by interposing constitutional safeguards such as requiring certain preliminary warnings or court orders, or requiring confrontation. Hearsay will not be received, although there are many exceptions to this rule. If the statement was reduced to writing, then that may have to be produced. Of course, what was heard must also be relevant to the issues and not immaterial or prejudicial. All of these matters are discussed and fully illustrated in this chapter.

§ 9:01 Witness Incompetent Because of Privilege

In a criminal case, a police officer was called by the People and asked by the District Attorney:

Q. *What is your occupation?*
A. *I am a policeman.*

Q. *On _____, 19___ where were you assigned?*
A. *I was assigned to the City Hospital to guard the defendant.*

Q. *What were your orders?*
A. *I was to remain inside the hospital room at all times and not to leave it unless relieved. I was not to leave him alone.*

Q. *Was the defendant under arrest at the time?*
A. *Yes.*

Q. While on duty there, were you present when Dr. _____, a resident physician, treated the defendant's injuries?

A. Yes.

Q. Were you in plain view of both the doctor and the defendant?

A. I was.

Q. And did you see and hear all that transpired during that visit by Dr. _____?

A. I did.

Q. Tell us what, if anything, you heard the defendant tell Dr. _____?

Defense Counsel: I object.

The ruling would depend upon whether, if the policeman were not present, the statement by the defendant to the physician would be privileged. This, in turn, would depend upon whether there existed a physician-patient relationship and whether the statement was necessary to enable the doctor to treat the patient.[1] Assuming that the statement would have been privileged, the next question presented is whether the fact that the words were spoken in the hearing of a third person who was known to be present, would nullify the privilege. In cases involving the attorney-client relationship, privacy is essential and the intentional presence of another person destroys the privilege,[2] but not so with respect to physicians. A physician may not testify although a member of the family was present at the examination[3] or where the patient had no choice but to speak in the presence of a third person.[4]

Of course, if the physician was not there to treat the defendant, or if the statement was not necessary or incidental to treatment, it would not be privileged.[5]

§ 9:02 Evidence Incompetent: Violation of Constitutional Rights

In a criminal case, the People called a detective, who was asked by the District Attorney:

Q. Did you arrest the defendant?

A. I did.

Q. And did you have a conversation with him?

A. I did.

Q. *What did he say to you?*

Defendant's Attorney: I object.

The objection should be sustained unless it first appears that the accused was advised of his constitutional rights to remain silent and to have counsel.[6]

§ 9:03 Interrogation After Indictment in Absence of Counsel

Defendant was being tried for robbery on an indictment obtained in February 19___. A police officer who had questioned the defendant while in jail on another charge was called by the People and asked by the District Attorney:

Q. *Did you question the defendant on June 15, 19___?*
A. *I did.*

Q. *Where did you speak to him?*
A. *In the county jail.*

Q. *What did he say to you?*

Defense Attorney: May I have a voir dire?

The Court: You may.

By Defense Attorney:

Q. *Was I or any other attorney for the defendant present when you questioned him?*
A. *No.*

Q. *At the time you questioned my client, you knew that he had been indicted, did you not?*
A. *I did, but he had not been indicted on the charge about which I questioned him.*

Defense Attorney: I object.

After the accused had been indicted, a confession or admission obtained on his interrogation by a law enforcement authority with knowledge of the indictment, in the absence of his attorney, is a violation of defendant's constitutional right to counsel and freedom from testimonial compulsion.[7] However, the mere fact that the defendant has been indicted on one charge as to which he is represented by counsel does not prevent law-enforcement officials from interrogating him in the absence of an attorney, about *another* and different crime, where he has been given the Miranda warnings and has waived his right to counsel.[8]

§ 9:04   Objecting When There Was a Wiretap

In a criminal case, a witness for the State was asked by the District Attorney:

Q. *Officer, are you familiar with the voice of the defendant?*
A. *I am.*

Q. *Have you heard him speak on various occasions?*
A. *I have.*

Q. *Have you spoken to him face to face?*
A. *I have, many times.*

Q. *Did you hear him speaking to someone on the telephone on May 19th last?*
A. *I did.*

Q. *Did you recognize his voice on the telephone?*
A. *I did.*

Q. *Tell us what you heard in that telephone conversation between the defendant and another on that day.*

Defendant's Attorney: *May I have a voir dire?*

The Court: *You may.*

By Defense Counsel:

Q. *Did you know who the other party to the conversation was?*
A. *No, I did not.*

Q. *Were you listening in with the knowledge and consent of the defendant?*
A. *No.*

Q. *Did you have an order of a court authorizing you to wiretap the defendant's telephone?*
A. *No.*

Defense Counsel: I object.

The objection should be sustained, under the common law eavesdropping is permitted.[9] Under Sec. 605 of the Communications Act, divulging conversations overheard by wiretapping was prohibited in both Federal and State courts.[10] Since the enactment of the Omnibus Crime Control and Safe Streets Act of 1968, it seems that this is no longer so, provided a proper warrant has been obtained by an authorized official.[11] If, however, the order was improperly obtained and illegal, the intercepted telephone conversations are inadmissible.[12]

Statutes in many jurisdictions permit wiretapping in certain instances when done pursuant to court order.[13] Statutory prohibitions are not violated by one listening in on a telephone conversation with the knowledge and consent of one of the parties to the conversation.[14] In the absence of either a proper warrant or consent, the testimony would be inadmissible.

§ 9:05   Hearsay: Declaration by an Unidentified Declarant

In a personal injury action a policeman was asked by the attorney who called him:

Q. *Did you investigate the occurrence which is the subject of this lawsuit?*
A. *I did.*

Q. *What did you do in the course of that investigation?*
A. *I spoke to the various witnesses.*

Q. *What did they tell you?*

Opposing Attorney: I object.

The objection should be sustained. Declarations made by unidentified persons are objectionable as being hearsay.[15] In some jurisdictions, a statement made by an eyewitness shortly after an accident, and while the eyewitness is still in a state of high excitement, is admissible as part of the *res gestae.*[16] But to justify admission, it is necessary to demonstrate that the declarant actually viewed the event of which he speaks.[17] Other jurisdictions will not admit such a declaration unless it was a spontaneous one, made impulsively and without any lapse of time between the event and the utterance so that there was no time to contrive it.[18]

§ 9:06 Hearsay: Telephone Conversation

The plaintiff, suing for breach of contract, was asked on direct examination by Plaintiff's Attorney:

Q. *When was your attention first directed to that property?*
A. *On January 10th.*

Q. *How was it brought to your attention?*
A. *By telephone.*

Q. *Did you make that call or were you telephoned?*
A. *I was called.*

Q. *Tell us in words or substance what was said.*

Defendant's Attorney: I object.

The objection should be sustained as hearsay because the speaker has not been identified nor shown to be a party to the action or his authorized agent.[19] The mere assertion of his identity by a person talking on the telephone is not sufficient, and additional evidence of his identity is required.

The witness may establish the identity of the speaker by testimony that he recognized the voice on the telephone.[20] Even if the witness was not acquainted with the speaker and did not recognize his voice at that time, the telephone conversation is admissible if the witness testifies that he met the speaker thereafter and then recognized his voice as the voice he had heard over the telephone.[21]

If the conversation reveals that the speaker had knowledge of facts that only he would be likely to know, or if his identity is corroborated by facts and circumstances tending to reveal his identity, then the message may be admissible.[22]

Where the witness did not receive the call, but it was an outgoing call made to a number supplied by the telephone company for the person in question, that additional evidence supports the assumption that the listing is correct and that the number is the one reached. If the number is a place of business, then the weight of authority allows the ensuing conversation if it relates to business reasonably transacted over the telephone, on the theory that the maintenance of the telephone connection is an invitation to do business without further identification. Otherwise, some additional identification of the speaker is required.[23]

§ 9:07   Declarations by Identified Third Person

The People called a police officer who was asked on direct examination by the District Attorney:

Q. *Did you, in the course of your investigation, speak to the defendant's brother, John, about the defendant?*

A. *I did.*

Q. *Who was present?*

A. *Just the two of us.*

Q. *What did the defendant's brother tell you?*

Defense Attorney: I object.

The objection should be sustained. The alleged declaration made by one who is not shown to have authority to bind a party, and made out of his presence, is hearsay and inadmissible. Thus, it is error to admit a declaration made by defendant's relative, for mere blood relationship does not confer the right to make binding admissions.[24] Similarly, when the father of an injured minor is testifying on behalf of his child, it would be improper to ask him, on cross-examination, as to whether the child's mother had ever warned the child about playing on railroad tracks, as this too would be calling for hearsay testimony.[25] And it was reversible error to admit, over objection, the testimony of one police officer as to what another officer orally relayed to him as to the speed of a test automobile used in making an experimental test run.[26]

Where, however, it becomes relevant to show that a certain statement was made (not to establish the truth or falsity of the statement itself), such proof is not hearsay and should be admitted.[27] Thus, in a proceeding involving a liquor license, a liquor control agent's testimony that a woman approached him for drinks and prostitution in a bar was admissible for the limited purpose of showing that proscribed activities occurred in the tavern.[28] Evidence concerning rumors as to an illicit relationship between testator's wife and another man was admissible on the issue of whether such rumors could form the basis for the testator's belief that the contestant of his will was not his child.[29]

Whenever the issue is whether or not certain words were uttered, any witness who heard the statement may testify to it, as this is not hearsay if offered merely to prove that it was made. For example, in an action for slander, any witness who heard the defendant utter the slanderous words may testify thereto.[30]

Witnesses have been permitted to testify as to what they heard another say when it was a "spontaneous declaration," "excited utterance,"[31] or "part of the *res gestae*"[32] or a statement of the declarant's then-existing state of mind, emotion, sensation, or physical condition.[33]

§ 9:08   Declarations by Servant After Accident

In an action brought against the employer of the driver of a truck to recover for personal injuries caused by the driver's negligence while driving the truck in the course of his duties, and within the scope of his employment, a police officer was called by the plaintiff and asked on direct examination by Plaintiff's Attorney:

Q.   *How long after you received the call did you arrive at the scene of the accident?*

A.   *In fifteen minutes.*

Q.   *Did you speak to Charles Butler, the driver of the truck?*

A.   *I did.*

Q.   *What did the driver of the truck say to you?*

Defendant's Attorney: I object.

The ruling depends upon whether an admission made by the driver after the accident is binding upon his employer or is considered as hearsay. Unquestionably, it would be received against the driver himself if he were a party to the action, but in many jurisdictions it would not be admissible as against his employer.[34] According to these authorities, the fact that the driver was acting within the scope of his authority in driving the truck, does not mean that he also had authority, after the accident, to make admissions which will be binding on his master.[35] There is a growing trend to make such a statement admissible requiring only that the declaration relate to a matter within the scope of the agency or employment and not that the servant be authorized to speak.[36]

The driver's declaration would be received if it was a "spontaneous declaration," "excited utterance," or "part of the *res gestae*."[37]

§ 9:09 Declarations by Alleged Agent as to His Authority

In an action for breach of contract brought against a corporation, the plaintiff was testifying on direct examination and was asked by Plaintiff's Attorney:

Q. *Did you speak to a Mr. Nathan on that day?*
A. *I did.*

Q. *What did you say to him?*
A. *I asked him whether he had any authority to speak for the defendant corporation.*

Q. *And what did he say?*

Defendant's Attorney: I object.

The objection should be sustained. Agency and authority cannot be proved by the declaration made out of court by the person whose agency it is sought to be established.[38] In an action against a corporation upon a contract made with its officers, direct authority must be shown from which such authority would be presumed.[39] Similarly, in an automobile accident case, the authority of the driver of the vehicle to use the automobile may not be established by the declarations of the driver although there is authority to the contrary.[40]

§ 9:10 Objection to Physician's Statement to Plaintiff as to His Injuries

In a personal injury action, the plaintiff, testifying in his own behalf was asked by Plaintiff's Attorney:

Q. *Did the doctor examine you?*
A. *He did.*

Q. *What did the doctor tell you?*
A. *He said I had suffered a brain concussion. . . .*

Defendant's Attorney: I object and move to strike out the answer.

The objection should be sustained and the motion granted. Any such statement by the physician, made out of court, would be hearsay and of no probative value.[41] Such testimony as to what a doctor said to his patient might be received as bearing upon his state of mind where that is relevant. For example, where plaintiff allegedly developed a neurosis after having suffered an injury to her breast, her testimony that her physician had told her to have x-rays taken regularly might be received on the issue of whether she developed a fear of cancer.[42]

§ 9:11 Prior Testimony of an Absent Witness: Availability

In the action of *Smith v. Roe,* which was being retried, a court stenographer was called and asked by Counsel:

Q. *Are you the court stenographer who took the testimony in the action entitled Smith v. Roe, tried in this court on May 10th of last year?*
A. *I am.*

Q. *Was Charles Butler, the driver of the truck, a witness at that former trial of the action between these parties?*
A. *Yes, he was.*

Q. *Will you please read the questions propounded to which answers were made by Charles Butler as such witness at such former trial?*

Opposing Counsel: I object.

Without more as a foundation, the objection should be sustained. Testimony given at a former trial is hearsay and is admissible only as an exception to the hearsay rule where permitted by statute and when the proper foundation has been laid. This has not been established in the illustration.[43] Before such prior testimony is received, it is generally required that the party offering it must establish (a) the identity of parties, (b) the identity of issues, and (c) the unavailability of the witness at the present trial.[44] This being a retrial of the same case, the first two elements are present, and what remains is to establish the unavailability of the witness. What constitutes unavailability is defined by statute and usually is established by (1) proof of absence of the witness from the hearing, coupled with inability to compel attendance by process and reasonable diligence,[45] (2) death or infirmity of the witness,[46] (3) the witness, whose testimony is sought to be read, is on the stand but claims his privilege not to testify[47] or simply refuses to testify despite judicial pressures to do so.[48] A witness is not unavailable if it is due to the procurement or wrongdoing of the party seeking to use the former testimony.[49]

Assuming the foregoing requisites have been met, it would also be necessary for the court stenographer to testify that the witness, whose testimony was to be read, had been sworn and that he had taken down his testimony in shorthand and that the transcript was a correct and accurate reproduction of his notes.[50]

The transcript is not absolutely necessary, and the best evidence rule would not prevent anyone who heard the prior testimony from testifying thereto if it was otherwise admissible.[51]

§ 9:12 Prior Contradictory Statement

The plaintiff's sister, Joan, had testified on behalf of the plaintiff as to the facts of the accident. She was not cross-examined in regard to having made a prior contradictory statement. During the defendant's case, a police officer was called and asked by the Defendant's Attorney:

Q. *Officer, did you speak to the plaintiff's sister, Joan, when you came to the scene of the occurrence?*

A. *I did.*

Q. *What, if anything, did she say to you?*

A. *She told me that she did not see the accident.*

Plaintiff's Attorney: I object and move to strike out the testimony.

The objection should be sustained and the motion granted because the proper foundation has not been laid for such a prior contradictory statement. Before a witness (not a party) may be impeached by a prior contradictory statement, he must first be warned and given an opportunity to admit, deny, or explain the alleged declaration. The witness Joan should have been asked when cross-examined whether, at a specified time and place, she had made a certain statement, quoting her language or giving the substance thereof.[52] It is only after the witness denies[53] or fails to recall such statement,[54] or gives evasive answers[55] that the impeaching witness may be called. The proper method of impeachment is to ask the impeaching witness the precise question which has previously been put to the witness sought to be impeached.[56]

In any event, even when testimony is admissible for the purpose of impeaching credibility, its admission is generally limited to that purpose, and the testimony is not admissible as substantive proof of the truth of what had been previously stated.[57]

There is a trend to receive the prior contradictory statement as substantive evidence and not as hearsay, the reason being that the inconsistent statement is more likely to be true because made nearer in time to the matter to which it relates and less likely to have been influenced by the litigation.[58] Of course, if the witness concedes that the prior testimony is true, it is received as affirmative evidence of the facts.[59]

§ 9:13   Self-Serving Declarations

In a personal injury action, plaintiff called a physician, who was asked by Plaintiff's Attorney:

Q. *Doctor, did you have occasion to see and examine the plaintiff at the City Hospital on January 13 of this year?*
A. *I did.*

Q. *When you first saw the plaintiff, what history, if any, did she give you?*
A. *She told me she was driving an automobile on January 13th and that a truck ran into her automobile while it was standing still.*

Defendant's Attorney: I object and move to strike out the answer.

The objection should be sustained and the motion granted. A narrative statement as to a past event made by a party to the action, on a prior occasion, to this witness which supports the party's claim, is a self-serving declaration and is generally inadmissible.[60] Were the rule otherwise, a party to litigation could create evidence for himself.[61]

Complaints of present pain made to a doctor for treatment would be received as an exception to the hearsay rule, it being deemed unlikely that a patient would mislead a treating physician as to his symptoms.[62] And the same rule has been applied to statements as to relevant past conditions and medical history to a treating physician (not one consulted for the purpose of testifying).[63] The doctor's testimony as to a spontaneous exclamation by the plaintiff would not be hearsay.[64]

§ 9:14   Objecting to Dying Declarations

During a trial for murder, a police officer was called by the People. After testifying as to the condition in which he found the victim, he was asked by the District Attorney:

Q. What was it that she said to you, officer, just before she died?

A. It was Jimmy who did it. If my husband finds out he will divorce me for sure.

Defendant's Attorney: I object and move to strike out the answer.

The objection should be sustained and the motion granted. A dying declaration is hearsay, but will be received as an exception to the hearsay rule if made by the victim of a homicide when, to his knowledge, he is *in extremis*.[65] Here, the answer itself discloses that the declarant's state of mind was not that of one without hope of recovery. "It is difficult to believe that one standing in the shadow of impending death and without hope of recovery would be concerned about procuring a divorce in the future." [66] If the dying declaration is sought to be proved in a civil case, it would not be received, as such a declaration is only admissible in a case of homicide.[67] However, there is a trend toward receiving dying declarations in crimes other than homicide and in civil actions because of the unavailability of the deceased as a witness.[68]

§ 9:15 Hearsay: The Confession of a Third Person

Defendant Smith, on trial for murder of Robert Davis, called as his witness Father Murphy, who was asked by Defense Attorney:

Q. Father, did you have occasion, in the course of your duties, to administer the last rites to one John Jones?

A. I did.

Q. Did he say anything to you with reference to the murder of Robert Davis?

A. He did.

Q. What did he say?

A. He said to me, "I want you to promise me that you will tell the court that Smith was innocent of the murder of Davis, that he (Jones) had killed Davis and he was confessing it so that he could die with a clear conscience."

District Attorney: I object and move to strike out the answer.

The objection should be sustained and the motion granted because the statement is by Jones, who is not the person charged with the crime, and it was made out of court while Jones was not under oath and not subject to cross-examination and, therefore, is hearsay.[69] It is not admissible as a dying declaration because only the declaration of the victim of the homicide can make a dying declaration.[70]

§ 9:16   An Admission Which Is An Opinion, Not a Statement of Fact

In a personal injury action, a police officer was called by the plaintiff and asked on direct examination by Plaintiff's Attorney:

Q. *Did you speak to the defendant, the driver of the automobile?*
A. *I did.*

Q. *What did he say?*
A. *He said, "It was all my fault."*

Defendant's Attorney: I object and move to strike out the answer.

There is a difference of authority as to whether the defendant's statement constitutes an admission of fact or only a conclusion or opinion [71] and as to whether, if received, it is to be used only as impeaching evidence or as substantive evidence.[72]

§ 9:17   Against Public Policy: Offer of Compromise

One of the attorneys for the plaintiff took the stand and was asked by Associate Counsel:

Q. *Are you an attorney-at-law associated with me in practice?*
A. *I am.*

Q. *Did you, before this action was commenced, communicate with the defendant regarding the plaintiff's claim?*
A. *I did.*

Q. *Did he subsequently come to see you at your office?*
A. *Yes, sir, he did.*

Q. *Did you have a conversation with him at that time?*
A. *I did.*

Q. Please tell us what he said to you.

A. He said that he had come up to settle the case and asked how much we wanted. I told him that we wanted $17,500 and he said that he would pay $12,500 and no more.

Defendant's Attorney: I object and move to strike out the answer.

The motion should be granted and the declaration stricken as a matter of public policy. An offer of compromise of a disputed claim should not be received as an admission of liability.[73]

However, an actual admission of fact, made by the defendant, not a mere offer of compromise, will generally be received, even though it was made during negotiations for settlement.[74] This rule has been criticized, as its effect is to inhibit freedom of communication with respect to compromise, as well as the fact that it gives rise to controversies as to whether a given statement is protected or not.[75]

The offer of compromise may be received if offered for another purpose, such as proving bias or prejudice,[76] negating a contention of lack of due diligence in presenting a claim[77] or in proving an effort to "buy off" a witness in a criminal case.[78]

§ 9:18   Silence by Others as Hearsay

In an action by a passenger on a bus for injuries caused by a sudden stop, the bus driver was asked on direct examination by the Defendant's Attorney:

Q. Did anyone else complain to you of being hurt on that bus?
A. No.

Plaintiff's Attorney: I object and move to strike out the answer.

The motion should be granted. Under the facts in this case, the question of whether or not anyone else complained or failed to complain would have no evidentiary value of the point in issue, to wit, whether this plaintiff was injured and would introduce an entirely collateral issue.[79] Similarly, where the quality of certain goods which had been returned was in issue, and it was sought to prove that the same goods were subsequently sold to others who made no complaint as to their quality, it was held that such proof of silence would be hearsay.[80] And the fact that a certain person said nothing when he had no duty to speak, is also inadmissible.[81] In a criminal case, evidence of silence would probably be inadmissible to prove guilt since the Supreme Court has held that no adverse inference may be drawn from reliance on the privilege against self-incrimination.[82]

§ 9:19   Parol Evidence of Written Contract

In an action for the breach of a written contract, a witness for the plaintiff was asked by Plaintiff's Attorney:

Q. Did you hear any conversation between the plaintiff and defendant as the contract was being prepared?

A. I did.

Q. What did you hear the plaintiff and the defendant say to each other?

Defendant's Attorney: I object.

Except under certain circumstances, the objection will be sustained. The agreement being in writing, the original writing should be produced or its absence accounted for under the best evidence rule.[83] If the contract has been marked in evidence, it speaks for itself, and what was said orally may not be received for the purpose of changing or varying what has been reduced to writing.[84] Parol evidence may, however, be allowed in certain instances for other purposes as, not to vary but to clarify an ambiguity or to complete the contract,[85] to establish that the contract was void by reason of want of consideration,[86] fraudulent misrepresentations, mistake, duress, or undue influence,[87] illegality,[88] alteration,[89] or delivery upon a condition precedent.[90]

§ 9:20   Evidence Is Irrelevant: Objecting to General Reputation Testimony

The defendant was sued for breach of contract. Defendant called a witness in his behalf and he was asked by Defendant's Attorney:

Q. Do you know the defendant, Mr. Jones?
A. I do.

Q. How do you know him?
A. We live on the same street for the past 20 years.

Q. Have you ever heard your neighbors speak ill of him?

Plaintiff's Attorney: I object.

Although, if the evidence were relevant, the good reputation of a person may be inferred from negative evidence that the witness had never heard anyone say anything derogatory about him,[91] the objection should be sustained because the general reputation of a party is not relevant in a civil action for personal injuries unless the nature of the proceedings puts it in issue.[92]

§ 9:21   Evidence which is Prejudicial: Insurance Coverage

In an action arising out of an automobile collision, the plaintiff was testifying when he was asked by Plaintiff's Attorney:

Q. *Did you speak to the defendant at the scene of the accident?*
A. *Yes, I did.*

Q. *Did he make any statement to you?*
A. *Yes, he made a statement.*

Q. *Tell us what he said.*
A. *He said, "I'm sorry this happened. I have plenty of insurance."*

Defendant's Attorney: I object and move to strike out the testimony.

The mention of insurance coverage is generally deemed prejudicial.[93] If, however, its mention was a part of an admission against interest made by the defendant, it would be received.[94] However, in the illustration, the words "I'm sorry this happened" is merely an expression of commiseration for the injured person and not an admission and the objection should, therefore, be sustained.[95]

Chapter Nine

FOOTNOTES

[1] See Section 8.04, "Physician-Patient Privilege."

[2] Baumann v. Steingester (1915), 213 N.Y. 328, 107 N.E. 578; by statute, an eavesdropper may be prohibited from divulging the conversation: N.Y. CPLR Section 4503 (a).

See also Coplon v. United States (3rd Cir. [D.C.] 1951), 191 F. 2d 749; cert. denied 342 U.S. 926.

[3] Denaro v. Prudential Insurance Co. (1913), 154 App. Div. 840, 139 N.Y.S. 758.

[4] People v. Decina (1956), 2 N.Y. 2d 133, 157 N.Y.S. 2d 558, 138 N.E. 2d 799, 63 ALR 2d 970.

[5] People v. Runion (1958), 3 N.Y. 2d 637, 170 N.Y.S. 2d 836, 148 N.E. 2d 165.

See also Section 8.04, "Physician-Patient Privilege."

[6] See Section 10.13, "Verbal Acts: Miranda Warnings," and Section 11.02, "Privilege Against Self-Incrimination."

[7] People v. Waterman (1961), 12 App. Div. 2d 84, aff'd 9 N.Y. 2d 561.

People v. Di Biasi (1960), 7 N.Y. 2d 544.

Massiah v. United States (1964), 377 U.S. 201.

[8] People v. Taylor (1971), 27 N.Y. 2d 327.

[9] *Wigmore on Evidence* (3rd ed) Section 2326.

[10] Lee v. Florida (1967), 392 U.S. 378, 88 S. Ct. 2096, 20 L. Ed. 1166.

Fuller v. Alaska (1968) 393 U.S. 80, 89 S. Ct. 61, 21 L. Ed. 212.

Coplon v. United States, *supra.*

Federal Communications Act, 47 U.S.C., Section 605.

Coplon v. United States.

[11] People v. Feinlowitz (1971), 29 N.Y. 2d 176.

Omnibus Crime Control and Safe Streets Act of 1968, 82 U.S. Stat. 197.

Wigmore on Evidence, (3d ed.), Section 2184b.

[12] Sarisohn v. Appellate Division of Supreme Court, Second Judicial Dept. (1967), 286 N.Y.S. 2d 255, 21 N.Y. 2d 36, 233 N.E. 2d 276.

[13] N.Y. CPLR, Section 4506; N.Y. CPL, Section 700.

[14] United States v. Kountis (1965), 350 F. 2d 869, 9 ALR 3d 420, cert. den. 382 U.S. 980.

Lopez v. United States (1963), 373 U.S. 427;

Westin, *Privacy and Freedom,* pp. 356–59.

[15] Brutman v. Lane's Department Store (1967), 28 App. Div. 2d 690, 281 N.Y.S. 2d 123; a declaration by an unidentified person to another uni-

dentified person, whose status was never shown to be such as would bind the defendant, will not be sufficient proof of notice.

Ungefug v. D'Ambrosia (Cal. App. 1967), 58 Cal. Rptr. 223; testimony of ambulance driver that he heard someone say that automobile, other than defendant's, had also struck decedent was improperly admitted over hearsay objection, where defendant failed to show, except by the remotest inference, conjecture or speculation, that one who made the statement about other vehicle had actually seen the accident.

[16] Nutter v. Dearing (Tex. Civ. App. 1966), 400 S.W. 2d 346.

Swenson v. New York Albany Dispatch Co. Inc.

Wigmore on Evidence, (3rd ed), Section 1745, *et seq.*

[17] Carney v. Pennsylvania Railroad Co. (Pa. 1968), 240 A. 2d 71.

[18] Greener v. General Electric Co. (1913), 209 N.Y. 135, 138, 102 N.E. 527.

Ingersoll v. Liberty Bank of Buffalo (1938), 278 N.Y. 1, 9, 14 N.E. 2d 828.

Wigmore on Evidence, (3rd ed.) Section 1750, *et seq.*

[19] A. T. Stearns Lumber Co. v. Howlett (1927), 260 Mass. 45, 157 N.E. 82, 52 ALR 1125.

Wigmore on Evidence, (3rd ed) Section 669.

[20] Mack v. State (1907), 54 Fla. 55, 44 So. 706.

[21] People v. Dunbar (1915), 215 N.Y. 416, 422, 109 N.E. 554.

Walker Discount Corp. v. Sapin (1965), 264 N.Y.S. 2d 841.

[22] Liberty Mutual Insurance Co. v. Preston (Tex. Civ. App. 1966), 399 S.W. 2d 367.

Wigmore on Evidence, (3rd ed) Section 2155.

[23] Matton v. Hoover Co. (1942), 350 Mo. 506, 166 S.W. 2d 557.

City of Pawhuska v. Crutchfield (1930), 147 Okla. 4, 293 P. 1095.

Zurich General Accident and Liability Insurance Co. v. Baum (1932), 159 Va. 404, 165 S.E. 518.

Proposed Rules of Evidence for the United States District Courts and Magistrates, Rule 9-01 (b) (6).

[24] People v. Smith (1966), 26 App. Div. 2d 588, 272 N.Y.S. 2d 174.

State v. Boscia (N.J. Super A.D. 1967), 226 A. 2d 643.

[25] Dickeson v. Baltimore & Ohio Chicago Terminal R.R. Co. (Ill. App. 1965), 220 N.E. 2d 43.

[26] Smith v. Frisch's Big Boy, Inc. (Fla. App. 1968), 208 So. 2d 310.

[27] *Wigmore on Evidence,* (3rd ed) Section 1789.

[28] State *ex rel.* 807 Inc. v. Saitz (Mo. 1968), 425 S.W. 2d 96.

[29] Kingdom v. Sybrant (N.D. 1968), 158 N.W. 2d 864.

[30] *Wigmore on Evidence,* (3d ed.), Section 1770.

[31] *Ibid.,* (3rd ed) Sections 1745–50.

[32] Hine v. New York Elevated Railroad Co. (1896), 149 N.Y. 154, 162, 43 N.E. 414.

[33] Proposed Rules of Evidence for the United States District Courts and Magistrates, Rule 8-03 (b) (1) (2).

[34] Roush v. Alkire Truck Lines, Inc. (Mo. 1957), 299 S.W. 2d 518.

Barcello v. Biel (1948), 137 N.J.L. 606, 61 A. 2d 42.

Gadd v. Universal Road Machine Co. (1942), 263 App. Div. 456, 33 N.Y.S. 2d 527.

Golden v. Horn & Hardart Co. Inc. (1935), 244 App. Div. 92, 278 N.Y.S. 385, aff'd 270 N.Y. 544, 200 N.E. 309.

Caulder v. Kivett Motor Sales (1942), 221 N.C. 437, 20 S.E. 2d 338.

[35] Northern Oil Co. v. Socony Mobil Oil Co.

[36] Grayson v. Williams (10th Cir. [Wyo.] 1958), 256 F. 2d 61.

KLM v. Tuller (3rd Cir. [D.C.] 1961), 292 F. 2d 775, 784.

Martin v. Savage Truck Lines, Inc.

Proposed Rules of Evidence for the United State District Courts and Magistrates, Rule 8-01 (c) (3) (iv).

Wigmore on Evidence, (3rd ed) Section 1078, *et seq.*

[37] See Section 9.07, "Declarations by Identified Third Person."

[38] Van Generen v. Paterson Wimset Thrift Co. (1942), 128 N.J.L. 41, 24 A. 2d 223, 224.

[39] Berwin & Co. v. Hewitt Realty Co. (1922), 199 App. Div. 453, 191 N.Y.S. 817, aff'd. 235 N.Y. 608, 139 N.E. 754.

[40] Cook v. Hall (Ky. 1948), 214 S.W. 2d 1017.

67 ALR 170, 150 ALR 623.

Hix-Green v. Dowis (Ga. 1949), 53 S.E. 2d 601, 616. *Contra* Golenterneck v. Kurth (Ark. 1948), 212 S.W. 2d 14, 3 ALR 2d 593.

[41] Blume v. Weaver (Tex. Civ. App. 1967), 412 S.W. 2d 760.

[42] Ferrara v. Galluchio (1958), 5 N.Y. 2d 16, 176 N.Y.S. 2d 249, N.E. 2d.

[43] Bivins v. Leath (1938), 236 Ala. 615, 184 So. 176.

Schofield v. Rideout (1940), 233 Wis. 550, 290 N.W. 155.

Wabash Railroad Co. v. Miller (1902), 158 Ind. 174, 61 N.E. 1005; followed in McCord v. Strader (Ind. 1949), 86 N.E. 2d 441.

Wigmore on Evidence, (3rd ed) Section 1669.

[44] Bulk Transport, Inc. v. Louisiana Public Service Commn. (La. 1968), 209 So. 2d 4.

[45] Barber v. Page (1968), 390 U.S. 719.

Proposed Rules of Evidence for the United States District Courts and Magistrates, Rule 8-01 (d) (4).

[46] Harris v. Reeves (Tex. Civ. App. 1967), 421 S.W. 2d 689.

[47] Wyatt v. State (1950), 35 Ala. App. 147, 46 So. 2d 837.

State v. Stewart (1911), 85 Kan. 404, 116 P. 489, 45 ALR 2d 1354.

[48] Johnson v. People (1963), 152 Colo. 586, 384 P. 2d 454.

People v. Pickett (1954), 339 Mich. 294, 63 N.W. 2d 681, 45 ALR 2d 1341; *Contra:* Pleau v. State (1949), 255 Wis. 362, 38 N.W. 2d 496.

[49] Proposed Rules of Evidence for the United States District Courts and Magistrates, Rule 8-01 (d) (4).

[50] Vander Veen v. Yellow Cab Co. (Ill. App. 1967), 233 N.E. 2d 68.

[51] Votos v. Petrocelli (1967), 28 App. Div. 2d 1145, 284 N.Y.S. 2d 725.

[52] Robertson v. M/S Sanyo Maru (5th Cir. [La.] 1967), 374 F. 2d 464.

Shallenberger v. Duncan (Cal. App. 1966), 53 Cal. Rptr. 77.

Kelly v. King (Miss. 1967). 196 So. 2d 525.

Hawkins v. B. F. Walker, Inc. (Wyo. 1967), 426 P. 2d 427.

[53] People v. Weldon (1888), 111 N.Y. 569, 19 N.E. 279.

Gayhart v. Schwabe (1958), 80 Idaho 354, 330 P. 2d 327.

[54] Williams v. Joslin (1965), 65 Wash. 2d 696, 399 P. 2d 308. *Contra:* witness may not be impeached if he does not recall the statement. Beam Motor Co. v. Loewer (1917), 131 Md. 552, 102 A. 908.

[55] Blackford v. Kaplan (1939), 135 Ohio St. 268, 20 N.E. 2d 522.

[56] *Wigmore on Evidence,* (3rd ed) Section 1029, *et seq.*

[57] Wilson v. Pennsylvania Railroad Co. (Pa. 1966), 219 A. 2d 666.

Spring Branch Bank v. Wright (Tex. Civ. App. 1966), 404 S.W. 2d 659.

People v. Johnson (1968), 68 Cal. Rptr. 599, 441 P. 2d 111.

[58] Proposed Rules of Evidence for the United States District Courts and Magistrates, Rule 8-01 (c) (2).

[59] People v. Anonymous B. (Co. Ct. 1968), 290 N.Y.S. 2d 507.

Moran v. Carignan (N.H. 1968), 238 A. 2d 735.

[60] Poumeroule v. Postal Telegraph Cable Co. (1912), 167 Mo. App. 533, 152 S.W. 114;

Crafton v. Livingston (Ga. App. 1966), 150 S.E. 2d 371.

Pacific Finance Corp. v. Rucker (Tex. Civ. App. 1965), 392 S.W. 2d 554.

Wigmore on Evidence, (3rd ed) Section 1722.

[61] Ingersoll v. Liberty Bank of Buffalo (1938), 278 N.Y. 1, 14 N.E. 2d 828, 830.

[62] McDuffie v. Root (1942), 300 Mich. 286, 1 N.W. 2d 544;

Hoffman v. Goldfield (1943), 129 N.J.L. 359, 29 A. 2d 876;

Proposed Rules of Evidence for the United States District Courts and Magistrates, Rule 8-03 (b) (4).

Wigmore on Evidence, (3rd ed) Sections 1718, 1719.

[63] Southeastern Greyhound Lines v. Webb (Ky. 1950), 230 S.W. 2d 99.

Floyd v. Department of Labor and Industry (1966), 68 Wash. 2d 938, 416 P. 2d 355.

[64] *Wigmore on Evidence,* (3rd ed) Section 1745.

[65] *Ibid.,* Section 1430, *et seq.*

[66] State v. Elias (1939), 205 Minn. 156, 285 N.W. 475.

[67] *Wigmore on Evidence,* (3rd ed) Section 1432.

[68] Thurston v. Fritz (1914), 91 Kan. 468, 138 P. 625.

Proposed Rules of Evidence for the United States District Courts and Magistrates, Rule 8-05 (3).

[69] Donnelly v. United States (1913), 228 U.S. 243, 57 L. Ed. 820, 33 Sup. Ct. Rptr. 449.

Greenfield v. People (1881), 85 N.Y. 75.

Wigmore on Evidence (3rd ed) Section 1476.

[70] See Section 9.14, "Dying Declarations."

[71] Eldridge v. Barton (1919), 232 Mass. 183, 122 N.E. 272.

Wright v. Quattrachi (1932), 330 Mo. 173, 49 S.W. 2d 3.

Wigmore on Evidence, (3rd ed) Section 1041.

[72] *Substantive:* Crowley v. Dix (1949), 136 Conn. 97, 68, A. 2d 366, 368; Wolfe v. Madison Avenue Coach Co. (1939), 171 Misc. 707, 13 N.Y.S. 741.

Impeaching: King v. Leeman (1946), 30 Tenn. App. 206, 204 S.W. 2d 384; Webb v. City of Seattle (1945), 22 Wash. 596, 157 P. 2d 312.

[73] Wilkinson v. Gerard (1940), 200 Ark. 125, 138 S.W. 2d 76.

Wigmore on Evidence, (3rd ed) Section 1061 *et seq.*

Proposed Rules of Evidence for the United States District Courts and Magistrates, Rule 4-08 (pp. 67–67).

[74] Firestone Tire and Rubber Co. v. Hillow (D.C. Mun. App. 1949), 65 A. 2d 338.

Mannella v. City of Pittsburgh (1941), 334 Pa. 396, 6 A. 2d 70, 73.

[75] Proposed Rules of Evidence for the United States District Courts and Magistrates, Rule 4-08; all conduct or statements made in compromise negotiations are inadmissible.

[76] 161 ALR 395. *Contra,* Fenberg v. Rosenthal (1952), 348 Ill. App. 510, 109 N.E. 2d 402.

[77] *Wigmore on Evidence* (3rd ed) Section 1061.

[78] McCormick Law of Evidence, *op. cit.,* Section 251.

[79] This objection was sustained by the trial court in the case of Huisward v. Good Humor Corp. (1947), 296 N.Y. 934, 73 N.E. 2d 45, at fol. 193.

[80] Thompson Co., Inc. v. International Compositions Co., Inc. (1920), 191 App. Div. 553, 181 N.Y.S. 637.

New York Canners, Inc. v. Milbourne (1928), 247 N.Y. 460, 160 N.E. 914.

[81] *Wigmore on Evidence,* (3rd ed) Section 1071 *et seq.*

[82] Griffen v. California (1965), 380 U.S. 609.

Stewart v. United States (1961), 336 U.S. 1.

Grunewald v. United States (1957), 353 U.S. 391.

Wayne Law Review Vol. 15 p. 1098, Note 14.

[83] Herzig v. Swift & Co. (1945), 146 F. 2d 444.

Butler v. Mail and Express Publishing Co. (1902), 171 N.Y. 208;

Wigmore on Evidence (3rd ed) Sections 1177–1280.

See also Section 6.06, "Contents of a Writing."

[84] Melton v. Ensley (Mo. App. 1967), 421 S.W. 2d 44;

Farmers State Bank v. Keiser (S.D. 1968), 159 N.W. 2d 388;

Wigmore on Evidence, (3rd ed) Section 2400 *et seq.*

[85] Thomas v. Scutt (1891), 127 N.Y. 133, 27 N.E. 961.

International Assets Corp. v. Alxelrod (1935), 245 App. Div. 300, 281 N.Y.S. 32.

[86] Baird v. Baird (1895), 145 N.Y. 659, 40 N.E. 222, 28 ALR 375;

I & I Holding Corp. v. Gainsburg (1938), 276 N.Y. 427, 13 N.E. 2d 532, 115 ALR 582.

Potter v. Grimm (1915), 248 Pa. 440, 94 A. 185, 12 ALR 349.

Wigmore on Evidence, (3rd ed) Section 2433.

[87] Blum v. Hoffkins (1924), 210 App. Div. 748, 206 N.Y.S. 587, aff'd. 244 N.Y. 531, 107 N.Y.S. 672.

[88] Houghton v. Burden (1913), 228 U.S. 161, 57 L. Ed. 780, 33 Sup. Ct. Rep. 491.

[89] Booth v. Powers (1874), 56 N.Y. 22.

[90] Admissible to show that contract never became operative; Vincent v. Russell (1921), 101 Ore. 672, 201 P. 433, 20 ALR 417.

But not to show that contract might be canceled on a certain future contingency; Jamestown Business College Assn. v. Allen (1902), 172 N.Y. 291, 64 N.E. 952.

[91] People v. Van Gaasbeck (1907), 189 N.Y. 408, 82 N.E. 718.

[92] Koonts v. Farmer's Mutual Insurance Assn. (1944), 235 Iowa 87, 16 N.W. 2d 20.

Bugg v. Brown (1968), 251 Md. 99, 246 A. 2d 235.

Beach v. Richtmyer.

Wigmore on Evidence, (3rd ed) Section 64, p. 472.

See also Section 6.07, "Character Evidence in a Civil Trial."

[93] Menefee v. Williams (Cal. App. 1968), 66 Cal. Rptr. 108.

Wigmore on Evidence, (3rd ed) Section 282a.

See also Section 6.11, "Prejudicial Testimony."

[94] *Ibid.*

Lindsey v. Rogers (Mo. 1949), 220 S.W. 2d 937, 939.

[95] Denton v. Park Hotel Inc. (Mass. 1962), 180 N.E. 2d 70.

TEN

PROOF OF ACTIONS
(WORDS AND CONDUCT)

TABLE OF CONTENTS

PROOF OF ACTIONS
(WORDS AND CONDUCT)

The words and conduct referred to in this chapter are those of the witness himself—not what he saw or heard someone else say or do. The trial attorney may increase the likelihood that his witness' version will be accepted by the jury by having the witness reveal the reasons and motives for his actions, establish that he had the capacity, means and opportunity to act and give a detailed exposition of his conduct rather than mere characterizations.

"Q. WHAT, IF ANYTHING, DID YOU DO?"

§ 10:01   Action Includes Both Words and Conduct

At first blush it may appear that words should not be included in the same category as conduct. Both are, however, types of action. To speak or to write involves the motor functions of the body just as do other actions. We are, of course, referring to the *act* of speaking or writing and not the *substance* of what was said. When a witness is asked Q. *"What, if anything, did you do?"*, the answer, A. *"I spoke to him,"* or *"I wrote him a letter,"* is just as proper and responsive as *"I went over to see him at his office."*

There are differences in the way words and conduct are viewed at law. For example, the First Amendment guaranteeing freedom of speech and of the press extends not only to speech but also what is written, printed, photographed, as well as to signs or posters carried in demonstrations, etc. By contrast, the Fifth Amendment, which protects an accused from being compelled to incriminate himself, has been construed to apply only to compulsion of the defendant to testify orally, and does *not* prevent the accused from being compelled to submit to fingerprinting, photographing, or measurements, to stand up to be identified,[1] assume a stance, to walk or make a particular gesture, or to try on a shoe to see if it fits.[2] The rationale is that, although this may tend to incriminate the accused, it calls for an act and is not "testimonial compulsion" and is, therefore, not within the purview of the Bill of Rights.[3]

The admissibility of testimony as to words spoken is subject to the extensive restrictions of the Hearsay Rule.[4] This rule will not apply, however, when the words are not offered to establish the truth of what they say but rather as constituting what Wigmore called "verbal acts." Thus, the fact that a police officer placed his hand on defendant's shoulder and said, "You are under arrest," constitutes one action in which the words explain the deed which might otherwise be ambiguous.[5]

§ 10:02   Effective Use of Words or Actions in the Courtroom

We sometimes hear questions commencing with the phrase, *Q. Tell the court and jury . . .*" This is redundant, as implicit in every question is an invitation to "tell the court and jury." However, it should be borne in mind that all testimony is an act in the form of a communication between the witness and the jury. The ability, or lack of ability, to communicate, the command of the language, the style and arrangement of the testimony, all have a bearing upon its weight and persuasiveness.

Less frequently, the witness is asked to do something in the presence of the court and jury. For example, the witness may be asked to reenact something performed in the past. Such reenactment is much more effective than mere testimony because the jury perceives the evidence directly through their own senses. Indeed, it is recognized that such demonstrations may be unduly effective and prejudicial. Thus, the trial court is accorded a great deal of discretion in deciding whether or not he will permit the plaintiff to show the extent of his disability or to reenact what took place, and may limit the proof to mere descriptive testimony.[6]

ILLUSTRATIVE THREAD OF TESTIMONY

Demonstration of Effect of Injuries

Q. With the Court's permission, will you please stand up and bend your right leg as far as it will go?

A. (The witness does so and the attorney describes the action for the record.)

Q. Is that the most you can bend that leg?

A. Yes, sir.

Q. Now will you be good enough to walk in front of the jury box?

A. (Witness does so).

Q. Now will you bare the right leg and show it to the jury?

A. (Witness does so).

The attorney should, whenever possible, state for the record a description of what the witness is doing or exhibiting to the jury.

§ 10:03   Testimony Relating to the Witness' Past Actions

By the question, "What, if anything, did you do?" the witness is being asked about his own actions and not the actions of another which he may have observed. The testimony considered in this chapter relates only to acts which the witness *himself* performed. He must himself be the actor or one of the participants. With regard to the acts (words or conduct) of another person, the witness may only testify as to what he himself *perceived* (saw or heard) the other person do or say.[7]

Where the question relates to the past, it is phrased in the past tense and, therefore, calls for the recollection of the witness as to an action which he had performed or in which he had participated. The question is then, in effect, *Q. What is your present recollection as to what you did?* Man has a way of forgetting many details and combining others so that what remains is foreshortened and distorted. When testifying as to some action performed in the past, we cannot retain and recall every little detail of every act. Many facts must be forgotten in order to be able to retain what is more important or vital information.[8]

§ 10:04   Using the Phrase "If Anything"

The phrase "if anything" is added to avoid an objection that the question is leading and suggestive. If the question was simply *Q. What did you do?*, it might be suggesting that something was done when that was not the fact. When there has been no prior testimony that the witness had, in fact, done an act, the question may be improper unless it contains the phrase, "if anything." Thus, the question *Q. What did you do before you started to cross?* would be objectionable as suggesting that the witness had done something, as that he had looked for traffic.

If the question is, "What, *if anything*, did you do before you started to cross?" the objection would be obviated because it gives the witness a choice in answering and does not tell him what the choice should be. A question such as, "Were you walking, running or standing still?" also gives the witness a choice of suggested answers. Similarly, the question *Q. Did you or did you not do thus and so?* might be acceptable.[9]

§ 10:05   Enhancing Testimony as to Actions

When the testimony of the witness as to some action, whether by words or conduct, is important, its weight may be enhanced by proof as to:

- Other related actions, reasons or motives to act.
- Prior habit of the witness.
- Capacity, means, tools and opportunity to act.
- Details of the act rather than mere characterizations.

§ 10:06   Other Related Actions, Reasons or Motives to Act

In the theatre, the stage is set and an insight given into the background of the characters or event before the drama is enacted. There may even be a prologue provided. So too, in court, the trial lawyer does not plunge immediately into the crucial action itself, but first elicits some background material. Very often, the act in question was but a reaction to what has previously occurred and, in turn, was the cause of another act which followed. By understanding the reasons or motives for the prior action, the jury comes to expect and accept what follows. Prior and subsequent acts often bear eloquent witness to the likelihood that the act in question also did occur. The reasons or motives which would be likely to induce an action by words or by deed, may be shown, therefore, as indicating the likelihood that the action in question was performed.[10]

Prior or subsequent acts may not be shown, however, unless they are deemed logically and legally relevant. Similar acts are logically and legally relevant where they indicate intent, motive, absence of mistake, identity, or a common scheme or plan.[11] A person's acts are more persuasive in making the factual determination of his intent than are the mere declarations or testimony of his intentions.[12]

Since intent with which an act is done is rarely, if ever, susceptible to proof by direct evidence, it must be ascertained from outward manifestations, that is, from words or acts of a party in accomplishing the act and from the facts and circumstances attendant upon the act.[13] Such evidence is also deemed relevant with respect to sexual acts. Sexual intercourse with the same person, before or subsequent to the time in question, is deemed to have probative value as indicating the likelihood that the act at issue was committed. Thus, in a prosecution for statutory rape, the complainant will be permitted to testify as to prior or subsequent acts of intercourse.[14]

§ 10:07   Establishing Prior Habit of the Witness

The importance and effect of habit has long been recognized by psychologists. ". . . a garment, after being worn a certain time, clings to the shape of the body better than when it was new . . . a lock works better after being used some time . . . it causes less trouble to fold a paper when it has been folded already. . . ."[15] Just so does the nervous system react to recurring excitements from without. *It is generally accepted at law that one's habit of doing or not doing an act in question increases or diminishes the probability of the act being done.* Thus, a notary public may testify as to his habit of giving notice on the same day as demand for payment.[16] An attorney who drew and witnessed a will, but who has forgotten the circumstances of its execution, is permitted to testify as to his habit of drawing wills in a certain manner in accordance with statute.[17]

The law will not, however, assume that a person will always and necessarily follow a habit and take such proof in lieu of direct evidence of what was actually done when proof of that is available. Thus, the fact that one was of careful habits will not be received as evidence that on a particular occasion he was careful in his actions.[18]

§ 10:08   Capacity, Tools, Means or Opportunity to Act

Generally, the possession of physical strength,[19] intellectual capacity, skill, technical knowledge and experience, requisite means, or opportunity to accomplish a certain act is of probative value to raise an inference that the act was done by the person in question.[20] But this rule is not universal and is applied only when there is a recognized relationship between the capacity to act and the action. For example, the fact that the defendant was in possession of adequate funds may not be shown on the issue of whether he had paid a certain debt because it is well known that wealthy people sometimes do not pay their debts promptly.[21] On the other hand, the fact that a person had no funds will be probative evidence as negating his claim of payment.[22]

§ 10:09   Giving Details Instead of Characterizations

A common difficulty met with in proving an act is that the witness uses a characterization in lieu of the act itself. It is not always improper or objectionable to do so, but, even when proper, it is not effective. At times the witness may use a word or phrase to symbolize the act. Such a word or phrase may be acceptable as what is termed "collective facts," or "a shorthand rendition of the facts."[23] But, if the doing of an act is an important issue, it may be required to be spelled out in detail.

Very often, what is testified to is not even a summary of facts but is no more than a mere characterization or conclusion. Sometimes, the characterization may be acceptable under one set of circumstances, yet be objectionable under another, depending upon the importance of the subject matter in the determination of the issues. Where the subject matter is of slight and incidental importance, such "shorthand rendition of the facts" may be unobjectionable and it may be left to the cross-examiner to probe into the details. Where, however, the performance of the act is at issue, it will not be sufficient merely to call it by name, but the specific acts will have to be elicited.

§ 10:10   Proving Whether Something Was Mailed

Testimony such as, "I mailed a letter to the defendant," might not be objected to. But, should the letter be important and the defendant deny receiving it, he is likely to object, and properly so. Under such circumstances, the testimony, "I mailed the letter to the defendant," would be a mere conclusion. To overcome the objection, the act of mailing would have to be broken down into its component acts and each established by sworn testimony. In order to prove that the defendant received the letter in the mail, it will be necessary to prove the details constituting the act of mailing before any presumption will arise that the letter had been delivered to him.

ILLUSTRATIVE THREAD OF TESTIMONY

Proof of Mailing

Q.   *You have told us that you wrote the letter. Tell us please, what, if anything, did you do with the letter?*

A.   *I put it in an envelope.*

Q.   *What, if anything, did you do with respect to that envelope?*

A.   *I addressed it.*

Q.   *What name and address did you write on the envelope?*

A.   *Mr. John Jones, 1 Main Street, New York City.*

Q.   *What else, if anything, did you write on the envelope?*

A.   *My return address, Charles Smith, 100 First Avenue, New York City.*

Q.   *What else, if anything, did you do with respect to the envelope?*

A.   *I sealed it.*

Q.   *What else, if anything, did you do?*

A.   *I put on an eight-cent stamp.*

Q.   *What, if anything, did you do then?*

A.   *I dropped it into the mail chute in the building where my office is located.*

Q.   *Who receives incoming mail in your office?*

A.   *I do.*

Q. *Did you ever get that letter back?*
A. *No.*

Attorney: *I call upon counsel to produce the letter pursuant to Notice to Produce served upon him.*

Opposing Attorney: *I do not have such a letter.*

Q. *Do you have a copy of that letter?*
A. *I do.*

Q. *Do you have it with you?*
A. *Yes, here it is.*

(The copy is marked Plaintiff's Exhibit 1 for identification only.)

Q. *When was this copy, Plaintiff's Exhibit 1 for identification made?*
A. *It is a carbon copy made at the same time as the original.*

Q. *What did you do with that copy when you mailed the original?*
A. *I placed it in the files.*

Q. *And has it remained there ever since and until you removed it to bring it to court?*
A. *Yes, it has.*

Q. *Has it been changed in any way?*
A. *No, it has not.*

Attorney: *I offer the copy, Plaintiff's Exhibit 1, for identification into evidence.*

§ 10:11 Detailed Acts Constituting Due Care

It is often necessary to prove not only the act but the manner in which it was done. For example, a pedestrian struck by an automobile while crossing a street must establish not only that he was crossing and was struck, but, more important, that he was using due care. The plaintiff is tempted to characterize his actions, indicating not only what he did but also his conclusion by saying, "I was crossing carefully." Of course, it is improper for him to express his own conclusion that he crossed "carefully," which is the ultimate question for the jury to decide.[24] More important, such an expression is empty and ineffectual. What he should do is testify as to all the pertinent details involved in his act of crossing, and these details must be such as will persuade the jury that he was indeed crossing in a careful and prudent manner.

Each of the many details pertaining to the place of crossing, observations made by him before and as he crossed, his gait, the relative speed and distances, and the surrounding circumstances all have significance as indications of due care and will help persuade the jury as to their findings.

By way of illustration, an effective direct examination of a pedestrian who was struck while crossing the street would call upon him for the details of what he observed as well as what he did. It would include the following:

- That he has a recollection of the facts; the exact place from whence he started across, the direction in which he was facing;
- detailed description of the crossing, its width, pavement, traffic;
- the atmospheric conditions and visibility, his observations made as to traffic *before* he started to cross;
- whether or not he saw what it was which later struck him;
- if seen, how far away it was when he first saw it (far enough to give him a reasonable sense of security in crossing);
- if not seen then, some good reason for this;
- the place of crossing and direction in which he walked (as straight across at a crosswalk where he would have the right of way);
- that he heard no signal or warning from the motorist;
- further observations made while crossing;
- that there was nothing between him and the vehicle to obstruct the operator's view;
- what he observed as to the approaching vehicle indicating that he would be able to cross safely;
- the distance he walked before being struck (the greater the distance, the greater the opportunity the defendant had to avoid him).

ILLUSTRATIVE THREAD OF TESTIMONY

Pedestrian Crossing a Street

Q. *Do you recall the details of the accident?*
A. *I do.*

Q. *Where were you just before you were hurt?*
A. *I was at the corner of Broadway and Chambers Street.*

Q. *On which of the four corners were you?*
A. *The southeast corner.*

Q. *In which direction were you facing?*
A. *I was facing north on Broadway.*

Q. *What would you estimate is the width of Chambers Street?*
A. *About 50 feet.*

Q. *Did you notice how Chambers Street is paved at that point?*
A. *Yes, it is asphalt pavement.*

Q. *What, if anything, did you do when you got to that corner?*
A. *I looked to my left and right for traffic.*

Q. *What, if anything, did you see?*
A. *I saw nothing on my left. I saw an automobile approaching the corner from my right, going west.*

Q. *About how far away was this automobile when you first saw it?*
A. *About 100 feet.*

Q. *Did you hear any horn?*
A. *No.*

Q. *What, if anything, did you do then?*
A. *I started to cross.*

Q. *In what direction did you cross?*
A. *I walked straight across.*

Q. *Was there anything between you and the automobile which might obstruct the view of the driver of the automobile?*
A. *No.*

Q. What was the condition of the weather?

A. It was very sunny.

Q. What, if anything, did you do then?

A. I continued to cross.

Q. What, if anything, did you do with respect to making observations?

A. I looked to the right again and saw the automobile about 50 feet from me.

Q. Where were you crossing, with respect to the crosswalk?

A. I was on the crosswalk.

Q. As far as you knew, who had the right of way?

A. My understanding was that as a pedestrian on the crosswalk, I had the right of way.

Q. What, if anything, did you do after seeing the automobile about 50 feet away?

A. I continued to walk across.

Q. What, if anything, did you see then?

A. I saw the automobile when it was a few feet from me, I saw it didn't stop, and then it struck me before I could get out of the way.

Q. About how far had you walked across Chambers Street before you were struck?

A. About 35 feet.

§ 10:12   Showing Details of Surgical Operation

Often the use of a characterization or name for the act, instead of detailed description of what was done, will be unobjectionable but ill advised as lacking in impressiveness. A mere characterization is not likely to bring as clear an image to each juror as a detailed description. For example, if the plaintiff in a personal injury action is content with having his medical witness testify to the fact that he performed a skin graft, the defendant's attorney will surely not object. But how much more effective and impressive it is to have the doctor describe his actions in detail as in the following illustration.

ILLUSTRATIVE THREAD OF TESTIMONY

Skin Graft [25]

Q. *Tell us what was done for the child on July 23rd?*
A. *By July 23rd we were able to apply skin grafts.*

Q. *From what part of her body were the skin grafts taken?*
A. *From her left thigh.*

Q. *And where were they applied?*
A. *To the abraded and destroyed areas of the lower left leg.*

Q. *Will you tell us how that was done; what procedure was followed.*
A. *The superficial layers of skin were removed after shaving and sterilizing the skin of the thigh from which the graft was to be taken.*

Q. *How were the layers of skin removed?*
A. *They were removed with a sharp, straight razor, peeled off in long strips.*

Q. *And what was done with these layers of skin?*
A. *These strips were applied directly to the areas which had no skin, after which the grafted areas were dressed every couple of hours for ten days.*

After such a description, even the most insensitive juror is likely to see the operation in his mind's eye and to give it the proper monetary evaluation when fixing the amount of the verdict.

§ 10:13 Verbal Acts: Miranda Warnings

As has been mentioned at the outset, the fact that a person speaks is an action on his part. The words that he utters may be inadmissible if hearsay or self-serving but not when they constitute part of what Wigmore calls a verbal act.[26] Under recent Supreme Court decisions,[27] a defendant's confession will not be received unless he had first been given the proper warnings.

It has become common practice to furnish police officers with printed cards setting forth the necessary warnings which must be given. The officer who gave the warnings to the accused testifies thereto.

ILLUSTRATIVE THREAD OF TESTIMONY

Miranda Warnings Given

Q. When you picked up the defendant, what, if anything, did you do?

A. I took out a card I had and asked him certain questions.

Q. What questions did you ask him and what were his answers?

A. I said to him, "I would like to advise you that I am a police officer," and asked him, "Do you understand that?" He said, "I do."
I said, "You have a right to remain silent and not make any statements or answer any of my questions. Do you understand that?" He said, "I understand."
I told him, "Anything you say can and will be used against you in a court of law. Do you understand that?" He said, "Yes, I do."
I said, "You have a right to talk to a lawyer and have him present with you during the questioning. Do you understand that?" He said, "I do."
I said, "If you cannot afford a lawyer, you have the right to have a lawyer appointed for you prior to questioning at no expense or cost to you. Do you willingly do without the services of a lawyer at this time?" He said, "I don't want a lawyer."
I asked him, "Knowing your rights in this matter are you willing to answer some questions or make a statement to me now?" He said, "I want to make a statement."

Q. What, if anything, did you do then?

A. (Witness gives details of how the statement was taken.)

§ 10.14   Oral Notice of Dangerous Condition

Oral notices are sometimes given in civil cases, for example, the giving of notice of an allegedly dangerous condition to a defendant or his agent. Here the words spoken are not received as proof that the danger did actually exist, but the words uttered constitute the act of giving notice from which we infer that the defendant thereby acquired knowledge that a dangerous defect was being claimed.[28]

Before any evidence of words which were spoken by the witness will be received into evidence, it is necessary that it appear that they were spoken either to a party to the action or his authorized agent.[29]

The witness first fixes the identity of the one addressed, the time, the place, and who was present, and then states the conversation constituting the notice.

ILLUSTRATIVE THREAD OF TESTIMONY

Oral Notice of Defect

Q. *Did you know the defendant Mr. R_____, prior to the ___ day of _____, 19__?*

A. *Yes, I did.*

Q. *Did you ever speak to him about the condition of the stairs?*

A. *Yes, I did.*

Q. *When was the first time you spoke to him about that?*

A. *On March 10th.*

Q. *What time of the day was that?*

A. *About 3 o'clock in the afternoon.*

Q. *Where were you when you spoke to him?*

A. *In his apartment.*

Q. *Who was present when you spoke to him?*

A. *He and his wife, Mrs. R_____.*

Q. *What did you say to him at that time, in words or substance?*

A. *I said to him that the pads on the stairs were loose and that he should fix it before somebody falls.*

§ 10:15   A Technique to Prove Notice by Telephone

Should the notice be given over the telephone, there is a dual problem of identity of the speaker as well as his authority. This problem has been overcome by the use of a presumption. It has been held that "under modern business practices and the law applicable thereto, a person who answers a telephone call at the place of business of the person called is presumed to be the person called. Especially is the identity presumed if the one answering the telephone responds to the conversation indicating that he has charge of the business in pursuant to which the call was made." [30]

In an action for personal injuries caused by a defect in the street, the plaintiff was required to prove that the municipality had actual notice of the defect. He called, as his witness, a person who lived near the scene who then testified:

ILLUSTRATIVE THREAD OF TESTIMONY

Telephone Notice

Q. On or about _____ 19__ did you observe the condition of the side-walk in front of your home?

A. I did.

Q. What, if anything, did you do?

A. I telephoned City Hall.

(Motion to strike City Hall was granted.)

Q. Did you look up a telephone number before you made the call?

A. I did.

Q. Whose telephone number did you look up?

A. I looked up the number for the Department of Streets and Highways of this City.

Q. Did you then call that number?

A. I did.

Q. Do you now recall the number you called?

A. No.

Q. I show you this telephone book and call your attention to a listing, does that refresh your recollection as to the number you dialed?

A. It does.

Q. What was the number you dialed?

A. (States number.)

Q. Is that the number which you found listed for the Department of Streets and Highways?

A. Yes.

Q. Did someone answer?

A. Yes.

Q.   *When you received an answer, did you ask for anyone in particular?*
A.   *Yes, I did.*

Q.   *Whom did you ask for?*
A.   *I asked for the person in charge of street repairs.*

Q.   *Then, what, if anything, did you hear?*
A.   *A voice said, "Hold the wire," then, after a pause, another man's voice answered and said "This is Street Repairs Department."*

Q.   *What, if anything, did you say?*
A.   *I asked him if he had charge of the repairs of the streets. He said he did.*

Q.   *Then what, if anything, did you tell him about Franklin Street?*
A.   *I told him there was a hole in the sidewalk in front of my house, 62 Franklin Street.*

§ 10:16   Words and Conduct: Rejection of Title and a Tender

The action may consist of a combination of both words and conduct. A good illustration is the proof of what occurred at the meeting of vendor and purchaser for the closing of title. If, for any reason, title does not close and a lawsuit results, the outcome will often depend upon the proof of the plaintiff that he performed all the terms and conditions on his part to be performed. He must show that he made a proper tender and demand and that if a deed was tendered to him, he had good cause to reject it. What each of the parties, or their attorneys, said and did at the closing is, therefore, of vital importance.

ILLUSTRATIVE THREAD OF TESTIMONY

Rejection of Title and Tender

Q.   *On _____, 19__, the date set for closing, did you attend at the office of Mr. Blackstone (vendor's attorney)?*
A.   *I did.*

Q.   *Who was present?*
A.   *The defendant (vendor), Mr. Blackstone, his attorney; the broker Mr. Johnson; the plaintiff and I, as his attorney.*

Q.   Did you at that time have a conversation with the vendor, or Mr. Blackstone, his attorney?

A.   I did.

Q.   With whom was this conversation had?

A.   With Mr. Blackstone.

Q.   Was it in the presence of his client, the defendant?

A.   It was.

Q.   What, if anything, did you say to them with reference to any objections
to the title?

A.   I said, "On behalf of my client, I am objecting to the title on the ground
that it is unmarketable by reason of the encroachments set forth in the
survey and also because of the inheritance tax which was a lien on the
property.

Q.   Was anything said as to an adjournment?

A.   Yes. I said that if the title could be cured, we would be willing to ad-
journ the closing to some other date.

Q.   What, if anything, did Mr. Blackstone or the defendant say to that?

A.   Mr. Blackstone said to me, "You are not justified in rejecting title and
you will have to take it as it is."

Q.   What, if anything, did you say?

A.   I said, "Under the circumstances I must reject title." I said, "I want to
make a formal tender of the balance we have to pay under our contract.
Here is a certified check for $15,000 payable to my client which he will
endorse over to you if you will remove the objections and tender a
proper deed.

Q.   What, if anything, did you then and there do with respect to the check?

A.   I exhibited the check to him. I said, "You don't question the form of
the tender that it is not the coin of the realm?" He said, "No, I don't
question that at all."

(The certified check was marked for identification.)

Q. *I show you Exhibit 1, marked for identification, and ask you what that is?*

A. *That is the certified check which I exhibited.*

Attorney: I offer Exhibit 1 for identification into evidence.

§ 10:17 The Use of Euphemisms

At times, offensive details are avoided by the use of a euphemism which has a well understood meaning, but this is not sufficient if an objection is made. Thus, in an action for divorce, the testimony of an alleged paramour that he had "sexual intercourse" with the defendant would be admissible.[31] However, in a criminal trial of a charge of forcible rape, the specific, though unsavory, details, such as to the fact of penetration, may have to be proven as an essential element of the crime.[32]

§ 10:18 Denial of Act

The witness may have the burden of denying an act instead of proving that he performed it as, for example, the denial of having committed the crime charged. The most effective testimony by a defendant who pleads innocence is his own simple, straightforward, sincere denial of the charge.[33] There is little he can add. If the jury believes him, his bare denial will be sufficient. However, the likelihood of belief will be enhanced if he can convince them that he had no motive or reason to do the act charged, that he lacked the means, capacity, tools, or opportunity necessary to perform it, as, for example, that he did not have the physical strength which would have been required to perform the act,[34] or that he was elsewhere at the time and so could not have done it,[35] that his reputation was that of a good citizen who had never been in trouble with the law and, therefore, was not likely to have committed the crime,[36] and that his conduct, subsequent to the time the crime was committed, was that of an innocent man.[37]

Chapter Ten

FOOTNOTES

[1] People v. Clark (1941), 18 Cal 2d 449, 116 P. 2d 56.

[2] People v. Van Wormer (1903), 175 N.Y. 188, 67 N.E. 299.

Schmerber v. California (1966), 384 U.S. 757, 86 S. Ct. 1832, 16 L. Ed. 1021.

[3] *Wigmore on Evidence,* (3rd ed) Section 2263.

[4] See Section 9.05, "Hearsay. Declarations by an Unidentified Declarant."

[5] *Wigmore on Evidence,* (3rd ed) Section 1772.

See Section 232, "Verbal Acts."

[6] Sullivan v. Minn. St. Paul & S.S.M. Railroad Co. (1927), 55 N.D. 353, 213 N.W. 841; scar on penis.

Wigmore on Evidence, (3rd ed) Section 1158.

[7] See Chapter 7.

[8] See Section 17.03, "Recollection of Insignificant and Routine Matters."

[9] McCormick, Law of Evidence, Section 6.

[10] *Wigmore on Evidence,* (3rd ed) Sections 117–19.

Ibid., Section 391.

[11] People v. Molineux (1901), 168 N.Y. 264, 61 N.E. 2d 286, 62 L.R.A. 193.

[12] Stein v. County Board of School Trustees of Du Page County (Ill. App. 1967), 229 N.E. 2d 165.

See also Section 281, "Intention Shown by Subsequent Conduct."

[13] United States v. H. M. Branson Distributing Co. (6th Cir. [Ky.] 1968), 398 F. 2d 929.

[14] People v. Thompson (1914), 212 N.Y. 249, 106 N.E. 78.

[15] James, *Psychology, The Briefer Course,* pp. 2–3.

[16] Miller v. Hackley, 5 Johns (N.Y.) 375, 4 Am. Dec. 372.

[17] Matter of Kellum (1873), 52 N.Y. 517;

Wigmore on Evidence, (3rd ed) Section 1511.

See Section 5.10, "Knowledge of Custom and Usage."

[18] *Wigmore on Evidence,* (3rd ed) Section 97.

[19] Thiede v. Utah (1895), 159 U.S. 510, 40 L. Ed. 237, 16 Sup. Ct. Rep. 62.

[20] People v. Molineux.

[21] Atwood v. Scott, 99 Mass. 177, 178.

[22] Pontius v. People.

[23] Shaw v. Sylvester (1960), 253 N.C. 176, 116 S.E. 2d 351.

[24] Winski v. Clegg (1924), 81 Ind. App. 560, 142 N.E. 130.

[25] Schwartz, *Trial of Accident Cases,* Section 2651 G.

[26] *Wigmore on Evidence,* (3rd ed) Section 1772, *et seq.*
[27] Jackson v. Denno (1964), 378 U.S. 368, 12 L. Ed. 2d 908, 84 S. Ct. 1774.
[28] Fitzgerald v. United States Lines (2d Cir. [N.Y.] 1962), 306 F. 2d 461, reversed on other grounds, 374 U.S. 16, 10 L. Ed. 2d 720.
[29] Connery v. Cass (1931), 277 Mass. 545, 179 N.E. 164.
Section 7.19, "Amissions by Agents Authorized to Speak for Party."
Section 9.08, "Declaration by Servant After Accident."
[30] Farris v. City of Columbus (Ohio 1948), 83 N.E. 2d 605.
Wigmore on Evidence, (3rd ed) Section 2155.
[31] Miller v. Miller (Pa. Super. 1941), 17 A. 2d 910.
[32] Barker v. State (1898), 40 Fla. 178, 24 So. 69.
[33] F. X. Busch, *Trial Procedure Materials,* pp. 202–4.
[34] People v. Galbo (1916), 218 N.Y. 283, 112 N.E. 1041.
[35] People v. Elmore (1938), 277 N.Y. 397, 14 N.E. 2d 451.
[36] *Wigmore on Evidence,* (3rd ed) Section 56.
[37] Moore *on Facts,* Sections 697, 701, 724.

OBJECTIONS TO
PROOF OF ACTIONS
(WORDS AND CONDUCT)

TABLE OF CONTENTS

OBJECTIONS TO PROOF OF ACTIONS (WORDS OR CONDUCT)

There are times when a witness should not be allowed to testify as to something he had said or done before trial. The Constitution may protect a witness from testamentary compulsion; public policy may prevent proof of non-access to rebut the presumption of legitimacy. A witness will generally not be allowed to pull himself up by his own bootstraps by testimony as to his prior consistent statements or as to his prior good habits or specific acts to show good character. Furthermore, testimony, as to actions, to be received, must be relevant to the issues and not immaterial or prejudicial.

Q. WHAT, IF ANYTHING, DID YOU SAY?

§ 11:01 Objecting When the Witness Is Incompetent: Public Policy

In a child support proceeding against the alleged father, it appeared that the mother was married at the time the child was conceived. The woman's husband was called and asked by Petitioner's Attorney:

Q. *When was the last date, prior to the birth of John, that you had intercourse with your wife?*

Defendant's Attorney: I object.

The objection should be sustained in those jurisdictions which hold, as a matter of public policy, that neither the mother nor husband may testify as to nonaccess to rebut the presumption of legitimacy in a paternity proceeding[1] or for the purpose of dissolving the marital status.[2]

§ 11:02   Privilege Against Self-Incrimination

In an action to recover for the wrongful death of plaintiff's decedent, a pedestrian who had been struck by an automobile owned by the defendant, the plaintiff's attorney called the driver of the defendant's automobile as his witness. The driver had been indicted for Vehicular Homicide. He was asked by Plaintiff's Attorney:

Q.   *Do you recall the occurrence in which an automobile you were operating came into contact with _____, deceased?*

A.   *I do.*

Q.   *Tell us, in your own words, what you did in the operation of your automobile, just prior to the impact.*

> The Witness: *I refuse to answer on the ground that it would tend to incriminate me.*

The court should sustain the objection. The objection has been made by the witness personally. The privilege to refuse to testify as to what might be incriminating is applicable to a civil as well as a criminal case.[3] The privilege is a testimonial one, i.e., it applies only when the witness is asked to give testimony and not when he is asked to do an act. Thus, a defendant may be compelled to stand up, put on a hat, or perform other acts in court.[4]

§ 11:03   When the Testimony Is Incompetent Due to No Opportunity to Cross-Examine

Defendant was being tried for assault with intent to murder. His alleged accomplice, Lloyd, had been tried separately and convicted, and his case was on appeal. Lloyd was called as the People's witness against the defendant and was asked by the State Solicitor:

Q.   *Where were you on the night of January 20, 19__?*

A.   *I refuse to answer on the ground it might tend to incriminate me.*

Q.   *Will your Honor declare him a hostile witness and give me the privilege of cross-examination?*

> The Court: *Yes, motion granted.*

> The Solicitor:

Q. I show you this paper and ask you if that is a confession signed by you?
A. I refuse to answer on the ground it might tend to incriminate me.

Q. Were you present when the truck was fired on?
A. I refuse to answer on the ground it might incriminate me.

Q. Did you state in this statement, "We intended to shoot at the truck?"
A. I refuse to answer on the ground that it might incriminate me.

Defense Counsel: I object to this line of questions.

Although Lloyd's refusal to answer and the Solicitor's reading of Lloyd's alleged statement were not technically testimony, in the jury's mind it was likely to be considered the equivalent of testimony that Lloyd in fact made the statement. The fact that Lloyd invoked his privilege in refusing to answer created a situation in which the jury might improperly infer both that the statement had been made and that it was true.[5] The defendant had no opportunity to cross-examine Lloyd as required by the Confrontation Clause of the Sixth Amendment of the United States Constitution. The objection should be sustained as this clause has been applied to the states.[6]

§ 11:04 Best Evidence Rule

Action to recover for brokerage commissions. The defense is that the employment of the broker was cancelled before he found a purchaser. The defendant was called to testify in his own behalf and asked by Defense Counsel:

Q. On January 19th last, what, if anything, did you do with respect to that property?
A. I mailed a letter to the plaintiff telling him the property was off the market.

Plaintiff's Attorney: I object and move to strike out the answer.

The objection should be sustained and the motion granted on two grounds. The statement, "I mailed a letter," is a conclusion and objectionable. The plaintiff can not be bound by the letter unless he received it. A presumption of delivery of mail in the regular course of business will arise, but only if the fact of mailing is established. The proof of mailing is set forth elsewhere in this book.[7] The second ground for objection is the testimony as to the contents of the letter, "telling him the property was off the market," without producing the letter itself as required by the Best Evidence Rule.[8]

If mailing is properly established and the plaintiff has been served with a notice to produce the letter and fails to do so, then it would be permissible for the defendant to give secondary evidence of its contents by testifying to what was stated in the letter.[9]

§ 11:05 Hearsay

Plaintiff seeks to impose a constructive trust upon land held in the name of the defendant which, plaintiff alleges, was paid for by him and was to be conveyed to him by the defendant on demand. Plaintiff called the vendor of the property as his witness and he was asked by Plaintiff's Attorney:

Q.   Before meeting the defendant, did you meet and speak to the plaintiff?
A.   I did.

Q.   And was that conversation with reference to the property which is here in litigation?
A.   It was.

Q.   Where did you speak to the plaintiff?
A.   At my office.

Q.   Who was present?
A.   Just the two of us.

Q.   Tell us what he said to you at that time?
A.   He said my asking price was fair and that he was willing to purchase the property at that price and that he was not going to take the title in his own name but that his son-in-law (the defendant) would be in touch with me and consummate the deal and take the property in his name but he was going to hold it in trust for the plaintiff.

Defense Counsel: I object and move to strike out the answer.

The objection should be sustained. The conversation between the witness and the plaintiff was not in the presence of the defendant and not binding upon him.[10]

§ 11:06 Hearsay: Self-Serving Declarations

Plaintiff sues for personal injuries sustained by her while riding in an automobile driven by her son which collided with defendant's automobile. The plaintiff was asked by Plaintiff's Attorney:

Q. *Before you got into the automobile to start on that trip, what, if anything, did you do?*

A. *Due to the downpour of rain, I cautioned my son to drive carefully.*

Defense Counsel: I object and move to strike out the answer.

The objection should be sustained and the answer stricken because it is a self-serving declaration and has no probative value insofar as the negligence or care exercised by the son is concerned.[11]

§ 11:07 Objecting to Evidence That Is Irrelevant: Good Character

A witness called by the plaintiff in a civil action is asked on direct examination by Plaintiff's Attorney:

Q. *Tell us about yourself, your background, activities, and antecedents?*

A. *I have lived in the same house in this community for 30 years. I am active in communal affairs, being president of the P.T.A., I go to church regularly. . . .*

Opposing Counsel: I object and move to strike out the answer.

Traditionally, there is a difference in attitude toward character evidence in civil and criminal cases. In criminal cases, the accused may introduce pertinent evidence of his own good character as this may create a reasonable doubt as to whether he was likely to commit the offense charged;[12] or he may introduce evidence of the character of the victim in support of a claim of self-defense in a homicide or consent in a case of forcible rape.[13] By giving evidence of his own good character, the accused is said to "put his character in issue" and the prosecution may then rebut with evidence of bad character.[14]

Good character is generally immaterial in a civil case. A person may have the finest character and yet be negligent or breach a contract, although it is less likely that such a person would commit a crime.[15] In a civil action, the fact that the witness was active in church matters or had distinguished himself in the armed forces[16] or other evidence of "good character" is deemed immaterial in determining what actually happened and may enable the jury to reward the good man or punish the bad because of their characters, despite what the evidence in the case shows actually happened.[17] The illustration being from a civil case, the motion to strike should be granted, the character of the witness not being directly in issue.[18]

§ 11:08   Prior Habit of Care

The plaintiff, a pedestrian, suing for personal injuries sustained when he was struck by defendant's automobile, was asked by Plaintiff's Attorney:

Q. *What, if anything, did you do when you came to the corner?*
A. *I stopped and looked for traffic. I always look before I cross a street.*

Defendant's Attorney: I object and move to strike out the last sentence.

In the illustrative given, the motion to strike would probably be granted for the reason that the plaintiff has testified as to what he did at the particular time at issue, and, therefore, what he did at other times is immaterial and not responsive to the question. Whether or not the plaintiff could testify so as to establish that he habitually did a certain act in a certain manner, presents more difficult considerations. There are differences of opinion. "The doing of the habitual acts may become semi-automatic."[19] The modern view is to permit evidence of the habit of a person or of the routine practice of an organization as relevant to prove that the conduct of the person or organization on a particular occasion was in conformity with the habit or routine practice.[20] There is a difference of authority as to what constitutes a habit and as to how often the act has to be done or how consistently the behavior must be followed in order to be deemed to be a habit.[21] In one case where the important issue was whether the pedestrian, returning home from church, had been struck while on the crosswalk or at a point east of the crosswalk, and there was a conflict in the testimony, the court received evidence of a defense witness as to the alleged habit of the plaintiff or crossing at a point east of the crosswalk when returning home from church.[22] On the other hand, testimony as to the religious "habits" of the accused, offered to prove that he was at home observing the Sabbath rather than out obtaining money through larceny by trick, was held properly excluded.[23]

In some jurisdictions, evidence of careful habits to prove freedom from contributory negligence will only be received in the absence of eyewitnesses in wrongful death cases,[24] but this rule has been criticized.[25] Testimony as to habit of care has also been held to be inadmissible as raising collateral issues.[26] While a man should live a careful life, no man is always careful and thus, evidence of habit is, it has been said, too uncertain upon which to base an inference of care or negligence on a particular occasion.[27]

§ 11:09   Prior Consistent Statement

A witness had testified as to the facts within his knowledge and was then asked as part of his direct examination:

Q. *Soon after this occurrence you were interviewed by a representative of my office, were you not?*

A. *I was.*

Q. *Did you, at that time, write out and sign a statement?*

A. *I did.*

Q. *I show you this paper and ask you whether that is the statement that you signed?*

A. *It is.*

Attorney: I offer the statement in evidence.

Opposing Attorney: I object.

The objection should be sustained. The testimony of a witness cannot be bolstered by proof that the witness had previously stated the same thing. The repetition of the same story does not increase its probative value.[28] Thus, a plaintiff may not be asked what history he gave his physician.[29] Nor may a police officer testify that a certain witness had identified the accused prior to the "in court" identification.[30]

If, however, the witness is a disinterested one and his testimony has been assailed on cross-examination as a recent fabrication, proof of any prior consistent statement, if made before there was any motive to deceive, might be received on redirect examination in order to repel such imputation as perjury.[31] In some jurisdictions, prior consistent statements are admissible after impeachment of any sort.[32]

§ 11:10   Prejudicial Conduct

In an action for personal injuries, plaintiff was on the witness stand and during direct examination he was asked by Plaintiff's Attorney:

Q. *Please describe your injuries, pain, and suffering.*

A. (The plaintiff burst into uncontrollable tears).

Defense Counsel: I move for a mistrial.

An emotional display by a party, engendering passion and prejudice, may result in a mistrial.[33] It is unnecessary that the display be deliberate or falsely simulated in order for it to be prejudicial.[34] The ruling is within the sound discretion of the trial court based upon whether or not the conduct was likely to cause the rendition of an improper verdict.[35]

On the other hand, it has been said that if any attorney is moved to tears during his summation, it may be his duty to shed them.[36]

Chapter Eleven

FOOTNOTES

[1] Eubanks v. Eubanks (N.C. 1968), 159 S.E. 2d 562.
Commonwealth *ex rel.* Leider v. Leider (Pa. Super. 1967), 233 A. 2d 917.
[2] Taylor v. Taylor (1908), 123 App. Div. 220, 108 N.Y.S. 428.
Gonzalez v. Gonzalez (Tex. Civ. App. 1943), 177 S.W. 2d 328.
[3] The Fifth Amendment to the United States Constitution.
Wigmore on Evidence, (3rd ed) Section 2250 *et seq.*
[4] Section 10.01, Note 2.
[5] Slochower v. Board of Higher Education (1955), 350 U.S. 551.
United States v. Maloney (2d Cir. [N.Y.] 1959), 262 F. 2d 537.
[6] Douglas v. Alabama (1965), 380 U.S. 415.
[7] See Section 10.10, "Proving Whether Something Was Mailed."
[8] See Section 6.06, "Contents of a Writing."
[9] Gordon v. Christenson (1921), 188 N.Y.S. 135.
[10] Hackin v. Gaynes (1968), 103 Ariz. 13, 436 P. 2d 127.
[11] Edwards v. Adams (Ga. App. 1968), 160 S.E. 2d 841.
[12] People v. Van Gaasbeck (1907), 189 N.Y. 408, 82 N.E. 718.
People v. Rodawald (1904), 177 N.Y. 408, 70 N.E. 1.
Proposed Rules of Evidence for the United States District Courts and Magistrates, Rule 4-04 (a) (1).
[13] *Ibid.,* Rule 4-04 (a) (2).
[14] People v. Sharp (1887), 107 N.Y. 427, 14 N.E. 319.
Proposed Rules of Evidence for the United States District Courts and Magistrates, Rule 4-04 (a) (1).
[15] Noonan v. Luther (1912), 206 N.Y. 105, 99 N.E. 178.
[16] Atlantic Coast Line Railroad Co. v. Daugherty (Ga. App. 1967), 157 S.E. 2d 880.

[17] See Judicial Conference Report (March 1969), on the Proposed Rules of Evidence for the United States District Courts and Magistrates, Rule 4-04.

[18] McKane v. Howard (1911), 202 N.Y. 181, 95 N.E. 642.

Beach v. Richtmyer (1949), 275 App. Div. 466, 90 N.Y.S. 2d 332.

[19] See Section 10.07, "Prior Habit of the Witness."

[20] *Wigmore on Evidence,* (3rd ed) Section 97.

Proposed Rules of Evidence for the United States District Courts and Magistrates, Rule 4-06 (a).

[21] Lewan, "Rationale of Habit Evidence," 16 *Syracuse Law Review* 39, 49, 1964).

[22] Glatt v. Feist (N.D. 1968), 156 N.W. 2d 819.

[23] Levin v. United States (D.C. Cir. 1964), 338 F. 2d 265.

[24] Wooster v. Broadway, etc. (1893), 72 Hun. 197, 25 N.Y.S. 378;

Zucker v. Whitridge (1912), 205 N.Y. 50, 98 N.E. 209.

[25] Frank, J., in Cereste v. New York, New Haven & Hartford Railroad Co. (2d Cir. 1956), 231 F. 2d 50; cert. denied 351 U.S. 951.

[26] See Note 24 above.

[27] Zucker v. Whitridge (1912), 205 N.Y. 50, 98 N.E. 209.

Lefcourt v. Jenkinson (1940), 258 App. Div. 1080, 18 N.Y.S. 2d 160.

[28] Rogers v. State (1908), 88 Ark. 451, 115 S.W. 156, 41 L.R.A. (NS) 857.

Crawford v. Nilan (1943), 289 N.Y. 444, 46 N.E. 2d 512.

People v. Buffington (1968), 29 App. Div. 2d 229, 287 N.Y.S. 2d 243;

Wigmore on Evidence, (3rd ed) Section 1122 *et seq.*

[29] Boston and Albany Railroad Company v. O'Reilly (1895), U.S. 334, 39 Law. Ed. 1006;

Davidson v. Cornell (1892), 132 N.Y. 228, 30 N.E. 573;

Wigmore on Evidence, (3rd ed) Section 1722 (a) and (b).

See also Section 9.13, "Self-serving Declaration."

[30] See Section 8.08, "Prior Identification."

[31] Commonwealth v. Retkovitz (1916), 222 Mass. 245, 110 N.E. 293.

People v. Katz (1913), 209 N.Y. 311, 103 N.E. 305.

Lynch v. L. B. Sprague, Inc. (N.H. 1949), 66 A. 2d 697, 700.

[32] *Wigmore on Evidence* (3rd ed) Sections 1126, 1129.

[33] See Note, 69 ALR 2d 954.

[34] Foster and Creighton v. St. Paul Mercury Indemnity Co. (1956), 264 Ala. 581, 88 So. 2d 825;

Lantex Construction Co. v. Lejsal (Tex. Civ. App. 1958), 315 S.W. 2d 177.

[35] Kuehn v. Hahn (Mo. 1964), 380 S.W. 2d 445;

Johnson v. Hansen (1964), 237 Ore. 1, 390 P. 2d 611;

Underwriters v. Foster (Tex. Civ. App. 1964), 383 S.W. 2d 829.

[36] Ferguson v. Moore (1897), 98 Tenn. 342, 39 S.W. 341.

PROOF OF STATE OF MIND (FEELINGS, BIAS, EMOTIONS, INTENTIONS)

TABLE OF CONTENTS

PROOF OF
STATE OF MIND
(FEELINGS, BIAS,
EMOTIONS, INTENTIONS)

A witness will be permitted to testify as to his own state of mind but such testimony is very weak and unconvincing unless it is bolstered by the witness showing that, by virtue of his background and antecedents, he is a person to be believed. Most important, the actions of the witness must have been such as are consonant with his alleged state of mind. This together with his apparent frankness and truthfulness, the logic and probability of his testimony as well as the vividness of the description of his feelings will go far to persuade the jury to accept such subjective proof.

Q. WHAT ARE YOUR FEELINGS WITH RESPECT TO . . .?

§ 12:01   The Oath Is a Matter of State of Mind

The question put to a witness in order to elicit his "state of mind" assumes many forms. For example, the very first thing we ask any witness is *Q. Do you solemnly swear, in the presence of the everlasting God, to tell the truth, the whole truth and nothing but the truth?* This is but another form of the question *Q. What are your feelings as to telling the truth?* "State of mind" is involved whenever the witness testifies to such matters as his feelings, emotions, beliefs, attitudes, pain, or any other mental state.

§ 12:02   Admissibility of Testimony as to State of Mind

Testimony of a witness as to his own state of mind might seem to be speculative and conjectural. Such testimony will, however, be received, where relevant, and given such weight as the triers of the facts feel is warranted.[1] Thus, the operator of a motor vehicle will be permitted to testify not only as to the manner in which he was operating his vehicle, but also as to his condition of mind just prior to a collision as this relates to his observations and conduct.[2] Such testimony is deemed factual. The witness may, so to speak, look within his own mind and report what he finds there. It is only when the witness tries to testify as to the state of mind of a person other than himself that he necessarily resorts to conclusions, speculation, or conjecture.[3]

A witness will be permitted to testify as to what his intentions were. The intent with which the witness did an act is known to himself and he is competent, therefore, to testify as to such fact.[4] So, a witness in a criminal case will be allowed to tell of his state of mind, his reasons, motives, or fears which would explain his failure to report certain matters to the authorities[5] or why an exculpatory note was written.[6] Of course, the testimony of a witness as to his own state of mind is not conclusive, but simply a part of the surrounding circumstances tending to support a finding thereof.[7]

Thus, in determining whether a driver had the owner's permission to use the automobile he was driving, the driver will be permitted to testify as to his own state of mind with respect to whether he believed that he had permission, or whether there was an intent on his own part to use the car unlawfully.[8] In one case, in which the issue was whether or not there was implied permission for an employee to drive a certain vehicle, the following testimony by the driver of the vehicle was held to have been properly received:

Q.   *Well, you didn't think you were stealing the truck, did you, when you drove off?*

A.   *No, sir.*

Q.   *Let us say you are out there working on the ranch and you need a shot of penicillin for some of the livestock and Mr. Herring isn't around, do you think you have permission to drive that vehicle and get that penicillin?*

Defendant's Attorney: I object to that question for the reason that it asks for the conclusion of the witness, invades the province of the jury.

The Court: I will overrule the objection.

A.   *Well, I don't know. If I thought they needed it I'd go and get it.*

In affirming the judgment for the plaintiff the court said, "We do not believe the court erred in admitting the above testimony. As a general rule, a witness may testify as to his own intention or other state of mind where the same is material." [9]

There are many other instances in which a witness has been permitted to testify as to his own intentions. The owner of an automobile, who was a passenger in it at the time of the collision, was allowed to testify that he had loaned the automobile to the driver with the intent that the latter be his bailee rather than his agent. And the driver could corroborate this by testimony as to his own intentions. [10] In another case, [11] a convicted murderer was granted a new trial because he was not permitted to testify as to what his intentions were when he went to the victim's home. *The court said, ". . . when the motive of a witness in performing a particular act, . . . becomes a material issue in a case, or reflects important light upon such issue, he may himself be sworn in regard to it, notwithstanding the difficulty of furnishing contradictory evidence, and notwithstanding the diminished credit to which his testimony may be entitled as coming from the mouth of an interested witness."*

Similarly, a prospective purchaser in an action by the broker for commissions, may be asked, on direct examination *Q. Were you, on that date, ready, willing, and able to sign a formal contract embodying those terms and to purchase the property on those terms?* [12] And a witness may testify that his intention, in turning over money, was that it was not to be a loan (at usurious interest) but security for money placed for investment. [13]

A witness will be allowed to describe his pain and suffering even though it was subjective and unaccompanied by any objective signs of injury. After all, no one knows better than the injured person whether or not he is suffering pain. The question of whether he is truthfully reporting the facts affects only the weight, and not the admissibility of the testimony. [14]

§ 12:03 Weakness of Testimony

All testimony by a witness as to his state of mind is necessarily subjective, and its value is lessened by the consideration that he is an interested witness and, even if completely honest, may be mistaken as to his true feelings by reason of some subconscious bias or prejudice of which he himself is unaware. The effect of unconscious fears, hopes, or rationalizations upon the conscious mind has not yet been fully explored or understood. Furthermore, the witness may be tempted to color or mask his feelings, believing that there is no way in which his true state of mind can be exposed.

§ 12:04 Enhancing the Weight of the Testimony

Because of the subjective nature of testimony of state of mind, it is especially important that such testimony be bolstered in every possible way so that the triers of the fact be persuaded that the witness is to be believed. The credibility of the witness is pervasive.[15] The mere fact that a witness makes an assertion does not mean that the triers of the facts are required to believe the matter asserted.[16]

WHAT TO SHOW TO ENHANCE THE WEIGHT OF TESTIMONY

The weight of his testimony as to his mental state may be enhanced by the following:

- His background and antecedents indicating credibility.[17]
- His acts and conduct corroborating his alleged mental state.[18]
- His disinterestedness and lack of motive to deceive.[19]
- The intrinsic probability of his testimony.[20]
- Appearance and manner of the witness on the stand.[21]
- The vividness of description of subjective feelings.[22]

§ 12:05 Background and Antecedents Indicative of Credibility

One way to reinforce such subjective testimony is to show that the witness is one who is likely to tell the truth. In the ordinary affairs of life, we arrive at our opinion of a man's credibility, character, and trustworthiness by studying him, his background, his friends and associates, his education, his marital status, or his community activities. It would seem to this writer that such evidence should be received in court on the issue of credibility. Unfortunately, the law has placed serious restrictions upon the admissibility of testimony by the witness regarding his antecedents as bearing upon his credibility.[23] *As a general rule, evidence of the background and antecedents of a witness which would indicate good character may not be received if there has been no prior impeachment of the witness.*[24]

There are, however, certain aspects of a witness' background, antecedents, and character which are received under various circumstances for certain limited purposes as follows.

§ 12:06 Disclosure of Bad Character of One's Own Witness: Anticipating Cross-examination

The trial attorney may find himself in the unhappy position of having to call a disreputable witness, as a matter of necessity, not choice. When this must be done, it is sound psychology and legally proper to disclose the facts *at the outset.* When an attorney calls a witness, he does not necessarily present him as a person of good moral character, but does vouch for his credibility and represent him as worthy of belief regarding the matters to which he testifies.[25] "The law does not limit a party to witnesses of good character, nor does it compel a party to conceal the bad record of his witnesses from the jury to have it afterwards revealed by the opposing party with telling effect. Such rule would be unfair alike to the party calling the witness and the jury. . . . But when a disreputable witness is called and frankly presented to the jury as such, the party calling him represents him for the occasion and for the purpose of the trial as worthy of belief." [26]

The adversary will not be heard to complain that this is anticipation of cross-examination. The proponent of a witness need not wait for the cross-examiner to damage his credibility.[27] The courts have gone so far as to allow the key witness in a trial for conspiracy to testify on direct examination that he had already pleaded guilty to conspiracy where the court adequately charges the jury that his guilty plea is not to be considered as evidence against the defendant.[28]

Such questions about the witness' past are to be asked at the outset and before any other testimony is given. If this is not done, and the witness later surprises the attorney who called him with his testimony, he may not then be questioned on direct examination in such a manner as to insinuate that he has testified falsely,[29] nor may his bad reputation then be shown.[30] It is one thing to disclose the witness' unfortunate past at the outset and another to discredit him by impeaching his credibility. It is generally improper to impeach the credibility of one's own witness.[31]

§ 12:07 Occupation as Bearing on Credibility

It is customary, by way of introduction, to ask the witness about his occupation or profession, the identity of his employer, the nature of his duties and how long so engaged.

Irrespective of any limitations placed upon the admissibility of testimony as to the witness' own background, antecedents, or good character, it is always permissible for the witness to go into the details of the nature of his employment or profession.[32]

If the witness is in the employ of one of the parties in the case, he is an "interested" witness, and this may affect the weight to be accorded his testimony, although it does not make him incompetent to testify.[33]

Some occupations or professions confer status and credibility while others carry a stigma. For example, a clergyman[34] or lawyer[35] are presumed to be truthful, whereas the testimony of a prostitute[36] or hired detective[37] is to be more strictly scrutinized.

§ 12:08 Professional Background as Qualifying the Witness to Express Expert Opinions

If the witness is an expert or skilled witness who is to be asked for his opinions, that fact furnishes a reason for going into his past accomplishments. The rationale is that this is admitted not as to credibility, but for the purpose of establishing the witness' qualifications to express an opinion by showing that he had specialized knowledge and experience.[38]

§ 12:09 Antecedents Which Are Directly at Issue

When the antecedents and background of the witness are directly at issue, he will be permitted to state what they are. For example, if the witness is suing for libel or slander or false imprisonment, his antecedents are pertinent in ascertaining the extent of his damage.[39] Where one of the elements to be established by the prosecution is the chaste character of the complainant who was allegedly seduced, she may testify in relation thereto.[40]

§ 12:10 A Child's Competency to Take an Oath

An oath will not be administered to a young child until he is shown, to the satisfaction of the court, to be competent to testify. There is no specific age below which capacity is deemed wanting as a matter of law.[41] The determination of whether or not a child is competent to be sworn is discretionary and is to be judged on the basis of a preliminary examination of the child conducted by the judge in court.[42]

Intelligence, not age, is the proper criterion to be used in determining the competency of a witness of tender years. The true test of competency of a young child as a witness consists of:

- His understanding of the obligation to speak the truth on the witness stand.
- His mental capacity at the time of the occurrence concerning which the child is to testify.
- His ability to receive an accurate impression of the occurrence.
- A memory sufficient to retain an independent recollection of the occurrence.
- A capacity to express in words his memory of the occurrence.
- Capacity to understand simple questions about the occurrence.[43]

It is not essential that the child have religious beliefs or convictions or even understand the meaning of the adult oath.[44]

In actual practice, the requirements are minimal and the finding of the trial court will not be reversed where all that appears is that the child knows that it is wrong to tell a lie.[45] If the child's testimony is to have any weight, however, more should be known about him than his age, or his knowledge of theology.[46]

It is to be expected that a young child, before he is sworn, will be asked questions concerning the following, amongst other matters, by the court:

- name
- address
- age
- birth date
- school
- location of his school
- grade attended
- teacher's name
- religious or Sunday school
- church attendance
- knowledge of difference between truth and lies
- the meaning of an oath
- consequences of lying.

ILLUSTRATIVE THREAD OF TESTIMONY

Voir Dire of Child

By the Court:

Q. *What is your name, little girl?*
A. *Anna Jones.*

Q. *Where do you live?*
A. *102 Main Street, Anyville.*

Q. *How old are you?*
A. *Ten years old.*

Q. *When were you born?*
A. _____.

Q. *What school do you go to?*
A. *Public School No. 6.*

Q.   Where is that?
A.   That is on Warren Street.

Q.   Near what street, do you remember that?
A.   Near 10th Street.

Q.   What class are you in?
A.   In the fourth grade.

Q.   What is your teacher's name?
A.   Mrs. May.

Q.   Do you go to Sunday School?
A.   Yes.

Q.   Do you go to any other school?
A.   Yes, to dancing school.

Q.   Do you go to church?
A.   Yes, I do.

Q.   Do you know the difference between the truth and a lie?
A.   Yes.

Q.   Is it right to tell a lie or is it wrong to tell a lie?
A.   It is wrong.

Q.   What happens to you if you tell a lie?
A.   God would punish me.

Q.   Do you know what it means to swear?
A.   Yes.

Q.   What does it mean?
A.   It means you promise to tell the truth.

Q.   What do you think the court will do to you if you swear to tell the truth
     and you didn't tell the truth?
A.   You would put me in jail.

The Court: I believe this witness is qualified to be sworn.

§ 12:11 Antecedents of a Defendant in a Criminal Case as Creating a Reasonable Doubt

In a criminal case, testimony by the defendant as to antecedents and background will be received. It is relevant, not as to credibility, but rather on the theory that it may indicate that his mental state and attitude was such that he would not be likely to commit the crime charged and thus create a reasonable doubt.[47]

§ 12:12 The Witness' Acts and Conduct Corroborating His Alleged Mental State

The clearest evidence available to indicate a "State of Mind" is proof of the acts and conduct of the witness which are consonant with his alleged mental state. It will avail a witness little to assert that he had certain feelings, emotions, or intentions if his actions have belied his words. A person's acts and conduct are the objective, outward signs of his inner feelings.[48] Prior, contemporary, or subsequent acts are equally pertinent. For example, the alienation of affections is shown by evidence of the little attentions and acts of kindness and courtesies paid the plaintiff by the spouse before and after the defendant came upon the scene.[49]

Love and affection, and any kindred or opposite feelings, is but a state of mind and, like other subjective matters, can only be evidenced by inferences arising from acts and conduct. The question *Q. Do you love your wife?* may glibly be answered by the witness, but the impact of his answer upon the court or jury will depend upon the actions of the witness from which the genuineness of the alleged feeling can be assessed.

§ 12:13 Intention Shown by Subsequent Conduct

The intention with which a party did an act may be inferred from evidence showing his subsequent conduct.[50] A good illustration is the testimony of a party to a matrimonial action to establish that when he had gone to a foreign jurisdiction to reside, it was his intention to be domiciled there. Intent plays an important part in the proof of change of domicile, as the mere intent to acquire a new domicile is not enough. To substantiate his claimed intention to change his domicile, the plaintiff should testify in detail as to all his actions from which such intent may be inferred. This should include:

- Testimony as to his abandonment of his original domicile, as, that he gave up his residence on a certain date and that prior to that date he had resigned from his position, closed his bank account, removed all his personal property and moved without any intent to return or resume his domicile there.

- That he took up residence in the new domicile, giving its location and description, that he obtained another position or went into business there, opened a bank account, took out insurance, registered as a voter and for the draft in the new domicile.

- He may state his intention of living there, his reasons for changing domicile, and that it was his intention of residing in the new domicile permanently.

ILLUSTRATIVE THREAD OF TESTIMONY

Intent as to Domicile

Q. *Until what date did you reside in the State of New York?*
A. *Until June ___, 19___.*

Q. *Then where did you go?*
A. *I went to Florida.*

Q. *On what date did you reach Florida?*
A. *About June 10, 19___.*

Q. *Previous to leaving New York, you were employed, were you not?*
A. *Yes.*

Q. *By whom?*
A. (Witness states.)

Q. *Did you resign from that position?*
A. *I did.*

Q. *When?*
A. *Before I left New York.*

Q. *Have you ever been employed there since?*
A. *No.*

Q. *At the time you went to Florida, did you intend to come back and work for your previous employer?*

A. No.

Q. Before you left New York, did you have a bank account at the _____ Bank?
A. I did.

Q. What, if anything, did you do with that account?
A. I closed it.

Q. Did you intend to reopen it at any time?
A. I did not.

Q. After you went to Florida, did you have any place of residence in New York?
A. No.

Q. Did you have any personal property in New York?
A. No.

Q. When you came to Florida, where did you live?
A. At _____ Street.

Q. What did you have, a room, or an apartment, or what?
A. I had a two-room apartment.

Q. Did you go into business in Florida?
A. Yes, I did.

Q. What business did you go into?
A. (Witness states.)

Q. Where was that business located?
A. (Witness states.)

Q. I show you this pad of stationery and ask you if that is the stationery you used in connection with that business?
A. It is.

Q. *Name some of the customers with whom you did business?*
A. (Witness names customers.)

Q. *Is this an advertising circular in connection with that business?*
A. *Yes, it is what is known as a throw-away pamphlet.*

The Court: What are you going to do with all those?

Defendant's Attorney: I offer them all as one exhibit, for the purpose of showing that this is an actual business.

Plaintiff's Attorney: I object.

The Court: I will receive it.

(Papers received and marked in evidence.)

Q. *Do you still own that business?*
A. *I do.*

Q. *Did you open any bank accounts in Florida?*
A. *I did.*

Q. *At which bank?*
A. *At the _____ Bank of Florida.*

Q. *Is this your deposit book with that bank?*
A. *It is.*

Q. *I show you three checks all drawn to the order of the plaintiff, all drawn on the _____ Bank of Florida, and ask you whether these were checks drawn on that account?*
A. *Yes.*

Q. *I show you this document and ask you what it is?*
A. *It is a certificate of insurance covering property damage and liability in connection with my business in Florida*

Q. *Have you voted the past three years?*
A. *I have.*

Q. *Where did you register and vote last year?*
A. *In Florida.*

Q. (Presenting same) *I show you this card, is this the card you received from your draft board in Florida?*
A. *That is.*

Defendant's Attorney: *I offer it in evidence.*

(Received and marked.)

Q. *Is it your intention to live any place else?*
Plaintiff's Attorney: *I object as self-serving.*

The Court: *Intention is a fact to be proven and such a declaration is not self-serving.*
A. *No.*

Q. *At the time you went to Florida, what was your purpose in going there?*
A. *I went there for a number of reasons. The paramount reason was to re-establish my earning power. Another important reason was that I knew that there was no estate tax there. Inasmuch as I had lapsed all my insurance except one term policy, it would be a most unfortunate thing for me to be caught dead in New York State.*

Q. *Were those your only reasons?*
A. *Frankly, the advantage of going to a state where divorce rulings are more liberal may have been a secondary objective, although not the primary one. I could have gone to Nevada or Arkansas.*

Plaintiff's Attorney: *I move to strike that out.*

The Court: *Yes, strike out "I could have gone, etc."*

Q. *When you went to Florida, how long did you intend to stay?*
A. *I intended to stay permanently and establish an office and live there.*

Q. Have you resided in New York since you left for Florida?
A. No, sir.

Q. Do you intend to leave Florida for purposes of residence?
A. No.

§ 12:14   Disinterestedness: Lack of Motive to Deceive

When the state of mind in question is truthfulness, it is helpful to show that there were no facts or circumstances which might tend to induce perjury—in other words, that the witness had no personal interest in the outcome of the action. The fact that the witness was disinterested may have some adverse effect on his testimony as to Perception[51] and Recollection.[52] On the other hand, this very negative quality of disinterestedness may add to the weight and credibility of the witness' testimony by reason of the fact that he speaks without any self-interest or motive to distort or deceive.[53]

The absence of facts indicating interest, bias or prejudice should be established at the outset of the direct examination of the witness. Disinterestedness may be indicated by testimony that the witness' knowledge of the facts came about fortuitously, as, for example, that he just happened to be at the scene of the accident; that he had never met either of the parties, nor their attorneys, nor had any relationship or dealings with them socially, in business or otherwise; that he was compelled to come to court by virtue of the service of a subpoena; that he did not receive and was not promised any compensation for his testimony; that he had no interest in the action nor in any similar action which might be pending which might be affected by the outcome of the case; that his appearance and testimony was equally available to both sides and that he was always ready and willing to cooperate with either without favor or bias; and, in general, that he had no motive, bias, interest, or prejudice one way or the other.

ILLUSTRATIVE THREAD OF TESTIMONY

To Demonstrate Disinterest and Impartiality of Witness

Q. Had you ever, prior to this occurrence, met any of the parties or their attorneys?
A. No.

Q. Did you give your name to the police officer at the scene?
A. I did.

Q. Did a representative from my office come to see you?
A. Yes.

Q. When he called upon you did you tell him what you knew of the facts?
A. I did.

Q. Were you also interviewed by a representative of the defendant's office?
A. I was.

Q. Have you been subpoenaed to come here by me?
A. Yes, I was.

Q. Have you discussed this case with me before coming to court?
A. Yes.

Q. When was that?
A. This morning, before court opened.

Q. Have you any interest in this action other than to tell what you know of the facts as you observed them?
A. No.

Q. So far as you know, do you have any interest, bias, or prejudice for or against either party?
A. No, I do not.

§ 12:15   The Intrinsic Probability of His Testimony

The witness' credibility will depend, on the one hand, upon his own personality, the apparent frankness and honesty with which he testifies, and the absence of any indication of reasons why he should distort or prevaricate. On the other hand, credibility is generated by the testimony itself and its logic and consistency in accord with the probabilities. If the testimony he gives is such as seems probable and logical, when viewed in the light of all the evidence, this will go far in helping the jury infer that he is a credible witness.

The testimony, to be believed, must have the ring of truth. To accomplish this, the proposed testimony should be scrutinized before it is given to see whether it is in accord with the other known or demonstrable facts or the testimony of other witnesses and with the probabilities.[54] It is possible for testimony to be strange and improbable yet true, but such testimony is less likely to be believed and special effort must be made to overcome this handicap by having the witness appear at his best by calling others to corroborate him or by creating some doubt as to the accuracy of the facts which seem to make his testimony improbable.

§ 12:16   Appearance and Manner of Witness on the Stand

The credibility of a witness depends as much upon the personality of the witness as on the content of his testimony. The advocate can help the witness make the best possible presentation and impression by his attention and advice with respect to the witness' dress and deportment as well as his insistence upon frankness and truthfulness in answering questions. The jury will be watching closely, and will note every mannerism, every grimace, and every inflection of his voice. Undoubtedly, as much will be learned by them from the fleeting expression, the twitching of muscles, and involuntary gestures, as from the words of his mouth. This is the reason appellate courts are so loathe to upset the findings of the court or jury who have seen the witness and observed his manner on the witness stand.[55]

§ 12:17   Vivid Description of Subjective Feelings

There are times when the ability to communicate the feelings of the witness to the jury may be most important. For example, the proof of pain and suffering by an injured plaintiff in a personal injury action may constitute a basis for a large award in damages.[56]

The plaintiff himself is the one who can best express how he felt. However, it is one thing to feel pain, and another, adequately to communicate such feelings to others. It is not enough to ask *Q. How did you feel?* and have the witness answer, "I felt very bad." Such an answer does little to convey the sensations of pain suffered by the plaintiff in such a way that the jury can fully appreciate what the plaintiff endured. The plaintiff can greatly increase the impact of his testimony in this regard in three ways:

- By the use of analogy in describing the pain and by making comparisons, whenever possible, to feelings which the jurors may have experienced. If the witness says, for example, that a particular pain felt, "like a dentist drilling and touching the nerve of a tooth," such a description will be meaningful to the jurors.

- By having the witness testify not only to the original pain but also as to his sensations at various periods after the time of the injury and up to the present. As time passes, memory of pain is foreshortened and tends to fade. A minute of excruciating pain may seem like an eternity, but once it is in the past, there is a natural desire to forget it. The plaintiff should recall it and let the jury know about it, for he is entitled to compensation for every moment of pain. This is not to say that he should testify as to how he felt day by day. On the other hand, the subject should not be dismissed with one reference. It will not be deemed repetitious to have him describe his sensations as of the time he sustained his injury, when he regained consciousness, when he was sent home from the hospital, while undergoing treatment, and presently while he is seated on the witness stand.

- If there are many manifestations or objective signs which accompany or account for the subjective feelings, they should be detailed. If, for instance, a young mother were to say, "I was very weak," that would not be nearly as effective as her testimony that, "I was so weak I couldn't lift my baby in my arms." If the plaintiff can relate embarrassing incidents which she lived through, that will be more meaningful than a mere assertion that she was embarrassed, as in the following illustration.

ILLUSTRATIVE THREAD OF TESTIMONY

Pains and Embarrassment from a Fractured Jaw [57]

The plaintiff, a young unmarried woman, suffered a fractured jaw. After telling of the fracture, the loss of teeth, the pain on injury and during treatment, the plaintiff went on to testify as to her present condition which included an impairment in speech, with saliva spraying from out of her mouth when eating or speaking, as well as pain on opening the mouth, laughing, chewing, or speaking.

Q. *Are you still in pain?*
A. *I am.*

Q. *Where do you feel pain?*
A. *In my mouth.*

Q. *Will you describe the pain in your mouth?*
A. *I can't chew on any food. It feels like I hit a nerve every time I chew and I have a tightening feeling in my mouth.*

Q. *Can you describe that feeling?*
A. *Well, it is an effort for me to open my mouth at all and every time I open it, it is quite painful. I get the pain all the way up here, on both sides of my face (indicating). I get the pain if I laugh or when I go to the dentist and have to keep my mouth open.*

Q. *What, if any effect has it had on your speech?*

A. *I have difficulty in speaking and I don't have too much control of my lower lip. When I speak my lower lip sort of quivers. My mouth is very uncomfortable when I speak.*

Q. *What is the difficulty?*

A. *Well, my lower lip droops while the left side stays up and my teeth buck up against the lip here and I am uncomfortable when I speak or eat.*

Q. *Is there anything else about the mouth?*

A. *Well, down here I have a lump or scar on the inside which my bottom teeth rub up against.*

Q. *Does anything else happen when you eat or talk?*

A. *Well, when I am eating or speaking at times, the saliva comes out of my mouth, which is the reason I don't like to go out in company.*

Q. *What happens when the saliva comes out of your mouth?*

A. *Well, when I am speaking, a spray of saliva will come out of my mouth and at times it has hit other people and that is very embarrassing.*

Q. *How often does that happen?*

A. *Quite often.*

Chapter Twelve

FOOTNOTES

[1] Longshaw v. Corbitt (Ariz. App. 1866), 420 P. 2d 980.
Hale v. Smith (Ore. 1969), 460 P. 2d 351.
[2] Osborn v. Lesser (Kan. 1968), 439 P. 2d 395.
Herrin Transportation Co. v. Parker (Tex. Civ. App. 1968), 425 S.W. 2d 876.
[3] See Section 13.01   "Witness Incompetent to Testify as to State of Mind of Another."

[4] People v. Levan (1945), 295 N.Y. 26, 64 N.E. 2d 341.

Medina v. Sherrod (Tex. Civ. App. 1965), 391 S.W. 2d 66.

Royal Indemnity Co. v. H. E. Abbott & Sons, Inc. (Tex. 1965), 392 S.W. 2d 359.

[5] State v. Mulero (N.J. 1968), 51 N.J. 224, 238 A. 2d 682;

Commonwealth v. Douglas (Mass. 1968), 236 N.E. 2d 865.

[6] State v. Durham (Mo. 1967), 418 S.W. 2d 23.

[7] Reed v. Reed (Tex. Civ. App. 1957), 303 S.W. 2d 460; rev'd. on other grounds, 158 Tex. 298, 311 S.W. 2d 628.

[8] Trejo v. Maciel (Cal. App. 1966), 48 Cal. Rptr. 765; the intent of the employee as to his final destination while on a special errand for employer and the subjective expectation of employer were elements to be considered in determining the terminal point of special delivery.

Darlow v. Dugan Bakery (1957), 2 N.Y. 2d 983, 163 N.Y.S. 2d 598, 143 N.E. 2d 338.

[9] Royal Indemnity Co. v. H. E. Abbott & Sons, Inc.

[10] Blount v. Sutton (Ga. App. 1966), 152 S.E. 2d 772; automobile operator's intention, being relevant to issue, was proof of a substantive fact and admissible.

Wigmore on Evidence, (3rd ed) Section 1965.

[11] People v. Levan.

Wigmore on Evidence, (3rd ed) Section 581.

[12] Ruling of trial court in Hubbard v. Rehill (1941), 262 App. Div. 753, 27 N.Y.S. 2d 513, fol. 268.

Wigmore on Evidence, (3rd ed) Section 89.

[13] Davis v. Marvine (1899), 160 N.Y. 269, 54 N.E. 704.

[14] See Section 9.13, "Self-serving Declarations."

[15] Wilkerson v. Randall (Miss. 1965), 180 So. 2d 303.

[16] *Wigmore on Evidence,* (3rd ed) Section 874.

[17] See Section 12.07, "Background and Antecedents Indicative of Credibility" *et seq.*

[18] See Section 12.12, "The Witness' Acts and Conduct Corroborating His Alleged Mental State" *et seq.*

[19] See Section 12.14, "Disinterestedness; Lack of Motive to Deceive."

[20] See Section 12.15, "The Intrinsic Probability of His Testimony."

[21] See Section 12.16, "Appearance and Manner of Witness on Stand."

[22] See Section 12.17, "Vivid Description of Subjective Feelings."

[23] See Section 6.07, "Evidence of One's Good Conduct."

[24] In North Carolina such evidence is received without prior impeachment.

Bridges v. Graham (1957), 246 N.C. 371, 98 S.E. 492;

State v. Brown (1958), 249 N.C. 271, 106 S.E. 2d 232;

State v. Moseley (1959), 241 N.C. 285, 111 S.E. 2d 308;

In two other states, a witness who is "a stranger" may show his good character although it has not been impeached.

State v. De Wolf (1828), 8 Conn. 93, 100.

State v. Lyle (1923), 125 S.C. 442, 118 S.E. 803.

[25] Vause v. United States (2d Cir. [N.Y.] 1931), 53 Fed. 2d 346.

[26] People v. Minsky (1919), 227 N.Y. 94, 124 N.E. 126.

[27] *Ibid.;*

People v. Bowman (Cal. App. 1966), 49 Cal. Rptr. 772; the people were entitled to show that at times witness for prosecution gave his statement and cooperated with the authorities he was subject to prosecution with respect to the alleged arson with which defendant was charged.

[28] United States v. Mahler (2d Cir. [N.Y.] 1966), 363 F. 2d 673.

[29] State v. Tilley (1954), 239 N.C. 245, 79 S.E. 2d 473.

[30] People v. Minsky.

Miller v. State (1930), 115 Tex. Crim. Rep. 388, 27 S.W. 2d 803.

[31] State v. Tilley.

Wigmore on Evidence (3rd ed) Section 896 *et seq.*

[32] Schwartz, *Trial of Accident Cases,* Section 1124.

[33] Zenith Transport, Ltd. v. Bellingham National Bank (Wash. 1964), 395 P. 2d 498;

Wigmore on Evidence (3rd ed) Section 949.

[34] Moore On Facts, Section 1016, note 180.

[35] Hudson v. State (Ala. App. 1966), 184 So. 2d 159.

[36] Brittain v. State (1905), 47 Tex. Cr. Rep. 597, 85 S.W. 278.

[37] *Wigmore on Evidence* (3rd ed) Section 969, Note 2.

[38] See Section 5.06, "The Expert's Background and Qualifications."

[39] *Wigmore on Evidence,* (3rd ed) Section 209.

[40] In some jurisdictions the good character of a complainant in a rape case may be shown without waiting for impeachment.

State v. De Wolf, (1928), 8 Conn. 93, 100.

Rogers v. Moore, 10 Conn. 14, 17.

Similarly, in a divorce: Warner v. Warner (1897), 69 N.H. 137, 44 A. 908.

[41] Jackson v. State (1940), 239 Ala. 38, 193 So. 417.

Wigmore on Evidence, (3rd ed) Section 1821, note 2.

[42] *Ibid.,* Note 3.

Muncie v. Commonwealth (Ky. 1948), 213 S.W. 2d 1019.

Perlin Packing Co. v. Price (Md. 1867), 231 A. 2d 702.

Rittenhouse v. North Hempstead; error to exclude infant's testimony without a preliminary examination.

State v. Peterson (W. Va. 1948), 51 S.E. 2d 78, 83.

[43] State v. Allen (Wash. 1967), 424 P. 2d 1021.

Artesani v. Gritton (1960), 252 N.C. 463, 113 S.E. 2d 895.

Collier v. State (Wis. 1866), 140 N.W. 2d 252.

[44] People v. McIntyre (Cal. App. 1867), 64 Cal. Rptr. 530.

People v. Berry (Cal. App. 1968), 67 Cal. Rptr. 312.

[45] Commonwealth v. Welcome (Mass. 1964), 201 N.E. 2d 827.

[46] Commonwealth v. Tatisos (1921), 238 Mass. 322, 325, 130 N.E. 495, 497.

Wigmore on Evidence, (3rd ed) Section 1821.

[47] *Ibid.,* Sections 891 and 1104.

The *accused* may at any time offer his own *good moral character, for the trait in question,* as evidence that he did not commit the crime. But he may not *as witness* offer his good character until it has been attempted to be impeached by the prosecution."

[48] See Section 10.06, "Other Actions, Reasons or Motives to Act."

[49] Knight v. Willey (1958) 120 Vt. 256, 138 A. 2d 596.

Wigmore on Evidence, (3rd ed) Section 211.

[50] Tranchina v. Arcinas (1947), 78 Cal. App. 2d 522, 178 P. 2d 65.

La Placa v. United States (1st Cir. [Mass.] 1965), 354 F. 2d 56.

Julian v. Kiefer (Mo. App. 1964), 382 S.W. 2d 723.

See Parker v. School District (Mo. App. 1959), 325 S.W. 2d 59; intent to abandon contract.

[51] See Section 7.03, "The Perceptive Powers of the Witness: Sight" and Section 19.32, "The Insidious Effects of Bias."

[52] See Section 3.05, "The Witness Had a Good Memory," and Section 17.09, "The Witness' Feelings and Emotions."

[53] See Section 12.07, "Occupation as Bearing on Credibility."

[54] See Section 22.23, "Inherent Improbability or Falsity of Testmony."

[55] Wheeler v. United States, (1895), 159 U.S. 523, 525, "The decision of this question rests primarily with the trial judge, who sees the proposed witness, notices his manner. . . . As many of these matters cannot be photographed into the record the decision of the trial judge will not be disturbed on review unless from that which it is presumed it is clear that it was erroneous."

[56] Schwartz, *Trial of Accident Cases,* Section 609 *et seq.*

The plaintiff is entitled to recover compensation for his pain and suffering and embarrassment from the moment of the injury to the time of his complete cure. Modern decisions allow recovery for shock, fear and neurosis due to the occurrence even when unaccompanied by any physical injury.

[57] *Ibid.,* Section 620

OBJECTIONS TO PROOF
OF STATE OF MIND

TABLE OF CONTENTS

OBJECTIONS TO PROOF OF STATE OF MIND

Q. HOW DO YOU FEEL AS TO . . .?

§ 13:01 Witness Incompetent: Testimony as to the State of Mind of Another

In an action for annulment of a marriage because of fraudulent misrepresentations, the plaintiff husband was asked by Plaintiff's Attorney:

Q. *Prior to your marriage, did you have any conversation with the defendant about the coming marriage?*

A. *I did.*

Q. *What did you say to the defendant?*

A. *I said to her, "I am not a youngster any more, I am 43 years old, I want to settle down and have children."*

Q. *What did she say?*

A. *She said, "Yes, of course, I want to open a home and have children."*

Q. *Now when she said that, did you believe what she said?*

A. *I did.*

Q. *Did you rely on those statements?*

A. *I did.*

Q. *Did those statements induce you to enter into this marriage with the defendant?*

A. *They did.*

Q. Were it not for the fact that she made that statement to you, would you have entered into the marriage?

A. No.

Q. Did the defendant, at the time she made those statements, have any intention of having children with you after marriage?

Defense Counsel: I object.

The objection should be sustained. The plaintiff is competent to testify as to his own state of mind as to his reliance on defendant's statements, etc., but he is not competent to testify as to the state of mind, i.e., the intention of the defendant.[1]

The plaintiff may testify as to defendant's conduct and conversations, after marriage, from which the defendant's intent may be implied.[2]

§ 13:02   Evidence Irrelevant as to Secret Intent

In an action for labor and materials furnished to build a cottage, the issue was whether the plaintiff had sold the materials to one Williams, the contractor, who was financially irresponsible, or to Seligman, the owner who was financially responsible. The plaintiff was asked on direct examination by Plaintiff's Attorney:

Q. Did you understand that you were selling the goods to Mr. Williams or to Mr. Seligman?

Defendant's Attorney: I object.

The objection should be sustained.[3] The identity of the purchaser must be established by evidence other than the secret intention of the seller.[4] A witness will not be permitted to testify as to his secret uncommunicated intention where the purpose is to change an expressed contract. For example, if in making the contract, the witness said in so many words that he was willing to sell something to a certain person at a certain price and agreed to sell it, he cannot thereafter testify that he had a secret intention not to sell.[5]

Chapter Thirteen

FOOTNOTES

[1] Dorsten v. Lawrence (1969), 20 Ohio App. 2d 297, 253 N.E. 2d 803, witness' opinion as to which driver was at fault and as to what one driver was thinking before the collision, was improper.

Medina v. Sherrod, (Tex. Cir. App. 1965) 391 S.W. 2d 66, and cases sited.

[2] Louis E. Schwartz, *Trial Lawyers Library, Matrimonial Actions,* (New York, Trial Attorney Publications, Inc. 1947), Section 113.

[3] Dillon v. Anderson (1870), 43 N.Y. 231.

[4] *Wigmore on Evidence* (3rd ed) Section 1971, Note 3, citing Bonfield v. Smith, 12 M. & W. 403 (England 1944); a question to plaintiff, "With whom did you deal" was rejected, because it amounted to asking, "With whom did you *believe* you dealt?"

Murray v. Bethune (1828), 1 Wend (N.Y.) 19. The mere private understanding of one party to a contract is immaterial and cannot be testified to.

[5] Conrad v. Conrad (1963), 275 Ala. 202, 153 So. 2d 635;

United States v. Walker (6th Cir. [Ohio] 1963), 313 F. 2d 236, 240;

Wigmore on Evidence, (3rd ed) Section 1985.

FOURTEEN

PROOF OF OPINIONS

TABLE OF CONTENTS

PROOF OF OPINIONS

Opinions are frowned on by the courts who want facts and will receive opinions only under certain limited circumstances. This chapter delineates when laymen may express opinions and when experts may do so. It also explains how the value of the opinion expressed is dependent upon proof of the qualifications of the witness, the factual basis upon which his opinion rests, and the logical rationale for his conclusions. It also deals with the use of the hypothetical question by the expert witness.

Q. WHAT IS YOUR OPINION AS TO . . . ?

§ 14:01   When Opinions Are Admissible

A witness is generally permitted to testify only as to facts within his personal knowledge. Opinions are frowned upon. No opinion will be received, whether from layman or expert, except out of necessity. It is for the jury to arrive at conclusions on the basis of the facts as established by sworn testimony and exhibits, and no witness will, ordinarily, be permitted to usurp that function.[1] But what is fact and what is opinion is often difficult, if not impossible, to distinguish, the difference being one of degree.

Much that is accepted as factual is actually an unconscious inference—a mechanically performed act of judgment.[2] The test of whether the testimony will be considered as fact or opinion depends on the nature of the operation of the witness' mind. When the operation of his mind is instinctive and automatic, his testimony is accepted as being factual. If, however, the testimony is obviously the result of deliberate reasoning or judgment, it is considered to be opinion evidence, which will be received only as a matter of necessity and then only when the proper foundation has first been laid.[3]

§ 14:02 When Laymen May Give Conclusions, Characterizations and Opinions

With respect to ordinary witnesses, testimony which is descriptive of the witness' sensory perceptions is considered to be factual.[4] Many seemingly conclusory statements are received because they are but "composite facts" or a summary or "shorthand renditions" of the facts.[5] Other conclusions and opinions are received when they pertain to facts which are so complex or subtle that they cannot be adequately and accurately conveyed to the jury in any other way than by giving conclusions.[6] Illustrations of such "composite facts" are, that an automobile was "zigzagging" and appeared to be out of control;[7] that defendant's vehicle struck plaintiff's vehicle;[8] that the marks on the road indicated that the motorcycle had skidded.[9]

Because of the difficulty in adequately conveying the facts without the aid of the conclusion of the witness who observed them, laymen are permitted to give their conclusions and opinions on these and numerous other matters. For example, an ordinary observer may be allowed to state that a person appeared to be pleased, angry, excited, friendly, affectionate, insulting, or the like.[10] Such a witness may express his estimate of age, size, weight and distance.[11] A witness has been permitted to state that a vehicle could be seen for 300 feet;[12] that a pedestrian was visible to an approaching motorist of normal vision;[13] a passenger in a bus may say that it made an "extraordinary, unusual, and violent stop";[14] that it was impossible for a motorist to pass to the left of an overtaken vehicle;[15] that there was sufficient room for an automobile to pass to the right of another vehicle coming from the opposite direction;[16] that an obstruction at a railroad crossing screened an approaching train from view;[17] that he saw no opportunity for the defendant to do anything other than what he did;[18] that plaintiff appeared to be waiting for a car and not about to cross the street.[19]

On the other hand, the witness will not be permitted to give his conclusion when the facts are capable of being fully presented,[20] nor where it is apparent that the testimony is a surmise or supposition of a witness with regard to facts as to which he is no better equipped than the jury to draw inferences.[21] Nor will the testimony be received if it is incredible, contrary to physical laws and common knowledge, or obviously mere conjecture.[22] Thus, a defendant motorist may not be asked, "Could you have stopped sooner than you did?"[23] or, "Was there anything that you know of that you could have done, that you did not do, to avoid the accident?"[24] Nor may a witness be asked, "Could the driver have avoided the accident?"[25] A truck driver's testimony that the oncoming automobile driver would have had plenty of time to go by if she had stayed on the truck driver's side, that she might have hit the trailer a little bit but she would have been alive, is conjectural and inadmissible.[26]

§ 14:03   How Far Laymen May Go In Testimony as to Bodily Conditions

The problem of drawing the line between laymen and experts is present with respect to opinions as to bodily or physical conditions. The plaintiff, a layman, will be permitted to state simple inferences drawn by him from his own conscious, though subjective, sensations as to his own health or physical condition and pain [27] and even as to impaired ability to labor.[28] The witness is not deemed to be expressing an opinion, but is stating a fact, when he testifies that he has suffered nausea or loss of appetite or loss of weight, or had backaches. Where the testimony relates merely to the physical condition of the plaintiff and not to the existence or character of a disease, it requires no medical training to perceive that a person is nauseated, lacks appetite, or is losing weight. These physical characteristics are incidents of everyday life.[29] A lay witness has been permitted to testify as to his ability to work without being caused pain.[30]

Similarly, a nonexpert witness who has had an opportunity to observe another is competent to express opinions as to such other person's general health, strength, bodily vigor, or his feebleness or apparent illness, or as to the change in his apparent state of health or physical condition from one time to another,[31] or that he was in pain or was suffering [32] or was conscious.[33]

A witness who, for years, worked side by side with an injured person, may be asked, "Please state what was his apparent physical condition as observed by you during that time?" A lay witness may testify as to the apparent physical condition of a person; he is barred only as to matters involving the existence or non-existence of a disease, the discovery of which requires the training and experience of a medical expert.[34]

This rule permitting nonexpert witnesses to testify to a person's apparent physical condition which is open to ordinary observations by persons of common experience does not extend to permit such witnesses to testify as to the existence, nature, or character of latent conditions or as to the existence of a particular disease which is determinable only through the peculiar experience, knowledge, and training of a physician.[35]

A nonexpert plaintiff who may testify as to his own physical condition and pain may have difficulty in trying to show a causal connection between his condition and pain and the injuries alleged to have been sustained in the accident. There are times when causal connection is obvious and no expert is needed.[36] No expert is needed to tell a jury that a "black eye" could come from a blow. One who has been run over and had his arm or leg dismembered needs no further proof of causal connection, nor does he need an expert to establish that he also suffered pain and disability. Where the causal connection is clearly apparent from the illness itself and the circumstances surrounding it, where the disability develops coincidentally with, or within a reasonable time after the negligent act; or where the cause of the injuries relates to matters of common experience or knowledge of laymen, an expert's opinion is unnecessary—although helpful.[37]

Sometimes it is difficult to draw the line as to the point beyond which the layman may not go. For example, the defendant was charged with mayhem in throwing a heavy water glass which struck the complainant in the face and destroyed the sight of his left eye. Opthamology is a medical specialty and the question of whether an eye is permanently blinded would seem to be one for experts. Nevertheless, the complainant was permitted to testify, when questioned as to what happened to his eyes, seven months after the event, that ". . . I have both of them but no sight in one . . . I still have my eye, but it is no good. It is just blank and I cannot see out of it." This testimony was held to be sufficient, without the aid of any expert's opinion to sustain a conviction.[38] But a plaintiff who had no objective injuries would need an expert to show the causal connection between the accident and, for example, an alleged psychoneurosis which followed.[39] An expert is needed when the causal relationship involves a subject clearly within the field of medical science.[40]

§ 14:04   When Opinions of Lay Witnesses Simulate Expert Opinions

There are instances when a lay witness may not be permitted to express a certain opinion because of lack of expertise, yet may be competent to express another opinion which will be acceptable and equally effective. Let us take proof of intoxication as an example. Whether a person was intoxicated or not may be the subject of scientific testimony.[41] This does not mean, however, that a nonexpert may not express an opinion on the subject. He may not be allowed to say that a person was intoxicated, but, if the witness has observed the appearance and conduct of another, he will be permitted to state that such other person *appeared* to be intoxicated.[42] To enhance the value of the opinion, the experienced trial lawyer will not only elicit testimony to the effect that the witness had observed the person in question, but will also establish the pertinent details which the witness observed which would indicate intoxication, as in the following illustration.

ILLUSTRATIVE THREAD OF TESTIMONY

A Layman's Opinion as to Intoxication

Q.   After the accident did you see the driver of the truck?
A.   I did.

Q.   Did you speak to him?
A.   I did.

Q. *What, if anything, did you notice about his speech?*
A. *It was thick and incoherent.*

Q. *How close did you come to him?*
A. *I came very close, to try to make out what he was saying.*

Q. *What, if anything, did you notice as you came close to him?*
A. *I smelled whiskey on his breath. His eyes were bloodshot.*

Q. *Did you see him walk?*
A. *I saw him try to walk, but he was so unsteady on his feet that he held on to the truck for support.*

Q. *Have you had occasion to see people who were intoxicated?*
A. *Yes, I have.*

Q. *And in your opinion, did he seem to be drunk or sober?*
A. *He appeared to be very drunk.*

Q. *On what do you base that opinion?*
A. *On his appearance and actions, the odor of alcohol on his breath, his bloodshot eyes, his manner of speech, his seeming inability to walk without support, and his general appearance.*

So, too, there is a difference of authority as to whether a lay witness may express an opinion as to whether a person he observed was sane or insane. In most jurisdictions, if the witness first states the facts which he observed regarding the person's actions, he may then express an opinion as to such person's sanity.[43] In other jurisdictions this is not permitted, but the observer may state that the *acts* and *statements* of such a person impressed him as irrational, but not that the *person* impressed him as irrational.[44] Similarly, after the state's witness had described the defendant's acts and conduct before he shot the victim, the witness was permitted to say whether the defendant *acted* like a man in his right mind.[45]

ILLUSTRATIVE THREAD OF TESTIMONY

Subscribing Witness: Opinion of Testator's Sanity

Q. *Did you know Mr. T_____ (the testator) during his lifetime?*
A. *I did.*

Q. *How long did you know him?*
A. *About twenty years.*

Q. Did you come to his home on the occasion that he executed his will?
A. I did.

Q. Who was present at his home at that time?
A. Mr. A_____ and Mr. B_____.

Q. Did you speak to Mr. T_____ before the will was executed?
A. I did.

Q. What did you say to him?
A. I said, "Good evening" and asked him how he was feeling.

Q. Did he talk to you?
A. He did.

Q. What did he say?
A. He said he was glad I had come and that he would like me to witness his will.

Q. What, if anything, was said and done after that?
A. I said I would be glad to be a witness. He then pointed to a paper he had in his hand and said, "This is my will," and he signed it in our presence.

Q. Then what, if anything, took place?
A. Mr. B_____ then took the paper and he read what was typed below the signature. I don't know what you call that clause.

Q. The attestation clause?
A. Yes, the attestation clause. Then he asked Mr. T_____ if that was his last will and he said it was. Then he asked me and Mr. A_____ whether we would sign and I signed it and Mr. A_____ signed it.

Q. I show you this paper, Exhibit 1, and ask you if that is your signature on there?
A. It is.

Q. And is that the paper that you refer to that Mr. T_____ signed and that you and Mr. A_____ then signed?
A. It is.

Q. *And did each of you sign in the presence of each other?*
A. *Yes, we did.*

Q. *And are those your signature and the signatures of Mr. T_____ and Mr. A_____?*
A. *They are.*

Q. *Did you then talk further with Mr. T_____?*
A. *I did. He asked me about my family and told me how much he appreciated my coming.*

Q. *Now, I ask you whether, at the time Mr. T_____ signed this paper, he appeared to be of sound mind and memory?*
A. *Yes, he did.*

Q. *Did he appear to be under any restraint at that time?*
A. *No.*

§ 14:05   When Experts May Give Opinions

Experts are used not only because of the intrinsic value of their testimony and their ability to "educate" the jury to understand the technicalities involved, but also because, when carefully chosen, they may add impressiveness to the case. An expert in a field beyond the experience, knowledge, or comprehension of laymen may aid the jury in arriving at a correct determination of the litigated issue.[46] However, there are limitations on the admissibility of expert opinions. No opinion will be received, whether from a layman or an expert, except out of necessity.[47] Expert opinions are necessary only when the subject matter relates to some science, profession, or business not within the common knowledge of the average man.[48] If the opinion is as to a matter of common knowledge, regarding which the jury is just as qualified as the expert, the opinion is unnecessary and will not be received.[49] For example, it would be error to ask a police officer for his opinion as to the meaning of a "No Turn" sign, as this is something which is comprehensible to any ordinary person.[50]

In recent years a new "science" has been developed. We now have expert "accidentologists" who have specialized in the reconstruction of accidents.[51] Many courts refuse to permit the testimony of "accident-reconstruction" experts,[52] either because the opinion asked for is of such a nature that the jury does not need expert aid [53] or because it is of the ultimate issue and would usurp the function of the jury.[54]

Some courts have shown a tendency to exercise their discretion liberally and allow the "accidentologist's" opinions as an aid to the jury.[55] Such a witness, if properly qualified,[56] has been permitted to express an opinion of a vehicle's speed at the time of the impact when based upon skid marks which indicate that the brakes were applied over a given distance on a dry, level road;[57] as to stopping distances at a given speed;[58] whether a vehicle was stopped or moving at time of accident;[59] the cause of the accident generally;[60] and as to the point of impact based upon observations of physical evidence shortly after the accident.[61] But, an opinion as to which driver was responsible for the accident is inadmissible.[62] Similarly, a witness will not be permitted to give his opinion as to whether a collision would have occurred if one vehicle had been traveling at a given speed;[63] or as to the speed of a vehicle based upon the extent of its damage alone;[64] or as to whether certain marks on the highway were caused by the vehicles which had collided.[65]

One type of opinion is generally deemed unnecessary and unacceptable; that is, the legal conclusion of the ultimate issue. In a vast majority of instances, once the facts have been set forth, the jury is then perfectly capable of coming to its own conclusion as to such things as which party was "at fault";[66] whose negligence caused the accident,[67] whether one was careful or careless,[68] that a condition was "dangerous,"[69] or that a speed was "unreasonable."[70]

There are rare instances, respecting matters understood only by specialists, in which the jury would be unable to arrive at any conclusion no matter how fully the facts were presented to them.[71] The opinion of experts, even as to the ultimate issue, will be received in such instances where not only the facts, but also the interpretation of the facts are beyond the comprehension of the jury.[72] An example might be the opinion of a medical expert as to the necessity of an emergency operation to prevent peritonitis in the abdominal cavity,[73] or as to non-parentage determined by blood tests.[74] Although opinions of experts are entitled to respect, they are not necessarily conclusive and may be disregarded by the jury.[75] There is, however, authority to the contrary if the testimony is unimpeached and uncontradicted.[76]

§ 14:06   Enhancing the Weight of an Opinion

When an opinion is to be called for, whether by a layman or expert, it is more likely to be received in evidence and accorded greater weight if the trial attorney will elicit testimony to demonstrate that:

- The witness is well qualified to express the opinion.[77]
- There is a solid factual basis to support the opinion.[78]
- There is a logical rationale for the opinion.[79]

§ 14:07   Establishing That the Witness Is Well Qualified:
          Lay Witness

The proof of the qualifications of a witness is a prerequisite for the acceptance of his opinion and is an important ingredient in determining the weight which should be given to it by the jury.

It is a common fallacy to think that only experts need be qualified to express opinions. No witness may give his opinion unless he is qualified to do so. There is, however, a vast variety of matters as to which every person is *deemed* qualified to express his opinion. There are other matters as to which ordinary laymen have little or no knowledge, which are the subject of "expert" testimony, and such opinions may only be given by "experts" who can demonstrate their special knowledge or expertise. In either event, both laymen and experts must possess that knowledge and experience which would qualify them to arrive at the particular opinion being expressed.

A layman's qualifications may be assumed as to certain matters. However, the experienced trial attorney is not satisfied with mere assumptions, but will endeavor to prove his witness' special qualifications to express an opinion whenever it is possible to do so. When the general qualifications of the witness are combined with an extensive knowledge of the specific facts and circumstances of a particular subject matter, then the opinion will have a greater impact upon the jury's thinking.

The qualifications of a witness are established by proof of his knowledge and experience. Reference should be made to Chapter Five, dealing with *Proof of Knowledge*.[80] Supplementing this, we shall here give further illustrations in which the witness' knowledge is adduced as qualification for his expressing an opinion as to the specific matters of speed and value.

§ 14:08   Qualifying the Layman for an Opinion as to Speed

Let us suppose that the witness is to express an opinion as to the speed of an automobile. A layman is permitted to express such an opinion out of necessity, for the witness cannot otherwise adequately convey the fact to the jury.[81] The qualifications required are minimal [82] and even a child who has never driven an automobile may give his opinion for whatever it is worth.[83]

Obviously, the weight of the opinion will be strengthened by the witness' testimony as to his qualifications, his driving experience both in time and number of miles of driving, and his observations of his own speed and the speed of similar vehicles checked with speedometers [84] as in the following illustration.

ILLUSTRATIVE THREAD OF TESTIMONY

Layman's Qualifications to Express Opinion as to Speed

Q. Do you drive automobiles?
A. I do.

Q. For how long have you driven them?
A. About 25 years.

Q. About how many miles have you driven in that time?
A. At least 250,000 miles.

Q. Have you observed the speed at which you were driving?
A. I have.

Q. Have you observed the speedometer from time to time as you drove?
A. Yes and for the past ten years I have had a buzzer signal which sounds when the speed reaches a set point.

Q. Have you ridden in automobiles driven by others?
A. Frequently.

Q. And have you observed the speedometers on those automobiles as they were in motion?
A. I have.

Q. Do you consider yourself a judge of speed of automobiles?
A. I believe I am.

Q. Did you observe the defendant's automobile as it approached the point of impact?
A. I did.

Q. How far away was it when you first saw it?
A. At least 150 feet.

Q. And did you watch it as it covered that distance of 150 feet?
A. I did.

Q. *Are you able to give us an opinion of the speed at which it was traveling as it approached the point of impact?*

A. *I am.*

Q. *What is your opinion as to its speed as it approached?*

A. *It was going at least 60 miles an hour.*

§ 14:09 Qualifying the Layman for an Opinion as to Value

A layman may express an opinion as to value, but only upon showing that he has sufficient knowledge of the subject matter to be of aid to the jury. Where the article is one which is commonly and frequently purchased, its owner need only show that he was familiar with its condition, that he frequently purchased similar articles, and he will be competent to express his opinion as to its value. This rule has been applied to such items as household articles.[85]

ILLUSTRATIVE THREAD OF TESTIMONY

Layman's Opinion as to Value of Household Articles

Action for conversion of linens used in a rooming house. The plaintiff was testifying in her own behalf when she was asked by her attorney on direct examination:

Q. *Did you own the bed sheets in question?*

A. *I did.*

Q. *When did you buy them?*

A. *In July of last year.*

Q. *What make of sheets were they?*

A. *Utica brand.*

Q. *Are you familiar with their condition as of January 14th of this year?*

A. *I am.*

Q. *What was their condition?*

A. *They were in perfect condition.*

Q. *Have you had occasion to buy sheets from time to time during the past twenty years?*

A. *Yes.*

Q. What, in your opinion, was the market value of those sheets on January 14th of this year?

The value of second hand automobiles is less a matter of common knowledge than household wares, nevertheless, the witness may express an opinion, provided it appears that he has knowledge of automobile market values. It will not be enough simply to show that the witness owned the automobile or that he had purchased automobiles, particularly if he bought them new. It must appear that he is familiar with the value of second hand cars. If he has such knowledge, then he need not be an automobile dealer in order to give his opinion.[86]

When a witness states that he knows the market value of an article, he is *prima facie* qualified to testify concerning it, even though he is not an expert witness.[87]

ILLUSTRATIVE THREAD OF TESTIMONY

Value of an Automobile

The plaintiff whose automobile was wrecked in an automobile collision sued to recover for its market value. While he was testifying, he was asked by his attorney on direct examination:

Q. Have you studied the market value of second hand automobiles?
A. I have.

Q. Have you bought and sold second hand automobiles?
A. I have.

Q. How many have you bought and sold in the past five years?
A. Four.

Q. Are you familiar with the market value of second hand automobiles as of the date of this accident?
A. I am.

Q. Do you know the market value of your automobile as of the date of the accident?
A. I do.

Q. State what, in your opinion, was the market value of your automobile just before this accident happened.

It has been held that an injured person could express an opinion as to the value of his personal services where it appeared that he was familiar with the wages paid to other persons of like vocation and earning capacity.[88] So too, a business man could express an opinion of the reasonable value of his own services to his business, provided he is qualified,[89] as in the following illustration.

ILLUSTRATIVE THREAD OF TESTIMONY

Value of Services of Restaurant Owner

Q. Prior to the accident, what work did you do in the conduct and management of your restaurant?

A. I ran the business from beginning to end. I did the buying, I did the cooking, I did the bartending, when we were busy in the dining room I was in the dining room, when there were repairs to be done, I was there to do them.

Q. Did you perform similar work over a period of years for other persons for compensation prior to the opening of your own restaurant?

A. Yes, sir.

Q. How long had you been in that line of business?

A. 20 years.

Q. Are you familiar with what others in the restaurant business were being paid for similar work?

A. I am.

Q. Did you have occasion to hire other persons to perform work similar to what you were doing?

A. Yes, sir.

Q. Do you know the fair and reasonable value of the services of the type you performed?

A. Yes, sir.

Q. What was the fair and reasonable value of services of a similar nature, in this city, as you were performing as of the date of your accident?

§ 14:10   Qualifying an Expert

When an "expert witness" is required, he must be one who, by reason of his education or specialized experience, possesses superior knowledge respecting the subject involved. This superior knowledge presumably enables him to draw correct conclusions and form accurate opinions, which persons having no particular training are incapable of doing.[90] In all cases, an expert opinion may not be given unless the witness is shown to have such skill, experience, or knowledge in his particular field as to make it appear that his opinion would rest on a substantial foundation and would tend to aid the trier of the facts in his search for truth.[91]

The expert and the skilled witness who is called upon to express an opinion will be permitted, at the outset of his testimony, to testify at length as to his background and antecedents with respect to his opportunity and means of acquiring knowledge and as to the nature and extent of the knowledge he possesses.[92] Incidentally, the opinion of the witness as to his own qualifications and expertise will be admissible as some proof thereof.[93]

Irrespective of what subject is involved, the pattern to be followed in eliciting the extent of learning and expertise is the same, the objective being to elicit everything about the witness which would indicate that he knows whereof he speaks and that his opinions are entitled to respectful consideration. The qualifications of an expert depend upon the extent of his knowledge of the subject matter, which has already been discussed.[94]

§ 14:11 The Factual Basis Is More Important Than the Opinion Itself

There is nothing more unreliable than mere estimates or conclusions.[95] No matter how well qualified the witness may be, that, in and of itself, is not enough to enable him to express an opinion. There must also be some factual basis for the opinion, and the jury should be aware of what the facts are upon which the opinion is predicated in order that they may properly evaluate it.[96]

The expert witness (just as the nonexpert) must base his opinion on facts established by competent evidence.[97] The facts may be presented in two ways: (a) the expert may himself furnish the basic evidence if he has personal knowledge,[98] or (b) the facts already in evidence may be incorporated into a hypothetical question and presented to the expert as his basic premise.[99] The expert may also base his opinion on a combination of both his personal knowledge and hypothetical facts.[100]

The expert who bases his opinion upon his perceptions rather than hypothetical facts is entitled to greater weight.[101] Thus, the treating doctor is entitled to greater weight than the medical expert who merely made an examination in order to give his opinion.[102] Too often we think that the only function of an expert witness is to express expert opinions. Actually, his testimony as to his observations may be more important than his opinion. By reason of his superior knowledge and skill, an expert witness may understand more of what he observes than an ordinary witness. There are details which are meaningful to the expert which the layman would not even notice.

His testimony, in which he clearly sets forth the significant facts which he found to exist, can be so illuminating to the jury that only one conclusion can follow, i.e., the one which coincides with the opinion which the expert will express.

The testimony as to the nature and extent of the expert's investigation of the facts, the details of his inspection or examination, his meticulous observations, his experimentation and scientific research and analysis which led him to his conclusions—all of these will bespeak the accuracy of his opinions and aid the jury in arriving at their own.

In the illustration which follows, an expert in building and construction testifies as to his observations and findings with respect to a defective window made on inspection on a given date. Before he may give such testimony, it must first appear that there was no change in the condition of the window between the date of the accident and the date of the inspection.

ILLUSTRATIVE THREAD OF TESTIMONY

Inspection and Findings by a Construction Expert

The witness is first duly qualified and then asked:

Q. *Did you, at my request, go to premises 1000 South Street and make an inspection?*

A. *I did.*

Q. *And at that time did you see Mr. L————, who testified here this morning?*

A. *I did.*

Q. *Did Mr. L———— show you a certain window?*

A. *He did.*

Q. *On what date did you make that inspection?*

A. *On September 10th.*

Q. *When did you make that inspection?*

A. *At about 10 A.M.*

Q. *How long did the inspection take?*

A. *An hour.*

Q. *Did you make notes as to what you saw on that inspection?*

A. *I did.*

Q. Have you refreshed your recollection from those notes?

A. I have.

Q. Tell the court and jury what you saw at that time when you examined the window.

A. I tried to raise the window and found that it was jammed when I raised it 12 inches. I looked closely and discovered that the window stripping was bent so that it would not slide evenly in the groove of the window. I saw that the window stop was too close to the sash and I found a nail bent over the metal weather strip which was rubbing against the side of the sash.

§ 14:12 Hypothetical Question as a Basis for Expert's Opinion

The expert is permitted to base his conclusions upon either personal observations or hypothetical facts presented to him in a hypothetical question, or upon a combination of both. In some jurisdictions, by statute, the expert may dispense with the hypothetical question, merely stating his opinion and leaving it to the cross-examiner to expose any lack of basic facts.[103]

Even if the hypothetical question is unnecessary, it should be used nonetheless. This gives the attorney an opportunity to select favorable facts, arrange them in a logical order, and state them in his question so that, in effect, the jury will be hearing a summary of his case or defense.

In framing the hypothetical question, it is perfectly proper to pick and choose among the facts. The facts chosen must, however, be in evidence. It is not necessary that it include all of the facts,[104] but the opinion must be based entirely on the facts which are set forth. The question should assume such facts in evidence as are relied on by the party and it may include any facts previously testified to by the witness from personal examination. The witness should first be asked as to whether he has an opinion on those facts. Upon receiving an affirmative answer, the opinion is called for.[105]

To enhance the chances of having the expert's opinion accepted by the jury, the attorney framing the hypothetical question should be careful to select those facts which have been clearly proven and to arrange them in a clear, logical order, and to ask for an opinion which is not speculative or conjectural. Not one which is merely "possible," but rather one which can be given with reasonable certainty.[106]

ILLUSTRATIVE THREAD OF TESTIMONY

Hypothetical Question to Treating Physician as to Cause of Injuries

Q. Doctor, assume [prior state of health] *that a man, thirty-five years of age, in good health,* [the accident] *on ＿＿＿, 19＿, was crossing a street when he was struck and knocked down by an automobile;* [the examination] *that he was brought by ambulance to the _____ Hospital, where you examined him,* [the injuries] *and found him to be suffering with the following injuries* [lists them] *as to which you have testified* [treatment], *and that you treated him for these injuries* [outline the treatment] *as you have testified to;* [has an opinion] *on the basis of these assumptions, do you have an opinion and can you state, with a reasonable degree of certainty, as to whether the occurrence set forth could be a competent producing cause of the injuries which you found and treated?*

A.   *I have an opinion.*

Q.   *Was it, in your opinion, a competent producing cause of the injuries?*
A.   *It was.*

§ 14:13   Rationale for the Opinion

A witness may be asked, "You have told us that thus-and-so is your opinion; tell us why this is so."[107] Such reasons should be fully and clearly stated by the witness, and, if they are logical and cogent, they will thereby increase the likelihood of the opinion being accepted by the jury. On the other hand, if the witness cannot give sound, logical reasons, but rests his opinion upon surmise or conjecture or on considerations which are not in the record nor included in the hypothetical question or contrary to the indisputable physical facts, then his opinion becomes vulnerable and may be stricken.[108]

§ 14:14   Comparisons Instead of Conclusions

Instead of the mere expression of an opinion by the expert, it is much more effective for him to furnish the jury with factual data and criteria which will enable them to make their own comparison and thus come to their own conclusions. For example, the ultimate issue may call for a determination of whether a party was at fault. This, in turn, may depend upon whether that party followed what is proper practice or the recognized custom and usage in the trade or profession. What constitutes the generally accepted practice or the recognized custom and usage is not a matter of opinion, but is a matter of fact which can be testified to by anyone who has knowledge of such fact.[109] Before the expert ventures an opinion, he should first place before the jury all the facts in his possession. These include, on the one hand, what approved practice or recognized custom and usage would require, and, on the other, what he found upon his personal inspection and investigation of the facts as they were *after* the occurrence. None of this is opinion evidence. Rather, he is giving the jury the facts, including some which only an expert would be able to fully understand and appreciate. Once the jury has these facts, they are then able to come to the proper conclusion on the ultimate issue of care or fault.

The jury, having been educated by him as to what was custom or usage or accepted practice, will be able to appreciate his testimony as to what he found upon inspection. As they listen, they will be able to compare what he found upon inspection with what should have been found, had custom and usage or the standard accepted practice been followed. Based on this comparison, the jury will arrive at the desired conclusion by themselves.

This can best be illustrated by an example. Let us assume that a workman in a trench was injured when the walls of the trench caved in. He sues the contractor who created the trench, charging negligence. A well qualified construction engineer is on the stand. How should counsel proceed after he has elicited the witness' qualifications and the fact that he had inspected the trench in question? The wrong way would be to ask the witness, *Q. Based upon your inspection, was the defendant negligent in the construction of the trench?* Such a question would usurp the function of the jury and, even if it was not objected to, the answer would have little persuasiveness. Rather, the examination of the witness should cover the following items:

(1) The witness is fully qualified.
(2) He is asked to describe the personal inspection he made after the occurrence.
(3) His familiarity with the custom and usage uniformly followed in the construction trade in digging similar trenches is established.
(4) What is the standard and approved practice, in particular that it called for shoring up the walls with planks of a certain size and strength.
(5) His findings upon inspection, in particular that it appeared that no planks or other shoring had been used.
(It will be noted that at this point, after the witness has testified as to the customary use of shoring and the failure to use it on that particular job, that the jury has enough data on which to find negligence even without the expert's opinion.)
(6) He is then asked whether he can state what was the competent producing cause of the cave-in.
(7) Upon receiving an affirmative answer, he is asked to state what, in his opinion, was the competent producing cause. The obvious answer is the failure to shore up the trench.
(8) He may then be asked for his reasoning and he can expound upon the nature of trenches, the forces which make for cave-ins, and the need for, and the effectiveness of shoring.

§ 14:15   Demonstrating Scientific Basis for Opinion

It is often possible to transform a mere expert opinion into incontrovertible fact by having the expert demonstrate, in court, the scientific tests by which he came to his conclusions. By use of modern technology and various scientific instruments such as micro-photography, ultra-rays, etc., the expert can compare a questioned document with a genuine specimen, fingerprints of the defendant and those found at the scene of the crime,[110] the marks on a bullet found in the body with the marks on a bullet shot from the murder weapon,[111] an x-ray of the injured bone with that of a normal bone, and many other similar matters. When the jury sees the various points of similarity or difference they are then able to reach a decision based on these facts and the opinion of the expert becomes surplusage.

Let us consider the determination of an issue as to whether a certain document was forged or genuine. It is not enough to have the so-called handwriting expert express his opinion as to whether or not it is a forgery. His opinion that the signature in dispute is or is not authentic is of slight value unless he is able to make the jury see with their own eyes each little difference in line, angle, shading, stroke, which differs or coincides, one with the other. To this end, the handwriting expert prepares enlarged photographs of both the genuine and the disputed document and points out to the jury the minute differences or similarities of the individual letters as well as the peculiarities of the handwriting itself.[112]

ILLUSTRATIVE THREAD OF TESTIMONY

Comparisons by Handwriting Expert

Before the handwriting expert is called to the stand, specimens of genuine handwritings as well as the questioned document are first introduced into evidence. The witness is qualified[113] and then asked:

Q. *Did you, at my request, examine and compare the letter, Plaintiff's Exhibit 1, with the writing on Defendant's Exhibit A, the concededly genuine handwriting?*

A. *I did.*

Q. *What process of comparison did you employ?*
A. *I photographed them together and enlarged the photographs.*

Q. *Have you those photographs?*
A. *I have.*

Q.   Will you produce them?
>   (Witness hands them to counsel)

Q.   Are these true and accurate photographs of the originals?
A.   Yes.

>   Counsel: *I offer the photographs in evidence.*
>   (Photographs were marked Defendant's Exhibit B)

*Q.   Will you tell us what you observed in comparing Plaintiff's Exhibit 1
with Defendant's Exhibit A, and point out on the photographs, Defendant's Exhibit B, the differences and similarities which you observed.*
A.   (Witness does so in minutest detail).

*Q.   As the result of your comparison of the two exhibits, have you an opin-
ion as to whether or not Plaintiff's Exhibit 1 was written by the same
person who wrote Defendant's Exhibit A?*
A.   I do.

Q.   What is that opinion?
*A.   The letter Plaintiff's Exhibit 1 was not written by the writer of De-
fendant's Exhibit A.*

Q.   What are the chief reasons for such opinion?
*A.   Because of the differences I have already testified to and because the
handwriting on the letter, Plaintiff's Exhibit 1, shows that it was written
slowly, carefully, and hesitatingly, and there are changes in some of the
strokes, whereas the writer of Defendant's Exhibit A was clearly accustomed to signing his name in bold, strong characters, he was very familiar with the act of signing his name, and the signature shows no
evidence of hesitation or careful, interrupted movements.*

Chapter Fourteen

FOOTNOTES

[1] Sozzi v. Gull (Cal. App. 1963), 33 Cal. Rptr. 221.
Loper v. Andrews (Tax. 1966), 404 S.W. 2d 300.
[2] "Helmholtz distinctly calls the perception of distance, for example, an unconscious inference—a mechanically performed act of judgment."
Wellman, *Act of Cross-Examination* (1962 ed), p. 158.
[3] See Note 35 ALR 2d 19.
[4] Caves v. Barnes (1964), 178 Neb. 103, 13z N.W. 2d 310.
[5] Kane v. Fields Corner Grille, Inc. (1961), 341 Mass. 640, 171 N.E. 2d 287; boisterous, arrogant.
Shaw v. Sylvester (1960), 253 N.C. 176, 116 S.E. 2d 351, speed.
[6] Finn v. J. H. Rose Trucklines (1965), 1 Ariz. App. 27, 398 P. 2d 935.
Redman Industries Inc. v. Morgan Drive Away, Inc. (1965), 179 Neb. 406, 138 N.W. 2d 708.
[7] McGrath v. Fash (1923), 244 Mass. 327, 139 N.E. 303.
[8] Land v. Bachman (1920), 223 Ill. App. 473.
[9] Rice v. Shenk (1928), 293 Pa. 524, 143 A. 231.
[10] McKee v. Nelson, 4 Cow. N.Y. 355, 15 Am. Dec. 384.
Bates v. Town of Sharon, 1873), 45 Vt. 474.
See also 38 ALR 2d 122.
[11] Ferderer v. Northern Pacific Railroad Co. (N.D. 1950), 42 N.W. 2d 216.
Montez v. Bailey County Electric Co. (Tex. Civ. App. 1965), 397 S.W. 2d 108.
[12] Altvater v. Battochetti (4th Cir. [W. Va.] 1962), 300 F. 2d 156.
[13] Conti v. Luchs (1947), 272 App. Div. 1025, 73 N.Y.S. 2d 763.
[14] Lombardi v. New York State Railway (1928), 224 App. Div. 438, 231 N.Y.S. 306.
Bergman v. Brooklyn and Queens Transit Corp. (1937), 163 Misc. 762, 297 N.Y.S. 727; sudden jerk or stop.
[15] Cannon v. Bassett (Mass. 1928), 162 N.E. 772.
[16] Shelley v. Norman (1921), 114 Wash. 381, 195 P. 243.
[17] Baltimore, C. & A. Ry. Co. v. Turner (1927), 152 Md. 216, 136 A. 609.
[18] Millhollan v. Watkins Motor Lines, Inc. (1967), 116 Ga. App. 452, 157 S.E. 2d 901.
[19] Lewis v. Steele (1916), 52 Mont. 300, 157 P. 575.

[20] S & S Construction Co. v. Stacks (1967), 241 Ark. 1096, 411 S.W. 2d 508.

Sturgis v. Garrett (Idaho 1963), 379 P. 2d 658.

[21] Pooler v. Klobassa (Tex. Civ. App. 1967), 413 S.W. 2d 768.

[22] Neil v. Mayer (Mo. App. 1968) 426 S.W. 2d 711.

[23] Taylor v. Lewis (1921), 206 Ala. 338, 98 So. 581.

[24] Sommer v. Martin (1922), 55 Cal. App. 603, 204 P. 33.

[25] Mann v. Woodward (1927) 217 Ky. 491, 290 S.W. 333.

Earl v. Edwards (Ga. App. 1968), 161 S.E. 2d 438.

[26] Scott v. Barfield (Fla. App. 1967), 202 So. 2d 591.

[27] Daniels v. Bloomquist (Iowa 1965), 138 N.W. 2d 868.

[28] Uris v. State Compensation Dept. (Ore. 1967), 427 P. 2d 753.

See also Note 30, this section.

[29] Quinn v. O'Keefe (1896), 9 App. Div. 68, 41 N.Y.S. 116.

Vincent-Wilday Inc. v. Strait (1948), 273 App. Div. 1054, 79 N.Y.S. 2d 811.

[30] Barnett v. Richardson (Okla. 1966), 415 P. 2d 987.

Pepsi-Cola Bottling Co. v. McCullers (Va. 1949), 52 S.E. 2d 257, 260.

Wigmore on Evidence, (3rd ed) Section 568.

[31] Tryon v. Casey (Mo. App. 1967), 416 S.W. 2d 252.

Richardson v. Wendel (Mo. 1966), 401 S.W. 2d 455.

City of Philadelphia v. Shapiro (1965), 416 Pa. 308, 206 A. 2d 308.

Phillips v. Stewart (Va. 1966), 148 S.E. 2d 784.

Fieldstein v. Harrington (1958), 4 Wis. 2d 380, 90 N.W. 2d 566.

[32] Cozine v. Hawaiian Catamaran, Ltd. (Hawaii 1966), 412 P. 2d 669.

[33] Miller v. Larson (N.D. 1959), 95 N.W. 2d 569.

[34] Travelers Insurance Co. v. Heppenstall Co. (Pa. 1948), 61 A. 2d 809.

[35] Phillips v. Stewart.

[36] Rowe v. Maule Drug Co. (Kan. 1966), 413 P. 2d 104.

[37] Straughan v. Tsouvalos (Md. 1967), 228 A. 2d 300.

[38] People v. McWilliams (Cal. 1948), 197 P. 2d 216.

[39] Daniels v. Bloomquist (1965), 138 N.W. 2d 868;

Harrison v. Weller (Mo. App. 1967), 423 S.W. 2d 226.

[40] Tyler Mirror & Glass Co. v. Simpkins (Tex. Civ. App. 1966), 407 S.W. 2d 807.

[41] People v. Tucker (Cal. 1948), 198 P. 2d 941.

See also 127 ALR p. 1513.

[42] City of Milwaukee v. Bichel (Wis. 1967), 150 N.W. 2d 419.

[43] Turner v. American Security and Trust Co. (1909), 213 U.S. 257, 29 S. Ct. 420, 53 L. Ed. 788.

Schatz v. Wintersteen (1949), 209 P. 2d 1136.

In re Schillinger (1932), 258 N.Y. 186, 179 N.E. 380; a lay witness who attested a will may express an opinion as to the sanity of the testator.

[44] Coral Ridge Clay Products Co. v. Collins (1918), 181 Ky. 818, 205 S.W. 958.

In re Coddington's Will (1954), 307 N.Y. 181, 120 N.E. 2d 777.

Wigmore on Evidence, Sections 1933, 1934, 1938.

[45] State v. Moore (N.C. 1966), 150 S.E. 2d 47.

[46] McKay Machine Co. v. Rodman (Ohio 1967), 11 Ohio St. 2d 77, 228 N.E. 2d 304.

Commonwealth v. Leslie (Pa. 1967), 227 A. 2d 900.

[47] Graham v. Pennsylvania Co. (1891), 139 Pa. 149, 21 A. 151, 12 L.R.A. 293.

[48] United States v. 60.14 Acres of Land etc. (3rd Cir. [Pa.] 1966), 362 F. 2d 660.

[49] Waggaman v. Frostman (D.C. App. 1966), 217 A. 2d 310.

State Road Commr. v. Darrah (W. Va. 1967), 153 S.E. 2d 408.

[50] Bedrosian v. O'Keefe (R.I. 1965), 215 A. 2d 423.

[51] Schwartz, *Trial of Accident Cases*, Section 814.

Lacey, *Scientific Automobile Reconstruction,* (New York, Matthew Bender), p. 5.

[52] Kapral v. Hartzelius (4th Cir. [Md.] 1968), 392 F. 2d 548;

Lopez v. Yannotti (1965), 24 App. Div. 2d 758, 263 N.Y.S. 2d 523.

[53] Collins v. Zediker (Pa. 1966), 218 A. 2d 776; speed at which pedestrian walked.

[54] Schoeb v. Cowles (1968), 279 Minn. 331, 156 N.W. 2d 895.

Stillwell v. Schmoker (1963), 175 Neb. 595, 122 N.W. 2d 538.

White v. Hunt (1968), 209 Va. 11, 161 S.E. 2d 809.

[55] Schwartz, *Trial of Accident Cases.* Section 813.

[56] Eldridge v. Pike (Ky. 1965), 396 S.W. 2d 314; qualifications inadequate.

[57] Saladow v. Keystone (1934), 241 App. Div. 161, 271 N.Y.S. 293.

White v. Zutell (2d Cir. [N.Y.] 1959), 263 F. 2d 613.

Andrews v. Moery (1952), 205 Okla. 635, 240 P. 2d 447.

Taylor v. Johnson (1966), 18 Utah 2d 16, 414 P. 2d 575. *Contra:* Willard v. McCoy (S.C. 1959), 108 S.E. 2d 113.

[58] Sigel v. Boston & Maine Railroad (N.H. 1966), 216 A. 2d 794.

78 ALR 2d 218, 135 ALR 1404.

[59] Farrow v. Baugham (1966), 266 N.C. 739, 147 S.E. 2d 167, 33 A.L.R. 2d 1250.

[60] 38 ALR 2d 13. *Contra:* Kelso v. Independent Tank Co. (Okla. 1960), 348 P. 2d 855.

[61] Gray v. Woods (1958), 84 Ariz. 87, 324 P. 2d 220; based on location of debris, marks on highway and damage to vehicles.

Starkey v. Bryan (Colo. 1968), 441 P. 2d 314.

La Fave v. Kroger Co. (1966), 5 Mich. App. 446, 146 N.W. 2d 850;

see 66 ALR 2d 1048, 77 ALR 2d 580. *Contra:* Woolner v. Ponicki (1966), 3 Mich. App. 590, 143 N.W. 2d 149.

[62] Hagan Storm Fence Co. v. Edwards (1963), 245 Miss. 487. 148 So. 2d 693.

Lombard v. Dobson (1962), 16 App. Div. 2d 1031, 230 N.Y.S. 2d 47.

[63] Wilson v. Perkins (Nev. 1966), 409 P. 2d 976.

[64] Deatherage v. Phipps (Okla. 1967), 441 P. 2d 1020.

Froemming v. Spokane City Lines (Wash. 1967), 427 P. 2d 1003.

ALR 726.

[65] Turcotte v. DeWitt (1954), 332 Mass. 160, 124 N.E. 2d 241.

[66] Beal v. Southern Union Gas Co. (1960), 66 N.M. 424, 349 P. 2d 337.
Southerland v. Porter (Tex. Civ. App. 1960), 336 S.W. 2d 841.
[67] Giamattei v. Di Cerbo (Conn. 1948), 62 A. 2d 519.
[68] Winski v. Clegg (1924), 81 Ind. App. 560, 142 N.E. 130.
[69] Bridger v. Union Railway Co. (6th Cir. [Tenn.] 1966), 355 F. 2d 382.
[70] Colebank v. Standard Garage Co. (1915), 75 W. Va. 389, 84 S.E. 1051.
[71] State *ex rel* State Highway Comm'n. v. Koberna (Mo. 1965), 396 S.W. 2d 654.
[72] Shepard v. Midland Mutual Life Insurance Co. (Ohio 1949), 87 N.E. 2d 156, 127 ALR 1513.
[73] Danielson v. Roche (Cal. App. 1952), 241 P. 2d 1028.
See Richardson, *Modern Scientific Evidence*, Section 5.5 *et seq*.
[74] Berry v. Chaplin (1946), 74 Cal. App. 2d 562, 169 P. 2d 442.
Saks v. Saks (1947), 189 Misc. 667, 71 N.Y.S. 2d 797.
[75] Equitable Life Assurance Society of the United States v. Neale (Okla. 1953), 258 P. 2d 654.
[76] People v. Taranto (1956), 4 Ill. 2d 155, 122 N.E. 2d 209.
[77] See Section 14.07, "Establishing that the Witness is a Well Qualified Lay Witness."
[78] See Section 14.11, "The Factual Basis is More Important Than the Opinion Itself."
[79] See Section 14.13, "Rationale for the Opinion."
[80] See Section 5.05, "The Witness has the Capacity to Know and Understand," *et seq*.
[81] Penny v. Rochester Railway Co. (1896), 7 App. Div. 595, 40 N.Y.S. 172, aff'd. 154 N.Y. 770.
[82] Taylor v. MacDonald (Wyo. 1966), 409 P. 2d 762.
Schwartz, *Trial of Accident Cases*, Section 743D.
[83] Murchison v. Powell (1967), 269 N.C. 656, 153 S.E. 2d 352; the fact that two of the witnesses who testified as to the speed of defendant's truck were young boys who had never driven an automobile would go to weight of their testimony but would not make it incompetent.
[84] Werth v. Tromberg (Idaho 1965), 409 P. 2d 421;
Schulman v. Roseth (1930), 227 App. Div. 577, 238 N.Y.S. 575.
Schwartz, *Trial of Accident Cases*, Section 743C.
[85] Watsontown Brick Co. v. Hercules Powder Co. (D. Pa. 1967) 265 F. Supp. 268.
McCurdy v. Union Pacific Railroad (1966), 68 Wash. 2d 457, 413 P. 2d 617.
Wigmore on Evidence (3rd ed) Section 716.
[86] Baker v. Goddard (Ga. 1949), 53 S.E. 2d 754.
Bruner v. Gordon (Ky. 1948), 214 S.E. 2d 997.
Louisville & N.R. Co. v. Hill, (1948) 307 Ky. 846, 212 S.E. 2d 342.
Cortez v. Mascarro (Tex. Cir. App. 1967) 412 S.W. 2d 342. *Contra:* United Transports v. Johnson (Ark. 1949), 220 S.W. 2d 814.
[87] Dallas Railway and Terminal Co. v. Strickland Transportation Co., (Tex. Cir. App.) 225 S.W. 2d 901.
[88] Southern Coach Lines Inc. v. Wilson (Tenn. 1948), 214 S.W. 2d 55.

[89] Kohl v. Arp (Iowa 1945), 17 N.W. 2d 824, 169 ALR 1067, and cases collated.

Lucia v. De Laye (La. 1948), 36 So. 2d 53.

4 ALR 1355; 32 ALR 706; 78 ALR 912; 169 ALR 1100.

Schwartz, *Trial of Accident Cases,* Section 636.

[90] Tryon v. Casey (Mo. App. 1967), 416 S.W. 2d 252.

[91] Bridger v. Union Railway Co. (6th Cir. [Tenn.] 1966), 355 F. 2d 382.

[92] See Section 5.06, "The Expert's Background and Qualifications."

[93] See Note 86, this chapter.

[94] See Section 5.06 for an illustration of the qualification of a medical expert; Section 5.10 an architect; See Busch, *op. cit.,* p. 467; an examiner of questioned documents.

[95] Nathan v. Duncan (Ga. App. 1966), 149 S.E. 2d 383.

[96] Lewis v. McCullough (Mo. 1967), 413 S.W. 2d 499.

[97] State *ex rel* State Highway Comm'n. v. Koberna.

[98] Turner v. City of Newburgh (1881), 109 N.Y. 301.

[99] See next section.

[100] Christastie v. Elmira Water, Light & Power Co. (1922), 202 App. Div 270, 195 N.Y.S. 156.

[101] Schwartz, *Trial of Accident Cases,* Section 1289, Note 2.

[102] Stuart v. Anheuser-Busch Co. (La. App. 1966), 187 So. 2d 442.

[103] N.Y. CPLR, Rule 4515.

[104] Schwartz, *Trial of Accident Cases,* Section 1214.

[105] 38 ALR 2d 20.

[106] Deaver v. Hickox (Ill. App. 1967), 224 N.E. 2d 468; courts will not permit speculation even by experts.

National Dairy Products v. Durham (Ga. App. 1967), 154 S.E. 2d 752.

Schwartz, *Trial of Accident Cases,* Section 215.

[107] Fox Wisconsin Theatres Inc. v. City of Waukesha (Wis. 1948), 34 N.W. 2d 783. See N.Y. CPLR, Rule 4515.

[108] ALR 2d 20.

[109] See Section 5.10, "Knowledge of Custom or Usage."

[110] People v. Jennings (1911), 252 Ill. 534, 96 N.E. 1077; 43 L.R.A.N.S. 1206.

State v. Kuhl (1918), 42 Nev. 185, 175 P. 190 see A.L.R. 1694.

Wigmore on Evidence, Section 417a.

[111] Evans v. Commonwealth (1929), 230 Ky. 411, 19 S.W. 2d 1091.

66 ALR 360.

State v. Martinez (N.M. 1948), 198 P. 2d 256.

[112] See Busch *Trial Procedure Materials* pp. 467–79 for excellent specimen of the direct examination of a questioned document examiner and pp. 349–57 for direct examination of an expert on ballistics.

[113] See Section 5.06, "The Expert's Background and Qualifications."

OBJECTIONS TO
PROOF OF OPINIONS

TABLE OF CONTENTS

OBJECTIONS TO
PROOF OF OPINIONS

The admissibility of opinions is the exception and not the rule. Before a witness, whether layman or expert, is permitted to express an opinion, the opposing attorney must ask himself these four questions: Is the witness qualified to express the opinion? Is there a sufficient basis upon which to arrive at an opinion? Is the opinion of the witness necessary or is there enough in the evidence for the jury to come to its own conclusion? Is the opinion called for more than mere speculation or conjecture? If the answer to any of these four questions is "No," then the opinion is objectionable.

Q. WHAT IS YOUR OPINION AS TO . . .?

§ 15:01 Objections When the Witness Is Incompetent: Comparison of Handwriting by Layman

At a murder trial, a witness was called by the State and asked by the District Attorney:

Q. *What is your business?*
A. *I own a pawnshop.*

Q. *I show you this paper and ask you what it is.*
A. *This is a certificate of purchase of a pistol.*

Q. *Was that signed in your presence?*
A. *It was.*

Q. *Who signed that?*
A. *The defendant, Vernon Loveall.*

(The certificate was marked in evidence, People's Exhibit 1)

The district attorney continued:

Q. *I show you this letter and this certificate of purchase, People's Exhibit 1, and ask you to compare the signature and tell us whether or not, in your opinion, they were written by the same person.*

Defense Attorney: I object to the competency of the witness.

The objection should be sustained in the absence of statute permitting a layman to make a comparison of handwritings.[1] It will be noted that the objection is to the witness and not to his testimony. This is necessary as otherwise the objection will not be in the proper form to preserve the point on appeal.[2] The qualification of a person to be a witness is determined by the judge.[3] The general rule permits identification of another's handwriting by a lay witness, provided that the witness is familiar with the handwriting by having seen the other write, by exchanging correspondence, or by some other means. However, authentication based upon a comparison with a genuine specimen of the handwriting is permitted only by an expert witness or by the triers of the facts.[4]

§ 15:02 Opinion of Value

The plaintiff, who claimed that his automobile was completely demolished in a collision with defendant's automobile, was asked on direct examination by Plaintiff's Attorney:

Q. *Were you the owner of the automobile involved in this litigation?*
A. *I was.*

Q. *What was its market value immediately after the accident?*

Defendant's Attorney: I object. The witness is not qualified.

The objection will generally be sustained. While the courts are not very strict as to their requirements as to the qualifications one must have in order to be permitted to express an opinion of the market value of an automobile,[5] it is usually required that the witness be shown to have some special knowledge on the subject which is not possessed by persons generally.[6]

Some courts will deem the owner of an automobile qualified to testify as to the value of his vehicle or other personal property *before* the accident on the theory that, being familiar with his property, he is presumed to know its worth in a general way.[7] Evidence of the price paid for the vehicle shortly before the collision has been received as some evidence of its value before the accident.[8] Generally, the mere knowledge of the price which was paid for the automobile is not sufficient qualification or basis on which to testify as to its market value.[9] The ordinary automobile owner is not presumed to know the value of his automobile in a *damaged* condition. Such knowledge must necessarily come from an expert witness, whose testimony must be produced directly, and not be hearsay.[10]

§ 15:03 Layman's Medical Opinion

In a personal injury action, plaintiff, who claimed loss of hearing, was asked by his Attorney:

Q. What, if anything, happened to you?
A. I hit my head on the right side.

Q. What effect did that blow have?
A. It made me deaf in the right ear and I suffered a concussion of the brain and my nerves were affected.

Defendant's Attorney: I object and move to strike out the answer on the ground that the witness is not qualified.

The objection to the question should be sustained because the plaintiff was not competent to express the opinion that it was the blow to his head which made him deaf, caused a concussion of the brain, and affected his nerves. This would be a medical opinion and plaintiff is not qualified to diagnose diseases or testify as to the causal relation between the injury and the disease.[11] A question involving the cause of physical or emotional disturbance is a complex one requiring expert testimony.[12]

Similarly, a question such as *Q. As a result of your injuries, when was it that you were able to return to work?* would be objectionable. By the use of the words "as a result of your injuries," the question calls for an opinion as to whether the continued inability to work resulted from the alleged injuries. This would be a medical opinion which a layman is not competent to express. The plaintiff may, however, testify as to how he felt, and the extent of his injuries, pain, and suffering so far as they were known to him. He may even be permitted to express an opinion as to when it was that he *felt able* to resume his work.[13]

Similarly, in an action for malicious prosecution, a lay person was competent to testify that nervousness, headaches, and upset stomach developed coincidentally with the institution of the criminal proceeding against him.[14]

The proponent of a will called a witness, qualified him as a psychiatrist, and asked him to assume certain facts indicating that the testator was senile. He then continued:

Q. *Assuming the foregoing facts, can you state whether or not, in your opinion, the testator was or was not capable of making and executing a valid will?*

Contestant's Attorney: *I object.*

The objection should be sustained because the witness is not asked his opinion of the mental condition of the testator, but as to his ability to make a valid will. The opinion called for, that is the competency to make a will, is more than a medical opinion as it also requires a knowledge of *law,* which the witness does not possess.[15] A question such as, "Did the testator have sufficient mental capacity to know the nature and extent of his property and the natural objects of his bounty to formulate a rational scheme of distribution?" would be allowed.[16]

§ 15:04 Testimony Incompetent: Opinion on the Ultimate Question

A police officer was called and examined by the Plaintiff's Attorney:

Q. *Officer, in the course of your duties, were you called to the scene of this accident?*
A. *I was.*

Q. *What time was it when you arrived there?*
A. *11 P.M.*

Q. *And did you, in the course of your duties, investigate the facts of the occurrence?*
A. *I did.*

Q. *Did you speak to the operators of both automobiles?*
A. *I did.*

Q. *And did you also interview witnesses at the scene?*
A. *I did.*

Q. *Now, after you learned the facts from these two operators and the witnesses and after your investigation, will you state who, in your opinion, was at fault in this accident?*

Defendant's Attorney: I object.

The objection should be sustained. The witness has not been asked to testify as to the pertinent, competent facts which he may have discovered in the course of his investigation or as to any admissions which may have been made by the motorists. Instead, he is merely asked for his own conclusion, which he may have based upon all manner of hearsay, surmise, and conjecture, as to who was at fault. Such an opinion is clearly inadmissible. The jury must formulate its own opinion as to fault based upon the sworn testimony as to the facts.[17]

§ 15:05   Ballistics

Trial for murder. The defense maintained that the victim had committed suicide and that the bullet wound in the head was self-inflicted. An eminent ballistics expert, after being fully qualified, testified as to his investigation and tests made. He was then asked by the District Attorney:

Q. I ask you to state the exact position in which you found the powder marks surrounding the wound in the head?

A. For a radius of one-half inch surrounding the opening in the scalp on the right side, a mass of powder grains, the larger amount of the mass being downward and forward, and towards the angle of the eye in relation to the opening in the scalp.

Q. Can you tell us whether or not this wound was or was not what we call a contact wound?

A. It was not.

Q. What is a contact wound?

A. A contact wound is one in which the weapon used is in direct contact with the skin at the moment of its discharge.

Q. You mean it is placed against the skin?

A. Yes.

Q. Why do you say it was not a contact wound?

A. The powder marks, instead of being centered at one point or being found inside the scalp, where they would have been had it been a contact wound, were disseminated in a circle, surrounding the wound for a radius of half an inch surrounding the opening.

Q. Can you state whether a revolver placed against the flesh when it was fired would tear the flesh?

A. It would. There was no bursting of the flesh from within outward.

Q. Can you tell with reasonable certainty from what distance this revolver was fired, and within what distance from the skull the revolver was held at the time of firing?

A. I can.

Q. Will you please so state?

A. At a distance from one to two inches from the surface of the skin.

Q. From your examination of the wound and the powder grains, and from your experience, can you state with reasonable certainty in what position this revolver was held at the time it was fired?

A. I can.

Q. Will you please so state?

A. In a position upside down (indicating), *with the sight in this direction and with the butt in this direction* (indicating).

Q. Now, taking into consideration the experience you have had with revolvers and gun shot wounds and powder marks, can you state whether or not you can tell with reasonable certainty whether or not this wound found on the deceased's head on the night of June 23rd could be self-inflicted?

A. I can.

Q. Was it self-inflicted?

Defense Counsel: I object.

The question posed in this illustration, it has been held,[18] was the ultimate question in the case, for, under the facts, the wound was either self-inflicted or else the defendant killed the deceased and, therefore, the objection should be sustained. This ruling seems questionable, assuming that the gun was held in a position which made it impossible that the wound could be self-inflicted. Such fact might not be obvious to the jury, but might be plain to the expert, who should be allowed to give his opinion that suicide would have been impossible.

In recent years, this "ultimate question" restriction has been greatly criticized as unduly restrictive, difficult of application, and depriving the court of useful information.[19] The restriction has been abandoned in some jurisdictions by case law [20] and by evidence codes.[21]

§ 15:06 Opinion Stated as a Fact

In a prosecution for murder, a ballistic expert was being examined by the District Attorney:

Q. *Doctor, I hand you State Exhibit 1, the gun found in the defendant's possession, and ask you to describe it.*
A. *It is a Colt Automatic #9202.*

Q. *Doctor, did you make any ballistic examinations and comparison of the bullet, State Exhibit 2, which was extracted from the body and the gun, State's Exhibit 1?*
A. *Yes, sir, I did.*

Q. *Will you please describe that examination which you made?*
A. *I fired this test shell which I have here, through the gun, State's Exhibit 1. The markings on this test shell were then compared with the markings on the bullet which was extracted from the body.*

(The test shell was offered and marked in evidence, State's Exhibit 3)

Q. *I hand you herewith State's Exhibit 2, the bullet that was extracted from the body of the deceased and ask you to state from what gun it was fired.*
A. *I can state positively that the bullet, Exhibit 2, which was extracted from the body of the deceased, was fired from this Colt automatic pistol #9202, State's Exhibit 1.*

Defense Attorney: I object and move to strike out the answer.

The question does not call for an opinion, but for a fact. The answer is a statement of fact. Although ballistics is regarded as a positive science by many, nevertheless, the witness has no personal knowledge and should only express his opinion. The objection should be sustained and the answer stricken.[22]

Along a similar vein, the plaintiff in a personal injury case had sustained certain fractures and suffered pneumonia thereafter. The question put to his physician, Q. *In this case were those fractures the cause of the pneumonia?* was held to be improper as framed in that the answer would usurp the function of the jury.[23]

§ 15:07   Opinion Contrary to Facts Judicially Noted

In an action against a retail butcher for alleged breach of an implied warranty that pork purchased from the defendant would be fit for human consumption, a physician was asked by Plaintiff's Attorney:

Q. Doctor, what was your diagnosis?
A. The plaintiffs were suffering from trichinosis.

Q. Doctor, can you state, with reasonable certainty, whether the eating of pork, after it has been properly cooked, is a competent producing cause of trichinosis?
A. Yes.

Defendant's Attorney: I object.

Judicial notice has been taken that trichinosis cannot be contracted from eating pork which has been *properly* cooked.[24] An opinion of an expert may be rejected, according to some authorities, when it is contrary to some well established scientific fact which is judicially noticed by the court or contrary to reason or common knowledge and experience. Under such authorities, the objection should be sustained.[25] There are also authorities to the contrary.[26]

§ 15:08   Lack of Factual Basis for Opinion

An automobile guest passenger was suing his host for personal injuries sustained when the automobile left the road. A traffic accident analyst was called, qualified, and asked by Plaintiff's Attorney:

Q. Based upon your investigation, what, in your opinion, caused the automobile to leave the road?
A. The driver fell asleep at the wheel.

Defendant's Attorney: I object and move to strike out the answer.

The objection should be sustained and the answer stricken. If there was evidence in the case that the driver had fallen asleep at the wheel, the jury is fully competent to determine whether that fact was the probable cause and whether the driver had been negligent. On the other hand, if there was no such evidence, then the opinion would be sheer speculation and an invasion of the jury's province.[27]

The mere circumstance that the subject is a technical one does not necessarily mean that the expert will be permitted to give an opinion. If the jury, with all the technical facts before them, can form a conclusion thereon, then it is their sole province to do so and the expert's opinion is unnecessary. Without the facts, there was nothing in the record upon which the expert could base his opinions as to the cause of the accident, which is the ultimate question to be decided by the jury.[28]

There are many variations of questions calling for opinions when there are no facts established upon which to base the opinion. To give but a few illustrations, a police officer who had arrived at the scene after the occurrence and described the damage he found on examining plaintiff's automobile was asked by plaintiff's attorney, *Q. Based on your inspection of the plaintiff's automobile and the damage you have just described, will you state how fast, in your opinion, the defendant's car had been going in order to cause those damages?*

Obviously, the objection should be sustained. The extent of the damage to plaintiff's automobile does not necessarily reflect the speed at which the defendant's automobile was traveling before the accident. The damage may result from many other facts, as the weight and the speed of the other vehicle with which it collided, the nature of the impact, or what occurred after the two cars came together. No expert, irrespective of his knowledge, is qualified to express an opinion of speed based only upon an inspection of the damage. Furthermore, the jury is just as qualified as the witness to determine what inferences the facts will permit or require.[29]

A question put to an eyewitness who was testifying on behalf of the driver of a vehicle which had struck a pedestrian, *Q. Could the driver have avoided the accident?* would be objectionable, as this calls for a conclusion which the jury can make on the basis of the facts in evidence.[30] Similarly, it was held that testimony by the defendant truck driver that the driver of the oncoming automobile would be alive if she had not changed her course was inadmissible as a supposition or opinion invading the province of the jury.[31] "The line of admissibility is crossed when the opinion of the witness is a reasoned deduction or surmise from circumstantial evidence, or from imagined facts, or is of the nature of a characterization predicated upon some standard in the mind of the witness."[32]

So, too, the operator of a car which was standing still and was struck in the rear by defendant's automobile, he who did not see the defendant's approach, would not be permitted to answer the question, *Q. How many miles per hour was that defendant's automobile going, in your opinion, at the time it struck your car?*[33] Such a witness, who did not *see* the car, but merely *heard* it coming down the highway, it has been held, was incompetent to testify that the automobile was traveling over 80 miles per hour.[34]

A mere mental impression that a witness may have had fails to rise to the dignity of admissible testimony if it consists of nothing more definite than guess or conjecture.[35]

§ 15:09   Improper Hypothetical Question as Basis for Opinion

At a hearing in Workmen's Compensation of a claim for death of John Jones from tuberculosis, a fellow employee of Jones, who was called in behalf of the claimant, testified as follows:

Q.   *What were the duties of John Jones?*
A.   *He was a grinder.*

Q.   *What was the custom of the workmen in that plant with respect to wearing masks?*
A.   *Some men wore masks, others did not.*

On cross-examination, the witness was asked by the insurance carrier's attorney:

Q.   *Isn't it a fact that the claimant always wore a mask when he worked?*
A.   *Yes, he did.*

The claimant's medical expert then testified and was asked by the claimant's attorney:

Q.   *. . . assume further, Doctor, that some of the workers wore masks and others did not, can you state whether, in your opinion, there was any causal connection between the death of the decedent and his work by reason of dust?*

Defendant's Attorney: I object on the ground that the fact that the claimant always wore a mask is omitted from the question.

The objection should be sustained. The only evidence in the record was that the claimant *always* wore a mask. This fact is omitted from the hypothetical question and this omission would vitally affect the opinion and makes the question objectionable.[36] While it is not essential that all the facts be included in the hypothetical question,[37] it must include all factors supported by the evidence which are necessary for a reasonably accurate opinion.[38]

It will be noted that the objection points out specifically the fact which should have been included in the question. Counsel who objects to a hypothetical question must advise the court in what respect the question fails to state the record properly and may not rely on a general objection.[39]

§ 15:10   Speculative Opinion Called For

The plaintiff claimed that as a result of an injury he developed a growth. The plaintiff's attorney asked the physician a hypothetical question and asked this opinion:

Q.   . . . *assuming the foregoing facts, can you give us your opinion as to whether such a fall was a possible cause of the lipoma?*

Defendant's Attorney: I object.

The objection should be sustained. An opinion regarding a "possible" cause has been held to be conjectural and speculative.[40] The objection may be overcome by asking for the opinion "with reasonable certainty"[41] or whether the occurrence was a "competent producing cause" of the condition.[42]

§ 15:11   Opinion Irrelevant—Character

In a personal injury action, plaintiff's fellow worker was called and asked by Plaintiff's Attorney:

Q.   *How long have you known and worked with the plaintiff?*
A.   *Fifteen years.*

Q.   *In your opinion is he a man who would make any misrepresentations concerning his injuries or be a malingerer?*

Defendant's Attorney: I object.

There are two possible reasons why the objection would be sustained. In the first place, character evidence is usually irrelevant in a civil suit for personal injuries unless plaintiff's good character for truth and veracity has first been attacked by the defendant.[43]

In the second place, even if character evidence was relevant, such evidence would not generally be allowed in the form of an opinion,[44] although common practice has permitted the character witness to be asked, Q. *Would you believe him under oath?*[45] The modern trend is to permit the use of an opinion as to character rather than reputation evidence.[46]

§ 15:12   Speed at Another Place

The plaintiff in an automobile accident case called a witness who was asked by Plaintiff's Attorney:

Q.   Did you see the defendant's automobile before the collision?
A.   I did.

Q.   Where were you when you saw it?
A.   I saw it when he passed me about three miles before the place of the collision.

Q.   At what speed was he traveling at that time?

Defendant's Attorney: I object.

The objection should be sustained. The speed of an automobile three miles from the point of collision would be too remote and irrelevant.[47] It is a matter of common knowledge that the speed of an automobile may be greatly increased in a short distance. Speed at a distance of a quarter of a mile has been held to be irrelevant.[48] However, the exclusion of testimony as to speed when the automobile was only 700 feet away has been held to be error.[49]

§ 15:13   Extraneous Opinions

The action was to recover for injuries suffered by plaintiff as a result of inhaling chlorine gas which escaped in the vicinity of a swimming pool operated by the defendant. The defendant called a medical witness, who testified at length as to the condition of the plaintiff, his examination of her and her x-ray pictures, and, in detail, his findings and opinion as to her condition. His direct examination was then continued by Defendant's Attorney:

Q.   Doctor, in addition to your general experience, I understand that you yourself have suffered with a bronchial ailment, is that correct?
A.   Yes.

Q.   How long have you had that condition?
A.   For several years.

Q.   What brought about your condition?
A.   Partly exposure and partly from irritation from the use of tobacco.
Q.   From your examination of the plaintiff and the x-ray pictures, can you state whether her condition is any worse than the condition from which you suffer?

Plaintiff's Attorney: I object.

It would be proper to sustain the objection. The trial court is vested with discretion in deciding whether to permit proof of extraneous facts. The comparison between the condition of the plaintiff and the witness has been held to be irrelevant.[50]

Chapter Fifteen

FOOTNOTES

[1] Breedlove v. State (Tenn. 1949), 221 S.W. 2d 801: "A lay witness may not make such a comparison. An expert may."
Wigmore on Evidence, Section 1997.
N.Y. CPLR, Rule 4536.
[2] Paris v. Carolina Portable Aggregates (1967), 271 N.C. 471, 157 S.E. 2d 131.
[3] Proposed Rules of Evidence for the United States District Courts and Magistrates, Rule 1-04.
[4] Wausau Sulphate Fibre Co. v. Commission of Internal Revenue (7th Cir. 1932), 61 F. 2d 879.
Desimone v. United States (9th Cir. [Wash.] 1955), 277 F. 2d 864.
Brandon v. Collins (2d Cir. [N.Y.] 1959), 267 F. 2d 731.
Wigmore on Evidence (3rd ed), Sections 1991–94.
Proposed Rules of Evidence for the United States District Courts and Magistrates, Rule 9-01 (b) 2, 3.
[5] Jamieson v. N.Y. etc. Railway Co. (1896), 11 App. Div. 50, (42 N.Y.S. 915); aff'd. 162 N.Y. 630, 57 N.E. 1113;
Wigmore on Evidence (3rd ed.), Section 463.
Ibid., Sections 714, 463;
Section 14.09, "Qualifying the Layman for an Opinion as to Value."
[6] Teerpenning v. Corn Exchange Insurance Co. (1871), 43 N.Y. 279.
[7] Merchants Motor Freight v. Downing, (8th Cir. [Iowa], 1955), 227 F. 2d 247.
[8] Larsen v. Long (Colo. 1923), 219 P. 1066;
Wentworth Bus Lines v. Sanborn, 99 N.H. 5, 104 A. 2d 392.
[9] *Wigmore on Evidence,* (3rd ed), Section 717.
[10] Stuart v. Rizzo (1968), 242 A. 2d 477.
Teitsworth v. Kempski (1956), 11 Terry 234, 127 A. 2d 237.

Alber v. Wise (1960), 3 Storey 126, 166 A. 2d 141.

[11] Matchem v. McGahey (Okla. 1969), 455 P. 2d 52.

[12] Harrison v. Weller (Mo. App. 1967), 423 S.W. 2d 226;

Peters v. Mutual Life Ins. Co. of New York (M.D. [Pa.] 1939), 26 F. Supp. 50; heart disease.

[13] American Fidelity and Casualty Co. v. Farmer (1948), 77 Ga. App. 166, 48 S.E. 2d 122.

Kirchof v. United Rys. Co. of St. Louis (1911), 155 Mo. App. 70, 135 S.W. 98.

Aetna Life Insurance Co. v. Wilson (1942), 190 Okla. 363, 123 P. 2d 656, 659.

Wigmore on Evidence, (3rd ed) Section 568, Note 1, and Section 1975, Note 21.

[14] Tully v. Dasher (Md. 1968), 244 A. 2d 207.

[15] Sase v. English (Ala. 1951), 52 So. 2d 216, 218.

Wigmore on Evidence, Section 1958, Note 1; notes that while a question as to whether the testator "was capable" of making a will is held to be improper, "there is great contrariety of ruling upon other forms of statement."

[16] McCormick, *Evidence,* Section 12.

[17] Giamattei v. Di Cerbo.

[18] People v. Creasy (1923) 236 N.Y. 205, 140 N.E. 563.

[19] *Wigmore on Evidence,* (3rd ed.), Section 1920.

McCormick, *Evidence, op. cit.,* Section 12.

[20] People v. Wilson (1944), 25 Cal. 2d 341, 153 P. 2d 720.

Schwergen v. Solbeck (1951) 191 Or. 454, 230 P. 2d 195.

[21] Proposed Rules of Evidence for the United States District Courts and Magistrates, Rule 7-04.

[22] State v. Martinez (N.M. 1948), 198 P. 2d 256;

Wigmore on Evidence, (3rd ed), Section 417a.

[23] The objection to this question was sustained by the trial court in Huisward v. Good Humor Corp. (1947) 296 N.Y. 934, 73 N.E. 2d 45, at fol. 303.

See also, Patrick v. Treadwell (1942) 222 N.C. 1, 21 S.E. 2d 818.

[24] Nicketta v. National Tea Co. (1949), 338 Ill. App. 159, 87 N.E. 2d 30, the court there said, "If the matter falls within the domain of judicial knowledge, it is beyond the realm of dispute."

[25] Bogard V. M. C. v. Henley (Ariz. 1962) 374 P. 2d 660.

[26] Judicial notice is not conclusive. Packer v. Fairmount Creamery Co. (1944), 158 Kan. 580, 149 P.2d 629, 631.

Wigmore on Evidence (3rd ed) Section 2567.

[27] Smaglick v. Jersey Insurance Co. of New York (Fla. App. 1968), 209 So. 2d 475.

Blind v. Rochester Aeronautical Corp. (1948) 273 App. Div. 1056, 79 N.Y.S. 2d 799.

See also Section 14.11 "The Factual Basis Is More Important Than the Opinion Itself."

[28] Alires v. Southern Pacific Co. (Ariz. 1963), 378 P. 2d 913.

Salem v. United States Lines Co. (1962) 82 S. Ct. 1119 on remand 304 F. 2d 672,

Waggaman v. Forstmann (D.C. App. 1966) 217 A. 2d 310.

[29] Farrow v. Baugham (N.C. 1966), 147 S.E. 2d 167.

Flores v. Barlow (Tex. Civ. App. 1962), 354 S.W. 2d 173.

Rumford v. Snyder (Wash. 1948), 197 P. 2d 446, 465.

Schwartz, *Trial of Accident Cases,* Sections 743 D and 814.

[30] Mann v. Woodward (1926), 217 Ky. 491, 290 S.W. 333.

[31] Scott v. Barfield (Fla. App. 1967), 202 S. 2d 591.

[32] 38 ALR 2d p. 19.

See Section 14.01 "When Opinions Are Admissible."

[33] Cartmel v. Williams (Pa. Super. 1965), 215 A. 2d 282.

[34] Meade v. Meade (Va. 1966), 147 S.E. 2d 171.

[35] Brown v. Spokane, Portland & Seattle Railway Company (Ore. 1967) 431 P 2d 817.

[36] Chapman v. Industrial Comm'n. (Ohio 1948), 81 N.E. 2d 626.

[37] Mallet v. Brannon (Ark. 1968), 243 Ark. 898, 423 S.W. 2d 880.

Ramsey v. Complete Auto Transit, Inc. (C.A. Ind. 1968), 393 F. 2d 41.

Allen Co. v. Grubb (Okla. 1968), 442 P. 2d 492.

[38] Brugh v. Peterson (Neb. 1968), 159 N.W. 2d 321.

[39] VanAernam v. Nielson (Iowa 1968), 157 N.W. 2d 138.

H. Perilstein, Inc. v. Stewart (Okla. 1968), 437 P. 2d 253.

[40] McCrosson v. Philadelphia Rapid Transit Co. (Pa. 1925) 129 A. 568.

Price v. Bates (Ky. 1959), 320 S.W. 2d 786, implying but not deciding that testimony that it was "possible" that some of plaintiff's symptoms "may" be permanent was insufficient.

[41] Walden v. Jamestown (1904), 178 N.Y. 213, 70 N.E. 466.

[42] McGrath v. Irving (1965), 24 App. Div. 2d 236, 265 N.Y.S. 2d 376.

[43] Argonaut Southwest Insurance Co. v. Pollan (Tex. Civ. App. 1968), 424 S.W. 2d 38.

Wigmore on Evidence, Section 104.

See Section 6.07 "Character Evidence in a Civil Trial."

[44] Section 6.07 *Ibid.*

[45] United States v. Walker (6th Cir. 1963), 313 F. 2d 236.

[46] Proposed Rules of Evidence for the United States District Courts and Magistrates, Rule 6-08 (a) (b).

[47] Shaw v. Skopp (1921) 198 App. Div. 618, 190 N.Y.S. 859.

[48] Stevens v. Potter (1925), 209 Ky. 705, 273 S.W. 470.

[49] Clay v. Monengton (1943), 266 App. Div. 695, 40 N.Y.S. 2d 108.

[50] Testimony excluded in Kiel v. Mahan (Tex. 1948), 214 S.W. 2d 865, 868.